the DEVIL
NEXT DOOR

Roberta Richards, Ph.D.
&
Rachel 2

SUNFLOWER INK - 37931 Palo Colorado Road, Carmel, California 93923

1 2 3 4 5 6 7 8 9 (paperback)

Library of Congress Catalogue Number 93-084894
ISBN 0-931104-38-6

To Sam,
beloved skeptic

Prologue

Do therapists create false memories of hideous abuse in their clients? Or do they successfully uncover forgotten memories of actual torture years after the terrible events?

What about Multiple Personality Disorder, a confounding, painful condition found in men and women abused as children? Can it be created by the overheated imaginations of therapists, or only by past torments which actually occurred? Controversy abounds. Television talk shows, magazines and books disagree. One moment we hear of terrible outbursts of satanic cruelty toward individuals, and in the next we are told that memories of this sort are false, imprinted upon clients through the clever manipulations of unscrupulous therapists.

Does any therapist have enough power over a vulnerable seeker to impose a form of mind control? Or is there a greater threat coming out of this question? Clients might once again become sure no one will believe them, continuing to suffer silently from the abuses they have barely survived.

Professionals deplore the idea that families may be torn apart by fabricated accusations. Parents are terrified that their children could be influenced to believe gruesome untrue stories about the past. But what if the stories are true?

Beliefs about satanic abuse are polarized, too, all the way from the existence of an international network of powerful people torturing children, to the certainty that there are no serious Satan worshipers anywhere.

This exciting story of Rachel, an abused child/woman with Multiple Personality Disorder, brings together the two sides of the quarrel between therapists, those who accuse them, and the existence of the Devil...next door.

Remember, this narrative is based on real life. It is more than simply story telling.

the DEVIL
NEXT DOOR

One

"It's hard to believe, but so were the reports about Nazi atrocities, then we found the concentration camps.

Bennett Braun, *director*
Dissociative Disorders Program
Chicago Rush-Presbyterian-St. Luke's Medical Center

It happens as we walk in an old, old graveyard in Plymouth, Massachusetts. Today is Memorial Day, so we are in a crowd. Here and there flags wave on their poles, and spots of color glow through the green and gray of the trees where the yellow of tulips warm the mounds of the dead. Occasionally, we hear the crunch of tires as a car drives slowly along the graveled winding roads, searching for a lost love or obligation. There is a worn-looking, white haired lady on her knees. She scrapes at the gray soil, planting a scarlet geranium bright against the speckled granite. The grass is green from yesterday's rain, but dry in the sun along the tops of the hillocks.

Rachel, my complex friend, and I wear our high-topped Nikes with our pants legs tucked in, no use contracting Lyme Disease from tiny brown ticks we fear lurk in the underbrush. Toeing in so as not to slip, we move downhill, away from the well-tended paths and the busy roads that wind through monuments. Thirteen stones make a series of small curved arches, only two or three feet high. Grouped on the steep slant of the hollow, these decaying markers are out of sight to passersby. On the hillside nearby the trees are tiny-leafed with spring. Through the veil of tender yellow green we can see the oaken trunks of the massive ancients. The younger trees below them bend and twist exactly as did the trees in Peeper's picture.

Rachel sinks to the ground. Her sobs are harsh. When she can tell me why she weeps, she says the distorted trees stand not just for her, but for the other children, who died there. It's just like Rachel (and her inhabitants) to give me this kind of double-duty symbolism. Nothing with Rachel just is.

Minds are wonderful and her's amazing. By now I know Rachel's depths may never be plumbed, because her mind is split vertically, like the deepest well, existing in up and down slices. Let me tell you what I mean.

In psychotherapeutic treatment in our gritty, desert home town, Rachel fused her alters Peeper, Lilith and Rachel 1 with herself. Well, that was more than a year ago. By now those three personalities seem to be fully integrated. You understand that fusion was the moment of coming together, as you've read in Sybil.

This is our big psychological adventure, Rachel's and mine, that we have planned for years. But you can understand why Sam gave us only his hesitant blessing, uneasy, as we climbed on the America West morning plane to bring us here through Boston.

Ours was a cheapskate flight, so we made two stops. I remember how I felt. On the first set down in Cincinnati, I found that I was now flying with a Rachel who had never flown before. The Rachel who left an overcrowded High Harbor Airport back in Texas said she was an old hand at air travel.

"I want to warn you to sit far enough front to avoid a bumpy ride over the plains. It's almost summer, remember, and storms are to be expected," she had told me then.

"Oh well," I thought, so far so good. Whoever this is still knows me and can carry on a conversation that has some continuity. She still gets all the names of her children right."

In the airport a smelly bus, complete with mouthy woman driver, took us to our rented car, a medium sized Toyota with a dark red finish. Nice looking, it had good enough control and was easy to drive out of the rental agency. Then, I was the one who split into fragments. My nightmare had come true: I was driving through darkening Boston during rush hour. I screamed in terror as waves of cars roared down upon us. I wanted to shut my eyes taking a sharp turn into the right lane out of Logan. I carped and complained as lines of cars slowed, creeping along in the growing dusk. It was raining. I hadn't seen rain for months and had forgotten how it reflects lights into confusion.

"Which way? Which lane? Oh, my God! The tunnel again. I just went through it . Are we going in circles?"

My companion was holding the map upside down, tracing the lines and colored shapes with her five year old finger.

Notes:

I expect this to be one hell of a trip. Sam was wary about our going, yet he, too, is curious about any information Rachel and I can find. O.K., he is more than wary. He is afraid for me. True, my pal and I can run into someone who is still dangerous. Terrible punishments were inflicted on Rachel forty years ago, yet our immediate danger is that I may not be able to keep Rachel and me safe from the emergence of a hostile personality. Neither of us knows who is still deep inside her.

Little by little I understand how Rachel works, or doesn't. She's not crazy. The peculiarities arise when executive control of her body is transferred from one to another of her personalities, the alters. Even Sam is sure this is not psychosis.

"The total Rachel is not out of touch with reality," he says.

She does, however, develop periods of amnesia with

blackouts, and Rachel still loses time. The voices she hears inside her head are not auditory hallucinations, but comments on what is happening at the moment. They are the thoughts and opinions of her other selves. Inside this woman, with whom I am to travel up and down the coastline of New England, there now live persons who intend to lead me on a search of woods and beaches. Someone, or more than one someone, has memories we need.

I understand I may never have met Rachel's original or core personality, the one that developed first after her birth, and then split off. Where did she go? Is she still in there somewhere, alive? Will she ever talk to me?

As traffic thins and the lanes ahead of me clear, I can think more calmly. I know intellectually that Rachel does not have separate people living inside one body, hers. These "people" are brain functions. However, I have reason to wonder if I can keep track of the several parts of Rachel, splitting and switching, some with two- way amnesia, and some with one- way only communication. It feels to me as if there are people who live inside her, just as she believes. I need to know if these parts of Rachel are co-present or co-conscious. These remaining "folk" may know and communicate with each other. Peeper and Lilith cooperated, but they are gone now, integrated into a much more whole Rachel. But who else remains inside? Do I dare find out?

There are so many unanswered questions in the developing field of traumatic memory. Memories are formed in an altered state of consciousness, created by terror, and Rachel had more than her share of that. Lilith, Peeper and Rachel 1 could recall every detail, color, shape, light, texture or shadow of the rooms in which they were tormented, tortured and frightened by staged rituals planned to unhinge their sanity.

Sure, I'm scared. I'm traveling down a strange highway with a little kid I don't know. She's where my friend used to be.

When I told him my plans for this trip, Sam asked me if I was prepared to meet some alter or two who contains Rachel's rage. Will such personalities be dangerous to me? A hostile alter owes me nothing. Under stress, can the grown up Rachel, my long time fellow explorer-detective, control and restrict a new personality's hate?

Will she be able to protect me from herself? Dear God, if that happens just don't let it be here in the car!

Rachel experienced such extreme violation of her physical and emotional boundaries, it makes sense that she is not always in charge of her own mental state, just as she could not protect herself when she was a little person. Helpless to direct her internal world, she sometimes finds herself once more helpless, as she was against early unpredictable parental assault. Split internally into people she does not know, she feels overwhelming confusion about her early life. Shame surges through her, then fear, anger, despair and a terrible wrenching grief. Her traumatic memories are now a part of her consciousness, her every day awareness. Her pain has been overwhelming, so of course she became suicidal and believed she was going crazy. No wonder she is still so difficult for me....and for herself.

The little girl beside me and I must have a serious talk.

"I must have your assistance. You must be a good girl and help me."

"I was good already," she says, "I packed."

That's why we are loaded down with so many plastic bags and various floppy sacks from dress shops.

"I couldn't decide, so I took a lot. Some of the others needed things."

I determine to remain calm.

"Sorry I'm cranky," I apologize.

There must be a hotel on the right hand side of the tell road. Here comes a neon sign, promising reasonable rates and cable TV. Just pulling into the parking lot floods me with feelings of relief. This "Wayfarer's Inn" turns out to be a shabby hotel, which is "remodeling" right now, and expensive. But I give up. I don't care.

5

This is no time for me to raise my voice again nor to start to cry.

Here in her room, the little girl is intrigued with the squat, brown room refrigerator/cupboard that holds miniature bottles of liquor, fat and sugary junk foods, plastic wrapped cheeses and cracker snacks. Finally, she chooses a giant candy bar and relaxes on the bed near the window to watch The Wonder Years. I remind her to take off her muddy shoes.

"You'll ruin the bedspread."

Downstairs in the coffee shop, an overpriced tuna salad with too much mayonnaise helps me compose myself. So does the long, hot shower later. I can't hear the sound of the television next door and coming out of the steamy bathroom I cross my fingers. Luck is with me. In 110 Rachel is back.

"Let's make some plans," she says, "Now that we are here we can't afford to waste time. Each hour is precious."

"We've got to organize our thoughts," I say, still annoyed as hell. First, I want to reach the little girl in Rachel.

"Bad girl! Do not come out," is what I want to say, but of course that would be the wrong thing. I try hard not to revictimize the victim, Rachel. Agreeing that we must "settle down and think," I remind Rachel that in the car I must have an adult traveling companion.

"You must be navigator and accurately read the map, calling out ahead where we will turn off." I sound very severe to myself.

"Otherwise, I will have a fit," I explain.

I realize I am asking something of Rachel that many fully developed, educated Americans cannot do. At the same time I must protect myself from another episode of my own East Coast traffic-terror-hysteria-disorder-syndrome.

My plea must have worked, because this morning Rachel and I are sitting in the back of the placid gray, stone church where she hid from Mommy, Daddy and the others. We have made it to our destination with a grown up and familiar Rachel in charge of directions. The ambiance here is in direct contrast to the gloomy black and red stone fortress we just visited across town.

There, we shivered in that giant edifice, towering grimly over the dark corridors and schoolrooms, where nuns educate little children as they did Rachel. That church school loomed high against the decaying tenements which surround it. A Sister let us in when we rang the bell, and grudgingly found Rachel's name in the files, which "you cannot take with you." There was no Xerox, but the stated permission, "You may take information by pencil," allowed us to copy information from the faded paper. We read that Rachel was undersized, as described on the height and weight charts, and "expelled," "unable to benefit" from school. The language spoken in her home was listed as "French." The address of her tenement was that of a house still standing.

My scanty notes, copied from those school records, form a scratchy paper wad in my purse which rests uncomfortably on my lap, here in this cool, safe church retreat. Maybe crossing my ankles chastely will help my body accept my restlessness and the hardness of this shiny pew. I look at Rachel, peaceful in her "sanctuary," and decide not to read over my pencil scrawls in front of her. I will spoil her mood. I haven't often seen her happy, as she looks now. The rosy light from the stained glass window creates an aura around Rachel's head, like that in a painting of a saint. How ironic.

Outside the church, it has become close to noon, sunshiny. From across the street the city hall of this little coastal town looks exactly like an armory. With childish awe Rachel likens it to a European castle.

"It is old and run-down," I agree.

She tells me the town is "picturesque," rather than shabby, and I am to concentrate on the blue sky and the coming-to-life trees. Lilacs in purple and lavender fill the air with sweet scent. However lovely the breeze and the perfumed air, we must go inside this forbidding building to its records department. Down the splintery hall and through two heavy dark doors, we discover a round-faced woman with friendly eyes who agrees to go "all the way" to the basement to help us.

That's where birth certificates from the early forties are kept. Like the library and the newspaper archives, this office is not yet automated. But here we make a find. An official looking paper with large swirling brown ink letters documents Rachel's birth, "at home." The date of documentation is a year later.

"That was not unusual," says the out of breath lady, up from the basement. But she cannot explain why the date of birth is not the day Rachel has always believed to be her birthday. Why would a baby be born, but not recorded? Is Rachel, Rachel? Peculiar. But then, so is our mission. So is Rachel's life. So is Rachel. So am I, for being here.

We have found no record of Rachel's family or her family's "friends."

Today the sun is gently warm on our shoulders, the morning breeze is cool off the blue ocean, just out of sight. Rachel has felt drawn to this cemetery and to a particular cluster of stones.

"I cannot explain why or how. Stop asking me. I don't know."

"Let's go further North, up the coast."

But Rachel cannot bring herself to leave. So we sit on the chill stones quietly, without talk. Hours later she is ready to trudge uphill, bending forward with each step, across the now slippery grass. Rachel hangs her head, watching her feet, forcing each step. The crypt ahead is gray granite, like most everything in this venerable spot. It has double doors and a tiny window. The name over the door spells out H-U-N-T-L-E-Y. Peering through the dusty window, I can just see the Huntleys, lined up at either end of the tiny room, sealed behind marble slabs carved with their names. Little Peeper once drew a picture for me of a building like this. She featured classic

Roman lines for the double doors and even managed to make them look like bronze. That was, of course, before she fused with Lilith and Rachel 2. Dear little despairing, artistic Peeper. How talented she was.

As I turn to look at Rachel, I can see she is... gone. The person who has taken her place reaches for my hand. Pulling me down to sit on the grass beside her, this young lady sobs quietly, chewing the pieces of her hair that float across her face with the spring wind. As tears spill from her eyes, she rubs them away with her fists. Her nose dribbles, unwiped.

A new child, Becky, is with me today. She jars me when she tells me she was buried alive in this very spot , placed in an open grave.

"Before the box is shut, I can see the moon up in the black sky. 'Cause I was caught by him... I ran as hard as I could. The man is wearin' horns. Horns like a deer, and a... I guess a dress made out of skins."

I imagine the moonlight and the child racing across the clearing. No five year old can run swiftly enough to outrace a grown man. "The Great Hunt" may have been sport for the man, and for who knows else. But for Becky, "runnin, hidin", being "caught" and "buried," are all "trials."

"Trials must be passed. I'm scared, Roberta. I'm cold."

Becky shakes, wrapping her arms around Rachel's thin woman's body. Her lips are blue. Minutes pass. Finally, color warms her cheeks, then her trembling mouth.

"Alive. I prove I'm strong." Becky is triumphant. "Smart! I know who the man in the fur thing is. But I will never, never tell."

Rachel is able to soundly sleep in her hotel bed tonight.

"This is the first night I can remember when I have no nightmares nor body pain and my eyes are not hurting. I do not have a headache or stomach ache to wake me."

Next day, Rachel thinks its a good idea to check records at the public school office. So I do what she says, or what someone says. On the copy of her attendance record there is a picture of a squinty eyed little girl, unfamiliar to Rachel, even though her own name is printed under it. This little girl's grades are dismal and her tardies and absences fill up almost all the boxes at the bottom of the page. A handwritten note says Rachel appears to read, but does not speak. Is there something the matter with this child, the paper implies? In those days teachers did not quickly assume parental abuse.

As Rachel studies the notations in the semi-darkness of the old records room, a voice speaks clearly inside her head. What she hears I cannot know, but I can see Rachel listening to something more impelling than the chatter of the records clerk. He is trying to tell her all the details about the night the school burned down, years ago.

"We think it must have started from the janitor who had a gripe..... the School Board... flames thirty feet high.....town was aghast."

"Come to the window," the voice tells Rachel. She obeys, walking directly away from the speaking man, holding her papers before her. On the top sheet, where white sunshine pours in upon it, she can see words forming in bloody red script. The letters spell out "Swan's Heaven," before they run together and drip from the page.

"I have to go there," Rachel whispers to me.

"Go where?" I ask, clumsily wading into the middle of the puddle which is invisible to me.

Rachel pushes me backward, looking disgusted. By my wrist she drags me around the red pool to the old, crackle-finished map on the wall. Straining to see the lettering on the yellowing surface, we find nothing that looks at all like "Swan's Heaven."

"Why Swan's Heaven? What are we looking for?" I whisper.

"A ceremonial spot."

From our hotel room Rachel calls the police. Her voice is strong and her questions clear and forceful. The detective who answers knows the name she gives him.

10

"Yeah, Swan's Heaven. I can get you started and you can ask for directions at the sheriff's office in that area. Look out, though, that you don't get lost. It's deep woods".

We drive though bogs and dunes, along marshes and through dark stands of oak and maple. I babble about how beautiful it must be in the fall with leaves burning scarlet and rust and gold.

"Yes, it is like that, exactly," Rachel says. She is not interested in my small talk and will not pretend. I don't care. I am happy to be away from six lane highways, rain, oil slicks and tunnels, in the open air and "getting somewhere." While Rachel is struggling to stay herself, I am in the middle of an adventure, believing I'm Nancy Drew.

At the rural police station made of half logs and flat limestones, we find a guide. She is six feet tall and not quite that wide-hipped, with a determined-to-find-out kind of curiosity about us and our search. She gives us advice, along with hot tea, then asks questions we won't answer.

"Yeah, I know Swan's Heaven. It's some clearin's in the woods, all surrounded by ponds and lakes. It'll be a community pretty soon. People are thinkin' of movin' in out there. But you couldna have been there in the forties. There wasn't nothin' there then, no houses, nothin'. Just woods. So I don't know how you really remember stayin' there when you was a kid, unless you was campin' with your folks. 'Cause there wouldna been any place to stay. There's still just a few new houses there, but they got hopes. It's a long way from anywheres. At least here, we got a post office."

With her big hand and thick fingers she draws an intricate, carefully executed map in green ink, putting in North and South, East and West, the mountains and the ocean. It looks mysterious and beckoning.

"Wish I could go with you. Even if you won't tell me what it's about. Easy to get lost, so I wish you luck." She grins.

11

This woman is aware we are scamming her. She's smart, as well as wholesome and big. Did she notice Rachel's shaking? If we get in trouble, I'd sure like to have her come get us.

We drive. Miles pile up, as we move through softwoods and along sandy marshes. I am numb, dreaming of home and Sam, when Rachel whispers,"Stop." Through the underbrush, I can see we are on the gravelly shore of a lake, surrounded by sand and trees. The water looks steely grey. White caps, pulled up by the wind, roughen the surface.

"I can't stop on this narrow road, Rachel, so I'm going to have to pull ahead".

The next wide spot is a surprise, a rocky parking lot. We pull in, grateful to the Veteran's of Foreign Wars, whose club house is our stopping place. Inside, a party is going on around the bar. The smell of beer floats off the walls of knotty pine and swirls toward the door. The music from the loud speaker blares, but the laughter is louder.

Past the knot of gray heads Rachel and I walk to the Ladie's room, trying to look like member's wives. As soon as we are relieved, we duck out the back door to the cold and windy water line. Walking the gritty shore, we are too cold to stare out across the water. I don't yet know much about who joined me here on this gravel beach.

Whoever it was does not stay long. Back inside the Veteran's hall, we are invited to sit down and drink strong, hot coffee out of white china mugs. The steam revives us, the heat from the cups is our reward. Over and over, we turn down beers. If these old fellows only knew how much Rachel can drink! I'm tempted to make bets, but that would defeat our purpose. I'm supposed to be helping Rachel get herself together. Listening to the tales of the old days around here, prompted by our questions, I imagine we are subtle and clever fact finders. My girl detective fantasy becomes more vivid. This is exciting.

Al is the fellow with the white whiskers, plaid shirt

and the climbing boots. I'll bet he sends for his clothes from the L.L.Bean catalogue.

"Mysterious doin's at one time."

What kinds of strange occurrences have been part of the history of this shoreline, the Veteran's can't say.

"It's the reputation."

The one in red plaid suspenders, Barney, insists there are no black sand beaches in these parts.

"Ladies, that's in Hawaii, that's the black sand she's asking about, " he says to me, "In Hawaii."

As we walked along the shore, someone in Rachel's head had remembered.

"The sand is black. Find the black sand," that someone begged.

"Aw, come on, have a beer!" the Veterans chorus. But Rachel has to get out of here this moment. Something is overtaking her. Or someone.

"No, thanks." I pause to say goodbye to our hosts, but Rachel disappears through the front door. In the parking lot I find a person curled up in the back seat of our car, someone who looks like Rachel.

"Ashes," she moans. "In a ring. The burnings make ashes, too. Oh, oh, the children burn."

I sit in the front seat, ready to drive away if one of those friendly old fellows comes out of the big wooden door to investigate, but the beery laughter goes on without interruption. From up here behind the wheel I can't see or hear what's being said very well, although I'm sure someone is "coming out" with a memory.

"I'm Seven."

"What? I can't hear you."

"They are tied together, my hands and my feet," she shouts to me.

The story is fragmented, torn from her chattering teeth. The rope connecting her tied wrists and ankles hauled her out of the lake, , back into the boat, she says.

"Just in time," Seven goes on, "cause I choked on the water. That man's face was white." Seven tells me more about the masked man in the black cloak and hood, who threw her into the moon reflecting water. I've got to get out and get closer. As I open the back door of the car, I can see that the child, Seven, is twisted into a tight knot. She looks in great pain.

"My side," she says, holding herself. "I banged it against the boat when he pulled me out."

Body memories torture Rachel now. Rolling from side to side, she clutches her side, her belly.

"I pass the test."

The child's voice continues though gusts of coughing, with a wheezy sound, reedier and shriller than Becky's whispery speech.

"Pneumonia is what I've got. They take me to the bad doctor, Becky's Mommy's friend."

Notes:
Well, Rachel came back to be with me an hour or so later. Back in town, we checked hospital records and were forced to accept the truth:; only one of her many surgeries, illnesses and "accidents" was on file in any authorized hospital or doctor's office.

That time was different. Something happened when a well meaning neighbor "interfered" with Mother and saved the little girl in an attic , found dying from a battered skull .

Notes:
In the margin of my notebook is written in red pencil: Ash and soot are traditional materials used to outline a witch's circle.

It's exciting to see it really standing there. The Victorian house elegantly molders away on this shabby street. Someone in Rachel remembers it, newly painted cream and tan. Inside the elaborate front door with its fancy etched glass, a truck driver paces, waiting to see the doctor. He asks questions about us and about Texas, impressed because we have come "all the ways from the plains."

His doctor was once Rachel's mother's Doc. Rachel explains, "That was before mommy's luck changed. The Mother had a lot of money then and so she got a new doctor."

In his eighties Dr. Brusque still carries on his small practice in the tenement neighborhood, where Rachel lived with her parents. On one special day Rachel walked down the street with her huge mother, waited in this very parlor, thrilled to see more than her own dirt yard and the chain fence which kept her separated from other children.

"What, oh, thank you. I will." The slick haired driver insists Rachel go in to see the doctor before him, even though she has no appointment. I'm surprised. He doesn't look like a gentleman, but he must be, because he is so courteous. I tell him so.

"I know how. My folks came from Portugal to fish here. We're all gents, us fellas."

I can't hear what Rachel and the doctor say to one another, but I can see Rachel holding out a piece of paper. I know it is the faded photograph, a picture of her mother, from years ago. When she steps back into the stiffly varnished waiting room, Rachel is pale and tense.

"He remembers the Mother and me. 'Insistent and hypochondriacal,' he calls her, and he implies... crazy. 'Until that day I had no idea she tried to raise a child,' he said."

Notes:

The stained glass portrait of a devil's face hangs in the front window. We struggle to find a parking place for the dusty Toyota, determined to visit the black painted building, the Witch's shop. Inside, other tourists, dressed as we are in jeans and tennis shoes, look through witch's lore in magazines like "The Green Egg." Dozens of books on the occult and magic fill carved shelves high over head. Books on witchcraft lean on one another. Elaborately wrought knives, swords and scabbards, some of silver or gold, many decorated with semi-precious stones, show off beside crystal balls and shining amu-

15

lets. The purpose of this shop is clearly commerce, but it reflects Salem's interest in the history of witchcraft.

Across the street is the Institute, a dignified building, housing a library filled with newspapers, books and records related to New England history. There, the library staff lady assigned to us refers to the killings of the innocents accused of deviltry as the "Witchcraft Delusion." What an island of sanity she provides! As American citizens, she wants us to be proud that only once did the rule of law break down in the colonies to the extent that well meaning people were hanged for imaginary crimes.

This library has trust-inspiring architecture, a beautiful example of traditional decor. Class, real class. Dark wood, marble sculptures in heroic poses and polished, well dusted brass glow beside the green glass of table lamps. Books, here, smell of real leather.

But Rachel and I can't rest from craziness long.We are here to look through newspapers from the forties, the years in which Rachel became a broken child. The United States of America is coming out of the horror and darkness of the Second World War, the papers say. The concept of individual liberty has been preserved and Americans can now settle into postwar consumerism. What excitement. Hotpoint ranges and Studebakers can be bought. In the black and white ads, women wear hats and long, full skirts, and only men smoke, while doctors proclaim Lucky Strikes are "soothing." There is no mention of the kind of violence we seek to learn about, of the new mind altering drugs from abroad or accounts of peculiar people banding together to violate human decency.

I give up on these newspapers. Moving to the dignified other side of the great room, I leaf through histories. Rachel pays little attention to the notations I have made and I am tired and ready for almost anything else. Beneath my restless fingers is a brief description filed under "Black Mass." The top card is a reference to ceremonies performed by a seventeenth century Abbe on the request of a Madame de Monespan. The account is of interest because there exists genuine evidence of its truth.

Madame was the King's mistress losing influence, daily or nightly, with her Monarch. To win him back magically into her arms, she lay naked upon an altar, while an evil ritual was said over her by a renegade priest. The ceremony culminated in the sacrifice of a baby, whose blood was caught in a chalice. A witness later confessed it was not a living baby, but *an* aborted three month fetus.

"Well, that's bad enough," I whisper to Rachel, as I show her the descriptive paragraph printed clearly on the cardboard, "At least it wasn't a living baby."

Rachel will not touch the paper. Instead she becomes rigid and pale. Now what? Her stiff lips whisper an explanation.

"French."

What am I to say now? So what, French? I'm quiet, thinking I hardly understand anything that is happening on this East Coast exploration. My functions are to drive, remind Rachel to eat and sleep, look through books, follow her as she darts here and there, listen, take notes and wonder. Where did these ideas of the ritual torture of children come from?

British writers claim the most heinous ceremonies of satanic worship came from France, traced back to the worship of the horned nature god. The French blame England. I am reminded the English once called syphilis the "French Pox," just as the French named the ailment "The English Disease." Modern writers suggest that Canada nurtured satanic families among its rebellious Catholics.

Moving along the anthropology shelves, I read Margaret Murray's notion that certain witch cults required a periodic sacrifice of a human representative to the witch's god. The male leader of the coven was that representative. On a Great Sabbat he would appear to his followers in "grand array," dressed in animal skins and a mask or horned helmet.

"Here's his picture. Do look here, Rachel. The Devil who appeared in person at the Witch's Sabbat was simply a man in ritual disguise. A man playing dress-up."

Rachel is standing still as stone. Her voice is hollow and deep as she says, "Fool! The Devil is not the sacrifice. He is the teacher." I know when to back off.

It has been at least an hour since she scorned me. Rachel is resting quietly now, flexibility coming back slowly to her body, while her head rests upon her folded arms on the library table. She looks like a little girl during first grade "quiet time."

Rereading these notes, I wait. I'm hungry, as well as insulted.

In 1735, England, the Witchcraft Act passed and was used as late as 1944, when the final witch was prosecuted in Old Bailey. As the second World War war ended, members of Parliament felt witchcraft was no longer a threat.

But back in the thirties, my own weary looking writing tells me, something magical and secret emerged in private circles, when occult fraternities started up once more. In 1947, sinister Aleister Crowley died quietly in his hotel room and was duly cremated. As a gesture, his ashes were sent to his followers on the East Coast of the United States, where some people held him in high honor. During his lifetime Crowley had been written up as the "Wickedest Man in the World," or "The King of Depravity." Some, on the outside edges of cultism, absolutely believed in his depravity and referred to him as "The Master Theron." That translates as "The Great Beast." Gullible admirers on both sides of the ocean continue to respect his name today.

Gerald Gardner further helped to repopularize witchcraft in the United Kingdom. His rituals were a great success, much discussed by the press. As he posed for reporters, describing the romance of his discoveries, his personal brand of witchcraft, British tabloids began linking witchcraft with Devil-worship. Lurid articles, poorly written, described satanist circles and rituals.

Articles in British newspapers described meetings in which worshippers sacrificed chickens and drank blood, the "blood of the devil." Reporters forgot to mention that great quantities of alcohol, were drunk along with only small amounts of blood. The reports of wild drumming, dancing and sexual orgies sounded like voodoo rather than witchcraft. These incomplete and exciting descriptions were read avidly in the USA.

About that time the English eccentric, Robert Cochrane, became famous, claiming he was a hereditary witch. His dark hair, tan skin and handsome face inspired his followers in France and America to imitate his exotic behavior. Robert generously initiated his young wife, as well as other women followers, into his coven. Unlike the Gardnerian witches, Cochrane chose not to practice flagellation and nudity. Instead, his devotees wore black robes and hoods while they worshiped in the woods around the traditional bonfires. He loved "mystification." Followers who dropped away called his practice of "grey magic" by a simpler name. They claimed he was lying.

Undaunted, Cochrane, excited by his personal influence, began to teach that the Horned God was the ruler of death and 'The Great Beyond'. As the Horned God's powers grew, so did Cochrane's. Soon the ancient god became once again the symbol of male fertility and with his amazing potency he carried "great terror and fearful dread".

Cochrane's rituals were clearly shamanistic. Terror began to follow in Cochrane's footsteps as he preached that "the Old One" was returning to his former importance. Devotees began to leave Cochrane out of fear, claiming he invented ceremonies to satisfy his cruel streak. Robert Cochrane became a specialist, focused on combining pain, sex and the fear of death, his own particuliar interests. He dedicated himself to the Horned God, the Lord of Death, and insisted that the rituals must be done exactly as he decreed.

Rituals were held in wooded hollows in the hills where they could not be seen. Chanting and dancing, "deocil" around the fire, continued until "religious wildness" set in. Together with yells and shrieks, sexual excitement triumphed, until the celebrants collapsed in sweat covered exhaustion.

Eventually Cochrane posed as an all powerful authority and threatened anyone who questioned the brutality of his interpretations. He began to order outrageous cruelties, demanding absolute obedience. Cochrane denigrated anyone who showed fear when he ordered branding or mutilation, so masochistic or sadistic followers cut, burned and humiliated themselves or one another.

Abandoned by those who were still sane, including his wife and family, Robert Cochrane committed ritual suicide on a Midsummer's Eve, as he had proclaimed he would do. In a magic death potion he had designed, he swallowed Deadly Nightshade. His dramatic death was described in detail in newspapers.

Followers in the United States venerated him "as more than a hero." They did not concern themselves with the coroner's opinion of "suicide, while balance of the mind was disturbed." I wonder if Cochrane's admirers carried on his beliefs here, where we are investigating.

It's time to be out the door, my notes with me, and a copy of this article. But here's a further piece of writing I found, by a man named Lugh. He, too, claims he is a witch.

"In America," Lugh writes,"the Hereditary Craft is made up of 'disparate factions', with differing practices. Although these groups 'keep to themselves," there are certain signs that hark back to early practice. 'Sexual induction' is one of them. Power is passed from one person to another in this way and is called 'The First Rite.' There may be a Second Rite, in which the empowered person passes authority to those who have earned it through tests of loyalty and personal strength. Three grades or rites have come down to us through French practice."

The English naming the French again. Heritage and

Rachel's personal history combined. To me, any ritual of "sexual induction" is just plain child abuse, pedophilia with an ancient revered name. Little children cannot resist domination by an older person, so no matter how "traditional" that behavior is, or how revered, it is criminal.

Maybe that's why Gerald Gardner insisted that a novitiate be at least twenty-one before joining his coven. Gerald seemed downright decent enough as cultists and sadists go, although into whippings and fancy costumes. How much could Gardner's rules influence a splinter group of child molesters in America?

It's time to insist Rachel walk with me to our hotel. Hot soup will help us both. Tomorrow we can begin our work again.

I guess the discovery of remembered sites of suffering is too much for Rachel. As Sam predicted, she splits further. Or, let's say, new-to-me personalities emerge, each holding a piece of Rachel's puzzle. Sam and I talked all this over before my puzzling client and I left home. He was readying me.

When a MPD person relapses, or continues to split, there are a variety of reasons. Since personalities are in some ways like real people, some of them may hide out, pretending to be gone so that therapy won't upset their lives (or end them). Like the rest of us, personalities have no desire to be confronted by terrifying memories. Or an alter may stay secret, insisting on separateness or, specialness. One or more may wait until therapy is finished in order to take over. Or an alter who never agreed to therapy in the first place, might feel forced by the other personalities to be treated and finally find a way to rebel.

Perhaps somebody in Rachel holds back, not wanting to be talked into anything, ever. A helper "self" may insist on staying hidden and available for protection. Then, if some alters conspire against others to please me, uncooperative or desperate personalities might come out at any time to stop therapy.

The phenomenon Rachel is experiencing seems to be what is called "layering." Groups of personalities, who have had no presence in the treatment up to now, are suddenly encountered. They may have been so deeply internal, that even Peeper, Lilith and Rachel 1 may not have known them.

Or perhaps they were creations suppressed by Rachel I, Peeper and Lilith themselves, and are now free to appear after hiding away for years.

I don't know what is happening here, but I understand there are so many memories not yet worked through, that too much pain lies in wait for Rachel and her alters.

Whatever the case, Rachel and I are not alone. Tonight, she is afraid of her bed. It is narrow and hard,traditional, and although just a twin, it is elaborate, a dark wooded two poster. The style is not the difficulty.

"I will sleep in the car," she says huffily. When Rachel looks down her nose at me like that she is afraid. "I could never be at rest in a bed of that sort."

She curls up on the window sill and her body slides into a position exactly like that of an barely adolescent girl. Quietly defiant, stretched out lazily, she looks unimpressed by anything.

"My name is Dei." Her voice is husky and insolent.

She volunteers to tell me more than I want to know about having sex with Daddy, just as a homely routine.

"He comes to my bed in the room next to his and Mommy's. But it's all right," she assures me, "It doesn't matter."

Then, with only an eye blink or two, a youngster, Jana, emerges to tell me her name and more about the places Rachel and I have explored this week, through these woods and along these shores.

"You are a good guide," I tell her, and she promises there will be more she can show and tell.

Becky listens in, then emerges to remind me how frightened she was in the cemetery.

"But I showed you the .."

"Crypt, Honey."

"Crypt. Am I good, too?"

"Of course, you are, Becky, and you're brave. I'm sorry I was so cross with you in the car. Please forgive me."

Becky gives me a sweet smile, then makes room for Joey.

"He's our boy," she explains. I hate to see little Becky go. I'm growing fond of her.

In his small boy's voice Joey says his job is to bury the dead baby parts. That seems to be all for Joey, as someone crowds him away from the surface. This emerging person is not a child, but a powerful someone who insists on all of my attention. Her eyes are dark with an angry light, beneath eyebrows drawn together into a fierce scowl. In a upside down grin, her mouth turns toward her chin in a curve, twitching as she tells me her name.

"I wondered when I would meet you, Revenge," I say, "Of course I can understand how much you want to punish all those people who hurt you."

Revenge looks confused. She knows little about Rachel's tortures or "all those people." I was wrong and overstepped. Angry Revenge seems to exist for one scene only out of all of events in Rachel's painful life. She repeats her story over and over like a recording, in the exact words she used just a moment ago.

"I use the knife on him, not on the baby. They didn't know I could kill him instead. There he stands behind me, looming up in his black and red, his paint and gold. At this moment I hold the knife high. I wheel. I strike. See the blood. He bleeds as others do, from many places. See his blood smear and dribble as they drag him away. I destroy him. I am more powerful."

Then silence. Concentrating hard, I prompt.

"What's happening now, Revenge? Do you kill him? Is he dead?" But Revenge is gone.

"My name' is Mara," the woman in front of me says. Suddenly her face twists into a screaming, widemouthed mask of pain. Mara's hands twist around each other, her arms rise high above her head.

"I am tied, tied to the bed," she moans to me, "They use

23

my body and my mouth. The men are here pushing one another aside. I must suffer them. I must suffer and satisfy. Punished. My rebellion. They will wear out their lust and their rage or I die."

"Mara, Mara!" I am horrified by her expression, the tortured movements of her body, bound by invisible thongs.

"Oh, poor Mara. Listen, Mara, it's over now, and you don't die. It's over." Mara fades into quiet.

I ask, "Who knows most about Rachel?"

My own Rachel opens her eyes. She has come back to help paste her story together. She speaks clearly, softly.

"I'm to tell you what happens in the tenements and later, when someone rich pays for the car in which I am taken for ceremonies. No one else we ever knew before owned a car. Never, never. I ride with a white faced person, whose eyes look black like holes. That is a mask made out of cloth and paint, I know. Some days later Daddy buys a car, too, so after that I ride in Daddy's shiny black automobile. It smells like leather and wax. I hate cars."

After a long pause Rachel goes on sadly.

In the country, where the trees are close together, children are kept in log stockades. Those are fences. I am not like the other children, but always separate. At home I am behind the high wire fence and in the woods I am shut up somewhere with no light, no windows. Always shut away. I am tested, tested to prove I am special, a chosen child. Ordeals. I prove I am gifted. 'Gifted' means I live. The other little children die."

Tears spot Rachel's shirt front. She pays no attention to the wet spots, but I do. I remember well the years when she couldn't feel.

"I am back to tell you about my birthday. That memory is given to me.Take notes. Quickly. Quickly! I remember. I have a party, but I know no one there. The people who come to celebrate me are all "friends" of Daddy and Mommy's. I have seen them before somewhere, somehow... I shiver when I see the people in my

24

mind's eye. After the party... something happens that separated me from the...cult. You say cult. I have always said, 'the family.'"

"Rest, Rachel. You have worked enough for today."

"After that I only remember the sweat shop."

"Stop, Rachel, I insist. You are worn out."

But Rachel is already asleep, clothes and all, in the bed she could not bear to lie upon. I take off her shoes and cover her with her raincoat. Lying on my bed late into the night, I outline future treatment. "Don't worry", I say to myself.

"I can sleep on the plane. I need to organize my thoughts, now."

Tomorrow is the important day when perhaps I'll find out just how Rachel distorts her past. I imagine, like all of us, she must exaggerate or distort her memories. Otherwise what the alters have told me might be literally true. I don't want it to be.

We plan to meet the aunt with the crinkled scar on her abdomen, the one who "had a falling out" with Rachel's parents. She is Auntie Lonnie, Daddy's sister.

Outside the steamy Fish House restaurant, "the Uncle" drops Lonnie off, but won't come in himself. Over and over, Rachel's white haired Aunt expresses shock at seeing us. She wears lace up shoes and what we used to call a house dress under her parka.

"I didn't know that after all these years you would even remember my name. I haven't seen you since, I figured it out last night, 1949. Think what a long time ago that is!"

Over a stoneware bowl of chowder thick with clams and floating a large rectangle of butter on top, Rachel tells Aunt Lonnie about her daughters and reveals part of her problem life.

"I can't remember my childhood, Auntie Lonnie. I guess I have amnesia. Maybe you can tell me what you remember about me, or about Daddy and Mommy."

The look Aunt Lonnie gives Rachel is hard to read. Is she frightened?

"Excuse me," she says "I have to go to the Ladies'." Rachel and I wait quietly.

"She's getting her courage up," Rachel says.

"Well," Aunt Lonnie wheezes on her return. "Your folks was a crazy young couple, all right, crazy about each other. That is, your Mom was goofy about my brother. Sixteen years old! I'm sorry to be the one to tell you this, Rachel, but they had to get married on account of you, 'cause all of a sudden there you was. That's just how it was. You know, back then, well...Maybe it was a mistake. Iris didn't take care of the baby, I mean, of you, and so me and some of the other neighbors helped out. But your Mom and Dad was always fighting and folks found out they was hard work to be around when they was drinking, you know. They'd get awful jealous, you see, and throw things.

Well, I never did understand my brother, anyway. He was a skinny little kid and he was mean. Tormented cats and dogs and set fires. Got people scared of him, cause you never knew what he was going to do next. I guess now we'd take him to a brain doctor, but back then we was all so poor, nobody much went to a real doctor. Except your Mom. She was there all the time, telling the Doc something was wrong with her. Well, we didn't take my brother anywhere, just hoped he'd get over whatever it was that was making him so pesky. We figured that something got messed up when he was born cause Mom was in labor with him for three days and nights and when he come out he was most dead, and tiny, such a little thing...and well, he never was just right. Violent, that's what he was. We got afraid.

But you know what? After he was married he was the one who was scared, scared of your Ma, I think, when I look back. She was such a big woman, twice as big as him, and she'd scream something awful. Put that bad hole in his forehead throwing the iron. When the police started coming regular, why, one night your Uncle and me just moved over to the other side of town.

I can remember way back to when Iris was just crazy

to marry Roy. She'd come over to my family's rooms nearly every day and finally she sure did get him. She was big then too, just a girl, but big and fat, both. You sure don't take after her. You're a nice looking woman, and thin, so its hard to think that you're her daughter.

I guess I got to tell you the truth. None of us much liked your Mom, even when she was a kid, and we was just sick when Roy had to marry her. We already had one person who was trouble and that was him, and now we was going to have two. I hope I don't hurt your feelings, Rachel, but that's the truth. As soon as Iris married Roy she didn't want to work in the shop no more, so one day she got in a big fight with me and got herself fired. Dragged out of there, I guess you heard. I still got the big scar on my belly. I was staying away from your folks by then, on account of what I already told you and what I heard. I been told that Iris wouldn't let Roy even see our own mother any more. As for me, I didn't want to spend any time with Roy anyway, let along Iris.

But I remember seeing you, a poor baby shut in the yard, all alone, trying to get a peek through the fence. I guess things got better for you after you got to go out to school, huh?"

"Auntie Lonnie, do you recall anything about a doctor Mommy took me to see? The one who took out my appendix?"

Thinking back over my notes, I understand Rachel is trying to find out more about the doctor who kept anesthetic from her.

"Just tied me down," she said.

Therapists hear from multiple personality clients that, sometimes, there is a personality who never goes under, even when anesthesia is given. Imagine that.

But I must carefully follow this conversation, and not allow my thoughts to drift.

"Well, there was a bad doctor we knew about cause Iris went to him. I can't think of his name right now. He was awful though, folks called him a quack. He sure liked to hurt people. Now I think he was...you know, high, like on something...maybe drugs, but of course we didn't know nothing about that then.

Boy, your Mom liked him a lot. She had went to the good doctor lots of times, too, back when we lived near, but he didn't tell her what she wanted to hear so she took up real close with the quack. There was always something wrong with her, but not what she thought and the quack didn't charge her nothing. She took him home with her...to visit. You know."
Auntie takes a bite and rests her voice.

"I wonder if he was a real doc? Anyway, he sure was strange, but you know what? He got richer than anything. About the time your Mom and Dad bought all that stuff. I'd moved a little while before, so I didn't keep track like I would have had I been living right next to them. Iris and Roy, your folks, started going out with some real expensive people. Fancy clothes and a car. Didn't have time for us no more, but by then that was just all right with us. We'd had enough of the screaming and hitting."

"Auntie, do you have any idea who paid for my Catholic school? When I was little I thought it must have been you."

"Oh, no, not me. I wouldn't, anyway. That scary old place. Not me. Besides, I never had that kind of money.

Say, I'd appreciate it if when you run into your Mom and Dad you just don't say anything about us getting together like this. Your Uncle don't want them to know. I guess I said some pretty bad things about them today, but that's how I feel. To tell you the truth, I don't ever want to see them or hear about them no more. After your Mom stuck me like she did, I had enough.

But I can still see your little face back of that fence and you wanting out so bad. So this is hush hush, if you know what I mean. I know they're still alive, and that's all I want to find out. I do wish you luck, Rachel, and I sure don't blame you for forgetting your Mom and Dad the way you have and that dirty old house way down there on the bad side of town. I'm glad you forgot. I'm going home now."

With a wave to me Auntie slides out of the booth and out the door where Uncle is pacing up and down. Our booth seems very quiet. In a little while Rachel and I will take up her life again, but not until after I have a vegetable plate.

"Hold It," I warn. "You can skip food, give in to your damned old anorexia, but your therapist insists on a more normal life for herself."

This is a warm place to talk through what we have heard, but Rachel needs to tell about her one romance while she remembers. She is in touch with an alter. I never know what is coming next. Just once I would like to be in charge of the conversation, but... I write:

Notes:
Her date, who is to become her husband, picks his new girl up at her tenement, but does not look directly at Mommy wearing her dirty transparent nightgown. Once out the door, Rachel's formal courtship consists of two nights out drinking and one episode of forced sex.

"Let's see," she reminiscences, "the first night I try seven drinks; a screwdriver, a martini, a manhattan, a gin and tonic, a margarita, a stinger, a bourbon and water and a rum and coke, but I do not get even a little drunk."

Her startled boyfriend loses status with his friends, when she easily drinks him under the table. The next day, some of the children in her head complain they are sick and have been unconscious. Rachel on her second date becomes more considerate to them, and drinks only two beers. End of notation.

It appears we have all the information we can find along the Atlantic for now. It's time for Texas and home. I have returned the rental car through the slippery rain and the roaring-down-on us traffic. Cramming all the little bags into two large ones made checking the luggage through easier. On boarding, we discover our seats are in the tail of the plane next to the restrooms. Here on the aisle, people bump each other as pushy lines of restless people already form. If I can keep my elbow in, I can sleep anyway. I can't remember being so tired or so eager to see Sam. I hope I can show him these notes systematically, and not just blurt it all out at once. If I do babble, he will get analytical and spoil my story. Excitement and relief may rattle me, but I want to impress him with my know-how and clinical poise.

There will be much to do. Time for medication again, while the alters are on such a merry go round. Rachel and I will have to make a new map of her internal geography, so we can chart recently emerged alters. I will need to interview each one, discover its function, help solve its problem, encourage her or him to be cooperative with me and friendly to Rachel . I may have to convince somebody inside, one of her saviors, to stop saving Rachel at all costs. Rescue entities are so intense and exaggerated. Their judgement is often bad, because they have so little experience at living outside. Each personality must eventually be integrated, even the ones filled with hate and lust. Disowning them or trying to drive them away will not work. Rachel needs their strength and energy. These particular alters parade themselves as reflections of Rachel's torturers, but underneath they are suffering children, theoretically only six, seven or eight years old. At the same time, these kids actually can be dangerous because of genuine conviction, they are evil. They are fascinated with knives, torture and killing.

I want to know which personalities are still tormenting Rachel after all our work. Together we must influence them to stop giving her torturous headaches, painful ulcers and throbbing muscle spasms. Who are the internal persecutors who keep her suffering?

In January Rachel will no longer be a multiple. She will be afflicted with a new name for her condition," Dissociative Identity Disorder." Will that help?

Our take-off is smooth. Rachel is asleep before me and she is dreaming. Another nightmare, I suppose.

Two

MPD is an experiment of nature that provides us insight into the range of possibilities for the human condition and a window into the psychobiological linkages between the mind and body...We need to take advantage of the lessons MPD offers rather than engage in meaningless debates about whether it is 'real'.

Frank W. Putnam
*Diagnosis and Treatment
of Multiple Personality Disorder*

Huddled, arms around bony knees, the child crouches trembling on the cold floor. In a corner of the dark empty room of her prison a small black candle burns, casts a swollen silhouette on unpainted walls. From far away the girl hears chanting. She waits. Mother has ordered her to be here. Mother commands absolute obedience.

As Chosen child she is bathed and anointed with special oil carefully applied over her skinny body, in readiness for consecration. Chuckling and clucking, colossal Mother slides the long, loose fitting white gown over the child's naked torso.

Now the girl hunches deeper over her bare feet. This lonely room, damp and drear, excretes a slow, energy stealing chill. Weakness quiets the little girl's body. As her heart beat slows, her thoughts leave her quietly in peace. She is hushed, indifferent.

She has fasted, as Mother ordered.

"No improper substance must enter my body to make it impure. I must be free from adulteration. Tainted offerings cannot be sacrificed."

31

The child's gray shadow slithers lower on the wall as she droops. Black wax oozing from the melting candle, slides into a black puddle smeared on the concrete floor. Time, too, slants, runs into a puddle. The candle, burned away now, allows blackness to settle softly upon her. So quiet, she, too, is a burned out candle. Melted away.

A tilting crack of blue light shocks her like a shriek. Through the open door, someone looms against the glow. It is the Messenger. The girl wills herself to stand, but cannot. The man's giant hand, closing on her arm, lifts her like a frightened kitten hoisted by a cat mother.

Along the murky hall, the acolyte steps rhythmically, deliberately, his black robe brushing his ankles with a scratching sound. A hood hides his eyes. Looking up as she is dragged along, the girl sees a pointed chin, covered with wiry black hairs.

Even with his tight hold, the little one stumbles up peeling wooden stairs. The shuffle sound of her uneven footsteps is drowned by chanting. A song peals out, nearer, pulsing. The child hears rhythmic knocking, then a deep hollow pounding, with a metallic echo. Sheet metal doors squeal open. She is pulled inside the place of secret worship.

She wakes. The child is alone, sick, bleeding. Shut in, deep in the shadows somewhere, insects crawl over her chilled feet. There is vomit on the floor.

Three

Rachel is caught up in one of her nightmare spells. I hope our fellow passengers believe she is simply sleeping. I close my eyes to erase the signs of strain I have seen in the mirror this week. How long have I been struggling with Rachel and her uncovering? Six, or was it seven years ago, when she became important to me, more challenging than just another student. In class she sat in the back row and refused to talk whenever we practiced self-disclosure. I remember how much I disliked her.

I say to myself, "Here comes that scowly Rachel woman." Clearly the little lady with the frown wants something from me. She's waited until everyone else has left and now appears determined. I'll listen to whatever she has to say, but from her expression it will probably be another complaint. Is she delivering the usual demand from the back row delegation? I'll bet it's either too hot or too cold back there or they can't hear what is going on.

No, I'm wrong about Rachel. It must be difficult for

her to ask to see me professionally. I can tell she strongly disapproves of everything I stand for. She even sniffs
through her nose when she has to talk face to face with
me.

"I'm sorry, Rachel. I'm full up with clients right now,"
I say, "But if you'll call me at my office, I'll find an opening as quickly as I can."

What a surprise coming from this thin little lady, so
desperately afraid of the high degree of intimacy in this
class. I expect her to drop soon. There's always a student
or two who can't tolerate this kind of honesty and fun.

At my home my answering machine whispers Rachel's tinny message, reminding me to look for an appointment time. I'll avoid her if she will do the same for
me. But, two weeks from now, on a late Sunday afternoon, I'll have an opening. We'll see what she does
when I offer that. Until then I'll forget about her.

Four

"Devils are a category of angels that slipped. There is a radical distortion there. They don't think right. They don't love right. Something that was created good, went wrong."

Father John Navone
Pontifical Gregorian University, Rome

Exactly on the hour, my potential client, Rachel, rings the doorbell. As I open the front door, I am comforted by the pleasant importance of my waiting room behind me. It's friendly. What a relief it is for me to work at home. I am a happy woman. No more plastic office cubbyhole in a busy medical clinic for me. No pervasive medicine smells. I have escaped the scurrying men and women in white coats and their bitter competition for a parking place.

This territory is my own. Like the '60's ladies in old issues of the Ladies Home Journal, I cut and arrange fresh yellow roses, feeling gracious. The flowers look lovely reflected in a hall mirror. I'm busy with clients and reading my therapy books. I like to remind myself I'm a professional and firmly believe I fit an 80's model of femaleness.

It's not that I can't function as a hostess, I still do. Waiting for me, a client can rest on my living room couch, if he chooses. In summer I hand out ice water, in glasses chilled in the freezer. To help people feel cared for, herbal teas, warm and fruity, are appropriate for

35

winter, and can be sipped in an easy chair next to the brown, rock fireplace. The smell of peppermint or apple, combined with the crackling of the fire, has to be therapeutic. I believe a healing atmosphere will speed along their work of recovery, because my genuine interest is in the people who come.

Clients hurt emotionally, of course. One man this morning needs to leave behind a person he once loved. Another man experienced the ripping pain of being left. A woman worries about a child. A boy is unexplainably sad. I want to help these likeable people. At last I am dealing with "problems in living," not the "disease model" of mental illness.

So here is Rachel, still insisting on biofeedback. She believes it is important to be "scientific," I'll bet, because a genuine doctor, a real M.D., has told her to "have it." Why can't she drop her insistence and accept my "no?"

"I don't 'do' biofeedback." No machines for me. But I can provide relaxation therapy which works, too. Improvement over anxiety problems is consistently reported, especially in stress related physical problems, like hypertension or migraine headaches. The results give us all reason to be optimistic.

Still standing at my door, trying not to argue with her, I can give her some encouragement.

"Rachel, the good news is that you can teach your body to feel better even without biofeedback machines."

Rachel appears to be an out-of-touch person. Too taut. Overcontrolled. Frightened. She will probably resist trance induction methods. In that case, I may have to listen to endless physical complaints, session after session.

Clients with little insight talk only about physical problems and ignore their emotions, unable to recognize negative feelings in themselves. I intend to teach them to enter into a trance state, at will, to get in touch with a deeper part of themselves, as Milton Erickson did. But real hypnotizability is inborn, a talent only an occasional client possesses. Those folks are a piece of cake for a hypnotherapist. They already know how to go into Alpha.

In many ways Rachel is the "wrong kind of client." But I might take a chance on her if she will take a chance on me.

"Systematic relaxation lessens. Pain from low back tension, colitis, or ulcers sometimes tends to drop away." I hope I'm not preaching here in the doorway. I'd better not oversell. I won't promise an amazing cure for anything.

"Will you come in now?"

Rachel stands still. Small boned, frail, transparent, she shines with a tremendous internal energy. Frowning, she finally steps inside, walking awkwardly down the hall to my beloved office. Rachel smells of soap and vanilla. Her hair is light brown and curly. From moment to moment her face shadows or glows. It's a winter day, of no concern to us, since we are citizens of the hot Southwest. It's still eighty degrees out. I have the air conditioning running on low.

Nevertheless, Rachel is dressed in a wooly turtleneck shirt, a sweater and two jackets, one short, one long. Her long sleeved sweater is ruffled. Now I remember Rachel always wears ruffles and high, severe lady-like necks to class. Under her wool slacks I'll bet anything she is wearing panty hose and a girdle. She walks stiffly.

Through the many layers of cloth covering her body still has little roundness, no hint of womanly curves. Narrow Rachel looks swaddled.

Here in my office she pauses, surveys the walls, pale disapproval on her face. Sitting rigidly, she glances about her, her mouth severe. I notice her back does not touch the back of the chair.

"If she is a genuine grouch, I won't take her," I promise myself.

When I work with clients, I rest in my father's faded red leather chair. It comforts me while I listen to their painful stories. The chair is worn where my Dad's hands and head rested over many years. Across from me, an Early American couch, covered in mustard-colored linen, squats heavily on a dark brown vinyl floor. This office was an extra bedroom. Now it is a "shabby genteel" therapy den. The coffee table is too large for the room, I know, but I don't shop for furniture. I've tried to care more about things than people and roses, but often I am unaware of my surroundings.

There is one possession of mine that I look at carefully each time. The cubist painting over the couch on the other side of the room depicts the bent and twisted figure of a mother. She has a green pointed face. On her lap she holds a little girl with what may be three legs. I'm attracted to this picture because it is strange, mysterious, provocative. Most people never see it at all.

Rachel's glances dart over my new volumes on child abuse, then move to my face. She says nothing.

"So, you're here, Rachel. I didn't believe you'd really come," I say, making a start. I feel awkward, tongue tied and thoroughly uncomfortable.

"In class I thought we weren't friendly. Are you sure I am the right therapist for you?"

Doubts about Rachel stir me. Referral is a way out for me. Preferably not to one of my friends. Looking at me carefully, Rachel nods. The nod is a yes.

So our adventure begins, an ordeal from which will grow a friendship requiring tremendous effort on both our parts.

Among Rachel's unusual speech mannerisms, I'm aware of her broadened A. Her refined Eliza Doolittle diction sounds overly cultured, contrived and just plain phony. Has she taught herself to speak from an etiquette book? Her hyperfemininity is expressed through ruffles and frills. Her firmly erect carriage and ladylike demeanor is distinctive, if not odd, in this casual, heavily perspiring Texas city. We wear boots and jeans. For dress we put on sequined satin shirts. I'm used to elegance, god-awful gaudiness or Western casual, but not the look of a nineteenth century governess. Rachel is a Mary Poppins lost in the tumble weeds.

"I understand, Rachel, from your call, you have four daughters. You've been active in your church, a superior student, a diligent worker. Does this sound accurate?" I sound stuffy, inhibited by this "nice" lady.

Rachel's frown softens when her children are mentioned.

"Yes, and yes again. I have four little girls. Melissa, Rebecca, Susan and Katherine. Their ages are nine, eight, five, and three. They are refined children. Each has red hair. They are all virtuous girls."

Virtuous? Back to you, Rachel, I think, thrown for a loop.

"How can I be of help to you?" This fussy, lady-like woman is not at all my cup of tea. Rachel makes me nervous and I'm the clinician who has training to keep her cool. Do I want to involve myself further with her?

However, I'm fascinated by the physical tension Rachel displays, embodying the old term "body-armor."

What could have happened to Rachel to turn her into such a tension-ridden size four?"

Looking upset, Rachel struggles with my question. Her shifting physical rigidities dominate the interaction between us. Still I avoid the obvious, too uncomfortable to be direct or honest with her.

I can't make myself say, "You appear to be in spasm, Rachel. What's the matter?"

"Tell me, more specifically, why you're here, please," is the best I can do at the moment.

"While I do not mind being here, Doctor, I have to admit I have been sent by my physician. I have pain in my lower abdomen and in my legs. My neck gives me agony. Hideous headaches keep me from sleeping. Or eating. My doctor tells me you will overcome my stress for me, control it."

"I can't do it for you, but I can help you relax."

Why am I so unresponsive? Is her anxiety contagious?

"Have you been in therapy before, Rachel?"

"Oh, no. No. No and no. Of course not. I've always been able to cope perfectly well. My church is a great blessing to me. I have a dear husband who loves me exceedingly."

What stilted language. Rachel's voice is soft, sweet, hollow, monotonous. Lifeless.

"I have all that life can afford. I am a terribly ungrateful person to complain, I know. My doctor thoughtlessly implies I cause my own illness. I do not. He does not understand. I am constantly afflicted. Things go wrong with my body with no rhyme nor reason. I have seen this same doctor for some years, but now he suggests I discontinue coming to him."

"Hmmmm." When in doubt I give a Rogerian murmur and wait.

"My doctor says I'm depressed."

Any admission of vulnerability must be especially difficult for her. Rachel is so perfect, so superior to the rest of us. Is this woman finally conceding powerlessness? I imagine how she struggles to keep from lapsing into even more severe depression.Somehow, physically, her body is acting out some hormonal messages from..... what? A damaged psyche?

But for now it appears I must listen to the wonderful make-believe world she has created.

"I see. Rachel, tell me a bit more about your husband. You refer to him with such affection."

"Well, he is very strong, a powerful big man. And tall. He is careful of me. He drives me wherever I need to go. He always knows what to do when I am in need. My husband will do anything, anything for me. I trust and revere him."

Rachel's listless voice murmurs on and on. Her mate is stronger than Atlas, wiser than Soloman, more generous minded than Galahad. Perfect in every way. Like Rachel, herself. If everything is so wonderful, why is she such a wreck?

I remind myself not to comment.

"My husband is the real reason I am here, Doctor. I strive never to think about myself. I do not want him to be upset. I attempt to be cheerful always, to overcome my pain. But he knows I am suffering. I must cure myself quickly. I must! It is wrong, wrong for me to worry

40

him."

Rachel trembles. Her eyes pale to grey.

"My Goodness! I can see how much you want to please him." I feel hypocritical. From whence comes my archaic outcry of "My Goodness!?" I haven't uttered anything like that since I practiced exclamations appropriate for the Woman's Movement. Exclamations with strength like "Bullshit!"

Rachel's aura of goodness, virtue, thoughtfulness and piety are striking. What motivates all this sugary self-lessness? Low self esteem? Feelings of unworthiness?

I have no idea of the monstrous evil hidden in Rachel. I'm confused by her superficiality, yet suspicious of her. In sweetness and light people sometimes hide a dark side, barely masked by a veneer of exaggerated socially rewarded behavior. Loudly protesting their hatred of the cruel and grotesque, they are nevertheless fascinated by pain. The mask of sanity expresses itself through exceptional concern about acting morally, properly. Having a keen sense of conformity to the trappings of society, these people exhibit exemplary behavior to others.

Their need for approval, and ability to second guess is so great, others do not comprehend their perversion of good into evil. We cannot easily understand these severely damaged creative spirits or their morbid fears. And we may not sense danger in time to save ourselves.

Rachel cannot help me know the truth about her. She is lost in her illusions.

An hour later I walk with Rachel past the package. It lies in the sun on my blue and yellow Mexican tile steps. In the car parked at the curb, Rachel's husband waits.

I want to meet this admirable man about whom I have heard so much in a short time. He must be a paragon, his eyes alight with intelligence and kindness. Surely he will have a handsome patient face. Unfortunately, he seems ordinary to me, just another guy. One with a trace of alcohol on his breath.

In my kitchen I take time to open the box I have brought inside with me from the patio steps. With a par-ing knife I cut the twine and peel back the soggy cardboard.

Inside, the disintegrating little body, eyelids sealed, fingers and toes sloughing away, is tacked onto an upside down cross. The odor is unforgettable. Police say the ugly, baby-like thing has been stolen from a hospital.

Five

*"i was a teenage creature
tonight there's a werewolf moon
come and hold my hairy hand
down at the black lagoon."*

Ric Masten, *Poet*

I like my clients, except for the fanatics. If I remain uneasy with a client more than a session or two I refer that person to another therapist. I'm beginning to know when I cannot work well with someone. I want to be effective for their sakes, and at the same time enjoy my work. Sam gives me permission to pass an occasional person on to someone else, but he sticks it out with his hard cases. He says that's how he forces himself to go on learning.

The client with me, here in my office, is my favorite today, a soft hearted investigator attached to the police department. He wants to quit his job.

"I won't follow the rules any longer. I've discovered my mission in life and the regs get in my way."

He pours out his disgust about his assignment to Devil worship investigation. Roger's voice is grating, his pitch uneven, grinding out his words. He is immensely angry.

"In America the worship of Satan is protected by the First Amendment. It guarantees freedom of religion. So only when worshippers commit crimes can I do anything about it. Only then." Roger actually snarls.

43

"Groups committing ritual crimes are mostly teens and a few people in their early twenties. Sometimes there will be one, maybe two sickies. Weirdo older people."

"You don't sound like you today, Roger. Language. 'Sickie'?. 'Weirdo'? I used to think of you as someone big on personal rights."

"Sure, I still am. Kid satanist crimes are just vandalism anyway, usually graffiti, most often on churches. Cemeteries get broken into. There's damage done to some graves or mortuaries. Big deal. But here's my other new word, Roberta. Depraved."

" 'Depraved'. Strong."

"Before now, I've had no particular reason to deplore satanism. I only read about it rather idly. I thought it was just kid stuff for emotionally retarded grownups. You know, I'm cool. But now I need to figure out what's my next move. I've got to untangle my thinking, Roberta. Help me. I'm going to have to go beyond the limits of my job."

As a psychotherapist I learn from my clients about the world out there. From me, they learn what's going on inside of them. Tonight, this pleasant, overly-polite lawman talks his troubles out to get some relief. He needs a new personal definition of what constitutes a crime. In police department records satanic mischief is listed only as "general vandalism" and that's not enough for Roger.

"Sometimes animal mutilations have specific marks indicating a particular cult. Once in a while the victim is a horned animal," Roger says, "but usually it is a cat. Around here large numbers of dogs are found ritualistically killed. Pet dogs are easily available, you coax them and they come to you, happily. Dogs are dumb, but ritualistic criminals are not. Hard to catch, they know what they do is wrong. They're careful not to leave evidence behind."

Scowling, Roger tells me there are three types of satanists. He counts them out on his fingers, to make sure I am paying careful attention.

"One: high minded New Age worshippers, intellectually atwitter with artsy   medieval symbolism. Two: "werewolves," that is, teenagers fascinated with satanism. Three: dangerous secretive cults. And my fellow cops don't know the difference."

I have a satanic dabbler in my psychotherapy practice, a blotchy faced kid named Philip. Maybe I can learn more about him from Roger.

"That's fascinating stuff, but much of it I can't take seriously."

"I can. I'm talking about harm to humans."

"Are you trying to scare me? I don't like this."

" It's time to be scared." Roger is firm. We have gone ten minutes over our therapeutic hour. My next client is waiting. I walk Roger to the door.

"Goodnight, Roger. See you next Wednesday. Feel free to call me. Remember to eat, sleep. Play with your kids."

Before he was a cop, Roger experienced two episodes of seious bipolarity, highs and frighteningly severe lows. It's important to remind him to take care of himself. People who look strong like Roger are sometimes vulnerable.

In thinking about satanism, I can see there are some reasons for the resurgence of interest in its practices. There are a growing number of nonconventional religions arising, as Americans seek to find expression for their spiritual feelings. Hundreds of cults or groups exist that have nothing to do with the occult or with satanism.

Witchcraft is growing as an old religion is redefined, new again. Often confused with satanism, Wicca is a religion about nature and the preservation of the environment. Reverence for life is a major tenet.

Mutilation of cattle and domestic animals has always been a source of consternation to ranchers and farmers in our parts, but in the past, it has been attributed to animal predators, not to satanists. Satanic symbols, like inverted crosses, bloody altars and pentagrams have been found in many places recently around our city.

However, there is no hard evidence of kidnapping of

children for ritual purposes, even though there are certain sick persons who "confess" to taking part in satanic ceremonies, either as perpetrators or as victims. These folks never provide any corroboration of their stories. If there is a genuine threat from satanism, it could be from the recklessness of small bands of mostly teenagers, possibly led by a sociopathic or psychopathic individual. These people could be foolishly dangerous to themselves and others, especially if they are using or distributing drugs.

Still, many of their narratives about satanic abuse are published and distributed by ultra rightist Christian religious publishing houses. Maybe its the Super Christians keeping satanism going.

I am angry, too, about the therapists who seem to jump to conclusions and dramatically spread these stories. Is treatment of satanic abuse becoming the latest wrinkle in psychotherapy? I think there is far too much accusation of child sexual abuse going on and innocent people are being unfairly accused. Families are destroyed by reckless charges of sexual exploitation by Daddy or Mommy. And now we are accusing them of trucking with satanism. What a terrible charge to make.

What is a reasonable position to take on this question? I talked through my hat when I was still innocent and ignorant. I was lucky then and foolish.

Philip, my half-baked devil worshiper, is a high school freshman. His manner with me is stiff, formal, but he's up front with his ideas.

"I began my enmeshment with Satan playing with a Ouija Board at a party."

Sometimes pedantic, Philip imitates his stuffy father's style of communication. Dad is the Chair of the Religious Studies Department in one of our Texas' most fundamentalist private colleges. Other times, Philip is all enthusiastic kid. Fitting squarely into adolescent tradition, he loves to be scared silly and rebellious at the same time.

Pimpled and muscularly underdeveloped, Philip,,

now, has found admiring companions, his fellow spooks.

"You should see the other kids. I didn't think it was the Ouija Board doing it, the magic talk, Dr. Richards. But secretly I believe there is something sinister happening. It's so mysterious. I don't know any kids who don't want to know about this stuff like I want to. I quit going to church when I learned about Satan.

My Mom listens to what I believe sometimes, although she doesn't agree. That's why she brings me here to see you, you know. My Dad would kill me if anybody really told him about me. All he knows is that I'm different. If you tell him, I better warn you.. .. Uh.... Someone could get hurt. You'd better not pass on what I tell you!"

Philip's face is red, his jaw tight. This kid is passionate.

"O.K., I promise, Philip. I'll keep my mouth shut. The rules of therapy say I can't tell, anyway. Confidentiality, remember? Of course, I have to do some warning, myself. If you tell me of plans to harm someone, I'll have to warn that person of danger. That's a rule, too."

We're off and running. Philip is eager to talk about his obsession. Six friends, boys, meet for rituals. On special nights they worship in the Greasewood Preserve, outside town, or come together in parks. Sometimes they meet behind the YMCA on the West side of the city. This last meeting place strikes me as funny, but Philip is solemn.

At worship ceremonies there is an older man, treated as leader and given much respect. A bonfire and a chant are part of the ceremony. When chanting, Philip feels himself changing, lighter on his feet, taller. He loves the expansive sensation repetition of ritual sound creates in him. Yet an appalling secret torments this sweetly ugly boy.

"I beat up an old lady."

But at the next session Philip tells the truth. "I didn't really do it. But I thought about it. And then I felt like I had done it."

"Thoughts and deeds are not the same, Philip. Please

47

always remember, thoughts are just thoughts." I lean toward him and squeeze his hand.

The kid's relief is tremendous. He's not heard this before. Philip holds himself very stiff and won't let himself cry, but his face is red.

Next time we meet he looks rounder, softer, more relaxed. I wonder if Philip will ever be handsome? I hope so. Someday, I'll mention a good dermatologist.

"We talk around the bonfire, about pleasing Satan," Philip says.

"Sometimes we sacrifice a cat, so the spirit can go to him. I intend to drink the blood of the next cat and eat some of its heart. Raw."

Philip's voice is still strong, insistent. Yet he spends long minutes looking down at the floor. At our first session he had unshakable 'religious' fervor. He stared directly at me, daring me to differ with him, youthfully dogmatic, fiercely insistent in his beliefs. He wanted me not only to understand him, but to agree with him. No deal.

"Satanism may be dangerous for some kids, but not for me. I know what I'm doing! Satan gives me security. He's always there for me."

Philip is silent for a few minutes. Silence is a good sign.

"O.K., my friends are secretive, and yes, you're right, they're angry kids. They have a right to be angry. Its a lousy world! But I don't think they're more rebellious than most kids. I think they're realistic. Toughminded. They don't care whether they live or die."

"I'm impressed."

"I like my friends angry. And I like 'black' music."

Together we listen to his blatantly satanic favorites. The lyrics glorify perversion, torture and murder. I don't react. Secretly, I'm bored.

"I've seen "splatter" and "snuff" films!" Philip shouts.

"Are you trying to shock me?" With unconcealed relish Philip reads to me grisly poems, and graffiti he has rewritten from his Book of Shadows.

"It's from an occult book store near your campus. One of my friends has Anton La Vey's Satanic Bible. He stole it from the Sagebrush branch of the library. I may be a satanist, Doctor, but you know what? I don't steal. I buy what I need."

Two weeks go by.

"Roberta, I've met a girl. Maybe I'll ask her out to a show. I'm not sure. She's pretty. No, she's beautiful. But I'm not supposed to hang around girls."

Philip is gazing carefully at the floor again. He does his best work looking at his feet.

"I don't want to turn into one of those 'casual' satanists, like Christians who only go to church on Sunday, and forget their religion the rest of the week. My Dad despises people like that. Hypocrites! They're worse than sinners!

Philip shows me his carefully devilish rituals and chants which come straight out of " The Satanic Bible."

"They have to be done right. Otherwise they have no meaning or power. I am protected, Doctor, I am protected! Remember, some kids die and God doesn't do anything to save them. Maybe Satan can keep people from dying, like from The Bomb or Aids. He can if he wants to. I'm going to find out how to keep from dying. I hate the cold and dark. Why do we have to die? I can't get used to the idea. There's so much crying, hurting and missing somebody. I've been to a funeral, you know.

Do you think people die from just too much pain to stand? My friend did. He was hit by a car and it took him two days to die."

"Who knows, Philip. I believe some people go out in a peaceful trance, others in their sleep, and there are those who die in pain. Dying doesn't seem to be any fairer than living. Tell me about the funeral. How do you feel when you think about it?"

"Awful. It was in his living room. A sick scene! Right at home, not in a church. My Dad wouldn't go. He was disgusted. Being at Buddy's house made it worse. Real.

49

The coffin was open and the window shades pulled down. There were bouquets of wilting flowers and two big lumpy holders with candles burning, but it was morning. Buddy had on a suit, dark blue, and a tie and a white shirt. I'd never seen him dressed up. He was in a casket and the inside was like a white satin bed. He looked alive, all pink in the face. His eyes were shut, like he was taking a nap. It was the way he looked at camp on his cot, but the bottom half of the coffin was closed. I know why. Down there he was all broken up from the car. Mangled.

Then they closed the lid forever and ever, took him to the cemetery, and put him in the ground to rot. Some guy talked about Life Everlasting. What he said was all lies."

"It's all right to grieve, Philip. You lost a friend. You found out about death."

Philip does his crying at home in the bathtub, with the radio turned up loud, at my suggestion. He makes sure his Dad can't hear him.

Lately I notice Philip protects himself with the rituals of psychotherapy, rather than those of satanism with our weekly meetings, serious talk about God and feelings of anger, jealousy, love, hate, hurt, lust, fear, loss, and grief. And with constant thoughts of death. He approaches each hour as a ceremony, carefully bringing notes. Adolescent dreams and visions crowd his journal. Philip's breast pocket keeps secret his personal diary. This little book reveals more about the girl and the "powerful" letter Philip is composing to her.

"I suppose you'll be glad to hear I declined a ride to the mountains for Black Sabbath."

"You did? Why?"

"The guy drives too fast."

"Sounds like you think your life is valuable after all."

It's no longer an honor for Philip to race along a narrow road at high speed, driven by a kid with a beer bottle between his knees. Philip still manipulates his mother to get her to force him to come to therapy sessions.

"Ah, Mom. A real waste of time, Mom!"

I like this kid. He won't give in easily. Integrity is important when you are fifteen years old.

Articles in newspapers, magazines and admonitions from the pulpit warn parents to pay attention to any withdrawn behavior of their children.

"Become aware of violent behavior, mood swings, radical changes in personality, or vagueness about whereabouts."

Mothers and fathers are exhorted to find out what their teen reads, to look for satanic symbols, the numbers 666, or pentagrams, the star-shaped Biblical sign for the devil.

Upset by all his reading about satanic ritual and regulations, Roger, in his therapeutic hour, is loud and speedy. He rants away his time.

"Drugs play an important role in recruitment of teens and then are used to control the kids once they are involved. Drugs work for Satan."

"Hey, wait a minute, Roger. Seems to me, drug misuse itself is what allows satanist notions, or any crazy ideas, to become addictive and dangerous to kids."

I forget to keep my opinion to myself. It's time again for Roger to leave and he is still focused on the Devil and Hi's presumed powers.

"Your hour is up, and then some. I promise I'll help you in any way I can. I'm on your side. I'll contact parents, speak to kid's groups. Let me know when I'm needed.

Meanwhile, since you insist on reading this stuff, take this book home with you. At least it is not as hysterical as the militant Christian material you have been pouring over. I've just finished it and we can talk about it next week. It's a graphic description of one drug ridden kid and, unfortunately, it's a true story. The boy is a satanist, one who commits murder. Right up your alley. It's called' Say You Love Satan.'"

Therapists, treating teenagers for involvement in satanism, used to handle this obsession/compulsion like any other psychological problem. Professionals believed adolescents getting into drugs for satanic reasons are the kids who would take drugs anyway.

Lately, therapists sound horrified about what they are hearing. What's happening to us as healers? Are we getting carried away with scary stories told us by hysterics and becoming hysterics ourselves.

Parents, who overreact, are hard to deal with, because they are often superstitious themselves. Professional care for the whole family is vitally important. Family members must communicate to develop agreement. Religious fanaticism has no place in successful treatment. Mothers and fathers must regain control of their teenagers. Each family member must become responsible for his own behavior and beliefs. That includes Mom and Dad. And the therapist must be responsible and reasonable, too.

I try to find the article I began to read, then lost somewhere in my office. It's not on my desk. Not in my old red chair. Something about a California satanic group linked to murder and mayhem. Is the paper in the cushions of the couch?

I think it claimed Geraldo's special on satanic crimes was the highest rated documentary in television history. Somebody else, Newsweek maybe, says satanism is to be the "crime of the nineties."

Supposedly, there is some kind of network of maybe a thousand police and therapists involved with the perpetrators and victims of satanic abuse. The ultra Christians are in on this too, urging police to investigate mockeries of their rituals. And now, the psychologists and therapists are caught up in the question of repressed memories and their truth or falsehood.

There is even a foundation formed to discuss "False Memory Syndrome." These folks claim that the interest in repressed sexual memories has much in common with the UFO abduction stories....a faddish wave of peculiar superstition, sweeping the country, stirred up by people whose lives are without excitement.

I remember a San Francisco woman's opinion:

"Satanists are already a few bubbles off center," she said simply. I can relate to her. Where did I put that paper?

U. S. Surgeon General, Dr. C. Everett Koop, has designated sex abuse a gigantic public health issue which requires serious involvement from everyone in the healing professions. But I don't know what to do about myself. Learning about sexual abuse is so repelling, I turn away, as if my own primal instincts dictate "tune out."

"Look away," my mind says.

Right now, ironically, I'm working too hard learning relaxation training. Intensity is my occupational hazard. I'm too insistent. I try to force clients to make major life style changes. I want their lives, not just their carcasses, to be user-friendly. Most clients change many things about themselves, but then, some don't. I am apt to press too hard, requiring effort and dedication from people who are unable to organize their thinking or feeling, let alone their lives or their payments. In my zeal, I am impatient, tired, cranky. That is why Sam is so good for me.

He is against zeal.

Rachel worries aloud that she isn't perfect enough for her husband. Her strongest desire is to be a worthy "handmaiden" to this "fine" man. But his protective devotion is not the casual interdependency we find in good marriages. This huge man hovers over Rachel, his sickly partner, like a gigantic bird force feeding her his energy. She leans upon him, flutteringly, chronically ill. Who is needier? She says their relationship is "nice." How can she be unaware of his drinking? Rachel's husband smells, as if he sleeps in heaps of juniper berries.

As Rachel's medical history unfolds, I am shocked even though in my work I am well acquainted with human pain. I listen to many a litany of suffering, as part

53

of my job. But   pieces of Rachel have been painfully stitched together from her head to her toes. Her surgeries have involved her spine, breast, abdomen, eyes and her head. Sickness and recuperating have been Rachel's life. Appalling.

"Why so much illness, Rachel? Why so many surgeries?"

"I have no idea." She is strangely nonchalant, indifferent to reasons for her suffering.

"How do you feel about all that medical care?"

"By now I should be functioning better."

"Yes, but how do you feel? Angry? Disappointed? Hopeful?"

"Oh, I have cramps from colitis, and my head aches terribly."

"Feelings, Rachel! Where are your emotions? You have only opinions and physical symptoms. Have a feeling, Rachel! Express despair, get happy, or something. Don't you know the value and purpose of emotion? People like you are unable to express feelings, because they have a disability, which is the incapacity to feel. I study feelings, Rachel, and you're not having any. I want you to stop analyzing and reach the poetic part of you."

Psychologists use three words for feelings. Emotion is the physical state, complete with chemical changes. Psychoanalysts use the word "affect," which describes how I look at Rachel from the outside. I call her "dull."

'Feeling' is a term for subjective awareness of one's own emotional state or how we sense ourselves from the inside. Emotionally bland, all Rachel's explosiveness is psychosomatic. She erupts into ulcers, rashes, bleeding bowels and twisting muscles. She has descriptive adjectives aplenty, but never for her own mood. Literal minded, she stays concretely in the present. Rachel is boring....and extremely ill. Is she so limited because of abnormal brain function? Her body responds violently to symptoms, but any comprehension of the feelings behind the body reactions is out for a walk.

I think, a concern with feelings is too close to the core

of our being for many practitioners. American society is technological. Since we do not have high tech tools for investigating a client's emotional insides, we're embarrassed by our lack of instruments. In some scientific circles feelings are still not respectable. Are feelings anti-intelligent? Are feelings neurotic symptoms?

In my work with Rachel I must pay attention to her absence of feelings. Emotions, even negative ones, are crucial to her development. Her physical pain tells her something is wrong. Stored somewhere in her brain her pain was meant to warn her to make wiser choices than she made when she was hurt. Her human feelings, intense to subtle, were meant to force her to make choices. Feelings prove she can learn. Because she cannot depend on her instincts, as do other animals, she must feel and remember.

Feelings can become exaggerated, of course, by any of us. We can feel so bad we eat ourselves into obesity. We can be so stubborn we become anorectic. Overwhelmed by shame we may wish to die. But feeling is its own reward.

"Rachel, our lives mean so much to us because we feel".

On this fourth visit Rachel finally talks about her family of origin. Nothing but sentimental trivia has filled earlier sessions, fanciful anecdotes about her perfect union with her husband. She has been long-winded, tedious, affectionate, unreal. Under pressure from me, Rachel describes her relationship with her mother.

"It was...strained." Rachel again is a master of understatement. Off handedly, she mentions Mother's many suicide attempts.

Depression runs in families vulnerable to mood disorders. If Rachel's mother was subject to depressions, no wonder Rachel is.

Twin studies demonstrate painful moods have strong hereditary components. Even mild forms of depression seem to be related to family trait patterns.

"I'm trying to recall, Doctor. It's true, I never invited

other children to my home. I was embarrassed about my, uh... mother. I think, perhaps, I had one friend, at one time, a teacher. Her memory is precious to me. To tell the truth, I don't know whether she really existed or not."

Rachel is coming closer. Slowly, slowly, she takes a risk to acknowledge a genuine difficulty in her past.

It is the middle of a session and suddenly color floods Rachel's face. She is vivid.

"I was kept from high school, forced to work as a factory girl."

Tears slide down her face.

"How do you feel?" Rachel looks at me vacantly. She shrugs slightly.

"You appear to be sad, Rachel."

"Sad. I remember school. Reading and writing."

"No wonder you cry, Rachel. You are mourning. You lost the happy part of your young life. And you are feeling sad."

Painful or not, I am pleased she has experienced an emotion. Quite the opposite are those clients who spend their lives stuck, reliving an old feeling from a forgotten happening. Unless they find out where this archaic feeling comes from and take a reading on its size and shape, the habitual feeling causes them to distort the world around them into ugliness.

"I am unable to tell what is real," Rachel confesses.

If a switch board operator doesn't know which plugs go where, she may panic. But if she knows how to turn off the switchboard and to ask for instruction she may still feel anxiety, but it won't be fear. I'm trying to show Rachel where some of her plugs fit. She feels chronically terrified because she's experienced something terrible, but can't remember what it is. Just like the switchboard novice without guidance, Rachel lives in confusion, expecting the worst any minute. She will get better, when she remembers what she is afraid of.

Not long ago she spoke only of "nice" things, all decency and conformity, unable to comprehend anger, hostility, jealousy, cruelty or hurt. Now, in her second stage of therapy she still has little ability to touch painful feelings. She believes her husband is her rescuer and that she can depend on him in this dangerous life. She refuses to recognize that he is an alcoholic. Noticing could upset her world, too much to bear right now. Some experience, somewhere, convinced her the world is a terrifying kind of place and she defends against taking a chance of being wrong. Because of fear, she misperceives the world and will only pay attention to evidence that supports that fear. Rachel, burned by a hot iron, believes all irons are hot.

I listen carefully. Rachel's vocabulary is extensive, sometimes elegant. Yet she speaks with hesitation, a peculiarly formal cadence and an occasional surprising mispronunciation. With unusual inflections, her language shifts from the sweet prattle of a little child to an occasional gemlike prose poem or a bookish passage filled with the polished language of carefully crafted fiction.

"I remember. I remember," she cries.

"Be there now," I urge.

"The long New England winters are harsh. There is a long, chill walk to school, when I am allowed to go. I am most unacceptable to the children and the teacher. Wearily, I urge myself home, forced by the frost to go inside the discomforting house. Long laborious afternoons and evenings are filled with housework, cooking, cleaning, setting the table, serving food, cleaning up. There are greasy dishes for me, in cold water, but there is no conversation. There are no games, no family evenings, no music."

"And no safety?" I ask on a hunch. My conviction grows, Rachel's childhood has been strangely difficult to bear in some way I cannot understand, and she cannot yet remember. I suspect she has survived some pathological enormity, wounded in body and mind.

Rachel's attention drifts away from the present. Her eyes, unconverged, fix on the ceiling.

"Be there, Rachel."

As she speaks her language is archaic, formal, like nineteenth century text read aloud.

"Not only passive, my father is 'peculiar.' Daddy's behavior is controlled by his wife, Iris, who is known by some as my mother. His preoccupation is the Catholic church. Attending obsessively, he manifests himself in the nave. The objects of the Mass mean power to him. They are hallucinatory metaphors around which he builds his existence. His reliance on rituals and totems persist, persist, persist and grow stronger. The church and fish, the church, fish. And, of course, the Devil. Oh, yes, Lucifer, most certainly.

Mother calls him fanatic and a fool. She attends Mass not at all. Not at all. This decision is of great importance. Something of primacy has happened. My lady mother is red with anger. There has been an affray with a Bishop or a Priest, a shrieking confrontation, a schism.

Oh, calamity! Mother's malice is focused upon me. I am the primary receiver of mother's hostility and wrath. Her fevered hatefulness."

Or mother's madness, I think. It's time to take a chance.

"Is Mother crazy, Rachel?"

Rachel's eyes focus on me. She is once more alert, poised, present, resuming her everyday manner while looking directly into my eyes. Then she cocks her head like a little child.

"Of course not."

Six

"Roberta, have I told you about the teenage boy who sacrifices his beloved dog to Satan, then swallows the knife himself."

Roger

Roger the Sleuth is pacing the floor. The back of his neck is American Beauty rose. His scowl, darkly fierce, hides what a softy he is, a loving father, delighting in his kids. I remember he was once a kind and tolerant man.

"I'm an inadequate parent. My son and daughter are bright, loving, precious, vulnerable kids and I fail them every day. Don't look at me that way. All right, I see I'm doing a number on myself."

"Why can't you be a Robert-Young-on-television father?"

"That's it. I want to be perfect."

This guy is already more conscientious than most. Yes, lately he sounds corrupted by his own perfectionism. He's overwhelmed with emotion. It takes him so long to say what he means, I forget my training and finish his sentences for him. His marching back and forth in my office isn't draining off his excess emotion, as I had hoped.

"Stop, sit down, Roger!" He stands very straight, still glaring.

"I'm waiting for a salute," I say, hoping teasing will

help.

It doesn't. I wish he wouldn't be extreme. It's a bad sign for someone with his mood disorder. I wonder if he's getting manicky now, as well as obsessive.

"Are you sleeping at night, Roger? Or do you ruminate about this stuff then, too?"

He doesn't hear me, still going on about justice, kids, Creeps, the American way and his fears of satanism. Until he's ready he'll just have to shout and pace.

"Maybe traditional religious satanists are honest about their beliefs. Maybe they are against criminal activity. Some could be good citizens. Don't tell me again the right to worship is protected. I know we have freedom of worship."

"So?"

"I also know there are satanists, right here in this neigborhood, who are dangerous. Out there right now, they're looking for lonely, thrill seeking high schoolers to invite to their parties. Then they'll get the kids hooked on nutsiness and drugs."

"Why do we have to talk about this again? We did this last week and the week before that and the week before that. What has that to do with you?"

"I intend to stop them. Me! I have to, Roberta."

Now Roger is able to collapse his big body onto the couch.

"Most satanists are just kids who outgrow this stage in a year or so. But I want all kids to have the chance to live to grow up. Young people are entitled to their usual familiar adolescent flirting with...."

"Frightening ideas, thrills, rebellion?"

"Yeah. They pick up bits and pieces from horror paperbacks, movies, videos, and..."

"Their own undeveloped religious backgrounds?"

"Sure. Like you, I wish they had healthy instruction from parents. But without that, they listen to lyrics of a heavy metal rock group and take them seriously."

"And needing a sense of belonging, as all adolescents do, they form their own groups and conduct rituals."

"That's right. But I'll reeducate these kids. And you'll help.Wake up to the danger, Roberta!"

"I've already agreed, remember. But I believe involvement with drugs and satanism have the same benefits for teens. At the beginning they both provide a sense of family. Without strong roots any adolescent feels lonely. Individualism is uncomfortable. Kids are adrift, empty, alone."

"And now satanism is marketed for kids as part of their subculture. Videos, music and clothing reflect satanic ideas."

"And as always, some kids need to shock their parents.

If you were into the bizarre, as punk kids are, dressing and talking in ways meant to shock, can you think of a better way than to adopt something as antisocial as satanism?"

"You're right. It's a sure way to get a rise out of Mom and Dad. Just look how upset I get." Roger can't keep himself from a smile.

"Hello there. Roger, you're back to reasonable."

Foggily, a hideous picture of Rachel's past life is emerging. Today, her recollection is of winter and biting, salt air. Included is hunger, neglect, cold, hate, superstition, and preoccupation with evil.

"Be there."

Rachel looks what I can only describe as "vague," then speaks with her odd mixture of erudition and childish error.

"Sinister, Roberta. Sinister. Sad is a feeling. Is sinister a feeling?

During "bad" times, Mother never abandons the house. Father shops, encounters persons only when necessary. Mother takes pills, pills, pills, depicting herself as a woman seriously and fascinatingly ill. Her moods shift from riotous hilarity to petty meanness. Often she excites herself into bouts of screaming. She shouts obscenities.

In her dreadful cellar Mother prowls. She arches her bulky body over the wooden apothecary table. Her dark rituals ex-

61

*press perverted meanings, known only to herself. Stinking
things fill fruit jars, baneful totems. Crouching, murmuring,
Mother mixes and boils, inaudibly murmurs the names of
those she hates. As she sings, her large tongue, with its deep
ridges, is visible. Her tongue thick, her toes long and clawed,
she is a dreadful beaked bird with folded wings. She shrieks,
but she is not a bird; she is a fat woman with soft strange ears.
She is my Mommy. In the cellar she becomes... Mother.*

As she relives her past, an hour at a time, Rachel's
motley, beautiful, private language is wrung from her, as
if she cannot stop.

On certain "wicked" days there is an especially time-
consuming brewing, she says.

"From the glowing hot plate in the shadowy dark below, there comes steam from an odious liquid. This is for
me to drink. It will cleanse me of the immoral thoughts I
contain."

Poor little Rachel, I sigh to myself. Is this symbolism,
or is Mother some kind of mutant? An anomoly? Rachel
is always consistent in her descriptions of Mother's ugly
physical self.

I muse further as Rachel falls silent, gasping. Rachel
has told me about "the Mother" and her fantasies. In my
imagination I see Mother, below the stairs, dreaming of
lust, feeling rage, passing judgement upon her enemies.

She repeats, over and over, her primal ritual. Someone
must be punished. Mother's violent fantasies are primitive, deeply buried, neurological short circuits, which
fire in her brain. She is desperate to satisfy a terrifying
need of her own. Rachel believes Mother has an evil private secret and must enact her unique morality play
turned inside out. For that purpose Mother uses her own
little girl.

How can Rachel understand all this. She does not
know mother's secret.

Suddenly, Rachel shrieks.

"You are possessed. You are an imp of Satan!"

"She's had a hard time today. It's a good thing you drive her home at the end of her session," I tell her husband. His wide and meaningless grin does not lessen.

Following each outpouring, Rachel's body moves stiffly, awkwardly, paying little attention to anything outside herself. As she moves to the car, her arms and legs like sticks, she is a crumbling scarecrow. Walking beside Rachel and her protector husband, I can see how he overshadows her with his big body. Once more, he says hospitalization for Rachel is out of the question.

I have finally found the newspaper for which I have been searching. It was under my desk with the dust balls.

"Dozens of children in California towns are telling authorities that they have been sexually abused by groups of adults, who forced them to take part in satanic rituals. They drank blood, ate human flesh and sacrificially murdered other children.

Law enforcement officers do believe the children. But, it's not only in California. We have learned of cases across the United States, where you can get these tremendously amazing similarities."

Evidence, however, is hard to find. Questions about satanism were asked when a five year old boy in Michigan testified one of his teachers at the day care center, where he was sexually abused, had dressed as a witch for a Halloween ceremony."

I fume, "What a big deal about nothing. Now even dressing up is labeled child abuse."

I sniff with disdain. A bad habit. Have I picked that up from Rachel?

"Therapists who treat sexually abused children are worried by the apparent similarity of the children's accounts. A well known psychiatrist says, 'I think anybody who works in this area ought to carry a badge and wear a gun. And not have a family. My car was blown up ten days ago.

Sexually abused children I treat speak of 'eating flesh, being forced to kill other children, ugly things like that.

At first I didn't believe them. I want to believe there is another explanation.'"

"This cheap-shot paper sells itself using sensationalism," I chafe.

Quickly, I look over the page to find an opinion less hysterical. Feeling frightened is something I don't need right now. God Bless people who are good to children.

"No bodies have been found."

I'm relieved someone sounds sensible. "Cheap journalism!"

A lawyer has an opinion:

"I think that probably some of these children have been molested in some way. By whom and when, I don't know. But the satanic aspect of it, that's when they lose me."

Me, too. This time I'll know where this disquieting article is. I'll put it in the trash.

Distracted, Roger sorts through his feelings, trying out on me his speeches for teachers and parents.

"Here goes. Are you ready? Try to look like a crowd.

Parents, Teachers and Guests: The usual satanic worshiper is someone who becomes involved because of low self esteem, someone who lacks confidence. Someone who is rebelling against strict discipline at home."

"In other words, a teenager," I interrupt.

"Yes, Asiatic and Black kids aren't intrigued. Just white middle to upper class youngsters. We can't spot satanists by the blood dripping off their chins. Or by a dead cat in a back pocket, but a butterfly knife is an indication.

Sometimes clothes are a giveaway. Teenage satanism has a lot to do with school. It's seasonal. Satan worship peaks when school is on, when kids are together. In summer, kids have to go on vacations with their parents. They are isolated and tend to forget religious fervor of any kind.

Satan is fashionable, and fashion is fickle, since it always comes and goes. Some kids can keep up their involvement with Satan for only a day, some kids with stamina can go a year, and the fascination with satanism in all but one in a hundred fades away by the beginning of college.

"Practicing like this is helpful, Roberta. I'm much calmer. I promise next week I'll have my material on secret codes or signs. The stuff about symbols is interesting."

Roger is all right today. Talking, talking, talking helps him control his feelings. He uses words to build a strong corral around wild fears that might trample him to death.

All right. Now I'm hooked on the topic. Between clients, on my well-used couch, I read up on satanic practices of old New England, Rachel's childhood neighborhood. As a Feminist, I'm interested in the politics of witch hunting, as reinterpreted by women scholars. I'm catching on to a bad rap.

"Although some scholars are more sympathetic than others to the plight of their subjects, witches are generally portrayed in the literature as disagreeable women, at best aggressive and abrasive, at worst, ill-tempered, quarrelsome, and spiteful. They are almost always described as deviants, disorderly women who failed, or refused to abide by the behavoral norms of their society."

Were these witches premenstrual and irritable? Lesbians? Why were they so disgusting to others? Mentally ill? Schizophrenic?

I'm in my office. The diplomas and honors arranged around the room are meant to reassure clients that I know what I am doing. A Phi Beta Kappa award and a doctorate from a fancy graduate school line up, placed deliberately at eye level. Above the couch, the large print of a mother and child, distorted, crookedly looks down.

Rachel is afraid of this picture. She can't stay in this room because of its twisted image. We've had to move her sessions to the room next door, the "blue room," where company sleeps on the hideabed when it serves as a guest room.

This battered office suits me. I think of it as warmly cozy and am insulted when clients refer to it as "small" or even "cramped." To me it's thoughtful, a place for feeling. It has the threadbare style I associate with Judd Hirsh in Ordinary People, my favorite flick.

Well, my job is to take care of Rachel, not scare her sillier. She can use the guestroom, if she wants to. The gazebo, anything. Rachel has had enough terror in her life. Sometimes she honestly believes her mother was a witch. But as a label for Mom, schizophrenic suits me better than witch. I live in the twentieth century and see nonconformity as a byproduct of disease. I've outgrown the diabolic. Something curative can always be done for our crazies, not by exorcism and ritual, but by medication and reeducation. Can't it?

Sam tells me twice a week I am idealistic.

If Rachel's mother sounds schizophrenic. Rachel's father does too. Not too long ago, even experts thought schizophrenia came out of family environment, but now almost everyone believes the cause of this terrible disease is biological and partly hereditary. Crippled by this severe illness, people cannot deftly handle life issues with which everyone must deal, money, food, clothing, shelter. That was true in New England when Rachel was little, just as is true, here, in Texas today.

Boy, Howdy! Today we are making progress.

"Rachel, be there." Once more her pale gray stare moves upward. Rachel gazes at the ceiling, her language becomes poetic.

"I'm there, Roberta. I'm there. Across the street is a vacant lot. Its a field, part cold clay clods, part overgrown with weeds, rising a little awkwardly, clumsily from the sidewalk. The smells are of dry grass and dog excrement.   In the middle stands my bare tree, with cordial shade for me in the scanty days of summer. My dearest tree. Rocks, like sacks of dirty laundry, push up from the hard scrabble. It is early evening. Far away from the feeble street lamp this block is surpassingly dark. It is a long way home from school. Tonight I sit on my special rock and know important things 'for sure'at last. Knowledge creeps its way into my bones. Moments slide by, the day slips away from gloaming into witching hour.

"I am not human. I am hateful. I must die and leave the earth. I know I am only masquerading as a child. In this dusky magical spot I recognize the wrongness, the sin of my existence."

Rachel is making more sense in her daily life. She has begun to question the peculiarly rigid, self-imposed severity of her newly adopted dogmatic religious training. Overly rigorous, when she was first a young mother, she forced herself to "be good." Her childish misunderstanding of her new belief system required her to put a "good face" on everything, even dreadful events. She cruelly punished herself and pretended perfection. She, who was always at fault in her own estimation, was more than a sinner. She was evil.

"Evil, Rachel? A nice lady like you? Bullshit." Rachel can laugh.

"Yes, Bullshit," she says, "And Horse hockey, too."

But in Rachel's dreams the conflict continues.

Why can't the girl be like Daddy who goes to Mass every day, receiving communion? Somewhere inside her there is terrible confusion. Catholic Daddy is good. But a different Daddy exists somewhere, a floating image of Lucifer, with bloody horns and malignant black eyes, piercing all the way through her soul.

Seven

"They felt that all the killing would draw a protective shield around them. It was religious craziness."

Jim Mattox
Texas Attorney discussing the Matamoros ritual murders

Fortunately for our furniture and dispositions, Sam, my colleague-sweetheart-business partner, works with his disturbed children in an imposing medical building miles away from our house. His unruly, ailing kids carve their names into his maple chairs, scuff his newly painted walls and pull loose threads from his linen upholstery.

Sometimes people make a blunder and inquire about the nature of our relationship. We define ourselves as "incorporated." Or Sam says I am his "Ummer," as in "Mom, Dad, I want you to meet my Um, um, um..."

That must answer the question. No one has pursued the subject further. Sam was married once and doesn't believe in it for himself. When repairing other people's marriages, he works hard to help them enjoy their union. I'm trained to analyze the institution, not defend it. As Sex Therapists we are also Marriage and Family Therapists, specializing in Group. With couples we work as a team. Since he is a man and I a woman, we intend to represent our genders fairly. Sex therapy makes more sense when someone who has grown up male and someone who has grown up female speak from their own life experiences. Until recently in psychology, as in life, men spoke for women.

I respect Sam's judgement, yet challenge him at every opportunity. Do I resent the authority he once had over me, as he says I do? Or is that just more of his Freudian dogma? Typically, a trainee is enamored of her supervisor. I was smitten with Sam at once, but persisted and outlasted my training and all the other women. For me the grand prize for steadfastness in this educational enterprise was winning the teacher.

So Sam and I are disentangling ourselves from the perplexity of the transition we made from supervisor/ supervisee to colleague/true love and professionals of equal stature.

Our role confusion quickly leads to a raised-voice professional consultation. To less informed ears it sounds like an argument.

"Rachel," I say in our next session, "why do you suppose your mother chose you to be the one to feel her rage?" Sam suggested this question.

"Something about me. I was a disgusting child, a gnome, skinny, stubborn, ungrateful. Maybe I was clamorous. I reflect on that question myself during each night, when I can't sleep, knowing I am galling. I am pondering that thought now, understanding that thinking is different than feeling, Roberta.

Why does Mother hate me? I do know. I was difficult. I know how very desperate, I mean, how very different, I was and am. Repulsive. Who would want a scrawny, wicked little girl with matted, tangled hair and dirty clothes?"

"It was your fault you were neglected?"

Suddenly, listening to Rachel, I am not simply angry, but furious. Rachel persists in thinking of herself as bad, sick or crazy. Now she looks at me thoughtfully, as if no one has ever before been angry on her behalf.

"When I wasn't doing housework, I crouched at home

in a corner, trying to stay out of the way. Crouching like an imp. An imp of Satan. Or sometimes I crouched at school. In a corner. It seems peculiar to me now that I sat bent over that way. Do you think it was strange?"

"I think it expressed the way you felt."

When she speaks again Rachel's voice is a woman's voice, deeper, melodious, unlike the wheezy sound of her thin childish whine. She takes a great risk .

"Sometimes I would go into a church to find peace in a quiet place to think. I would like to say 'feel', but that would not be true. You use that word 'feel' often. But what is feel? I am in pain, but I don't feel pain. I don't feel what other people talk about. Emotions."

At last.

"Feelings are not thoughts," Rachel says. This time she's got it.

I'm convinced Rachel's lack of affect exactly corresponds to her degree of muscle tension. Excited, yet attempting to appear calm, I make a mental note that Rachel has discovered she's missing something important.

Of course, we're dealing with emotions! Although pain comes first, eventually Rachel will recall some happy childhood feelings as well. In spite of my impatience, I remind myself to go slowly. I know it will take a long time for Rachel to revive, come alive, melt, to become an emotionally developed human being.

Slowly, and as carefully as possible, I review her psychosocial history. On the subject of sexuality, Rachel is adamant. She has none. She never did. Rachel grew no breasts, never masturbated, nor felt sexual desire.

"No sexual fantasies?"

"Never." Rachel's sexuality is untenanted, empty. Nobody home."Sex is of no interest to me, Roberta, simply not worth discussing. I have important things to talk to you about, however, not that sort of thing."

Rachel wants powerful methods to influence "The Girls" to be even more tractable.

"By learning the principles of obedience, the girls can become worthwhile persons."

"Ho hum."

This is one of the days when Rachel is certain of everything. She delivers her insistent ideas in the style of a small child, unconvincingly pretending to be grown up, a complete switch from the demure lack of confidence she projects most often. Is this another pattern for me to monitor? Rachel is opinionated, then cautious, grandly dogmatic, next wary and timid. I don't get it.

"The Girls must become adept at homemaking. They will learn to be successful wives and mothers," Rachel insists.

I bite my Feminist tongue and wait.

Lately Rachel falls quiet more often, thinking, evaluating ideas. At this point in her therapy she will not openly disagree with me, although, I can see she disapproves of my ideas about "The Girls."

"The little women."

"The what'"

"You know, Doctor, like the girls in 'Little Women,' the book. Jo and Amy and Beth! Marmee. Don't you remember?"

Animated now, Rachel's pale face shows traces of pink. Her voice is high, her eyes wide. She is aroused. What is this? Passion at last?

"I'm glad I have no boys. I don't know what I would do with a child who isn't a little woman."

Looking puzzled, frowning, Rachel hears herself.

Did Rachel learn about family life from that particular idealistic novel written a hundred years ago? Don't tell me she learned her parenting from the Louisa May Alcott model of family management.

Sobbing now, Rachel struggles to make her views sound rational.

"People are supposed to do what they are told. Good people obey! That is how one knows someone is a good person!"

Gaining courage, Rachel defends her rules from me. Patiently, but firmly, she explains to me in how many ways I am wrong. My ideas, which I believe democratic and generous, she sees as silly. Her views are her husband's. Rachel quotes him at great length and on many occasions, particularly regarding right and wrong. I think of his drinking and evasiveness. Her denial of his behavior is a wall between us.

"How did your husband become your authority?"

"A husband is automatically an authority. Quite correctly, he is interpreter of how things should be. Think how fortunate I am to have someone who will explain and to enforce rules. A family with rules is guaranteed high functioning."

I look dubious. Rachel is insulted.

"Rachel, what are we doing here? Are we wasting your money and my time? If we are going to argue we can do that with other people, cheaper."

Relaxation training with Rachel is a bust. With my most soothing professional voice and exercises which work easily and well for other clients, she remains sitting straight up in her chair, tense, wide-eyed, staring. Rachel's thin fingers bend inward into clenched fists.

I am annoyed. Why won't she let go? Hopefully, someday Rachel will open her fortress gate. We resume the "talking cure."

Modern therapy is a process of self-examination, emotional awareness and growth. People still imagine a client to be a Sybil-like character whose multiple personalities suffer fascinating emotional tortures, while a distant parent figure, the remote therapist, usually male, writes in a long series of notebooks. Only a miniscule percentage of therapy, today, fits that image. Feminist therapy, which sprang from the human potential movement, appeals to me. Women are strengthened most, I believe, when backed up by feminist perspective.

"Educate men and empower women," I hear Natasha Josephowitz say.

Lately I've been wondering why am I "seeing" so many men in therapy? Maybe liberation is good for them, too.

Actually, Rachel fits the Sybil stereotype more than I like to think. She also fits a stereotype I have discarded in myself, that of the servile handmaiden, the Pleaser. It's hard work to keep myself from scorning anyone who reminds me of a part of myself I have outgrown. I don't like her type. Why am I still seeing Rachel? Working with her is riding a psychotherapeutic roller coaster, holding on with both clinical hands. Somewhere along the bumpy ride, Rachel is teaching me about stamina, the power of imagination and human courage. There is someone deep down in Rachel I want to meet.

Psychological knowledge of human behavior is growing and developing here in Texas. Therapists have changed to fit contemporary people. We have vast variations in our personalities and approaches, but our goal is always the same. Changes in attitude, feeling and behavior will enhance a client's ability to enjoy life.

An overwhelmed client, like Rachel, has no one to whom she can express her most personal thoughts and painful feelings. Crisis drives men and women, protestingly and hesitantly, into my office. Like patients of a dentist, no one wants to come to see me at first. It takes the loss of a relationship, stress to the point of exhaustion, a psychosomatic illness or heartbreak over a child to bring someone in. Most clients grow tired of dealing with their same old problems. They hate their boring relationships, chronic guilt feelings, lack of assertion, family conflicts, job dissatisfaction, or day after day depression.

People who make the best use of therapy are those who want their lives to be richer and more meaningful. Fortunate folk, who use therapy well, develop new careers or hugely increase their self-esteem. Therapy is not only about relieving emotional pain, but about enlivening the experience of living. I can be enthusiastic and creative with people who want growth and adventure, not simply relief from distress. There are those who say "therapy is wasted on sick people."

My clients are interesting, thoughtful individuals with

personal issues on their minds.

Most are hungry for intimacy. Some have suffered upsets in identity and trite as it sounds, do "find themselves." Both men and women require pre-nuptial or divorce counseling. Couples seek help with parenting issues. Dissatisfied people want sex therapy for themselves or their partners. And you would be surprised how many grown children bring their aging parents in to have them "fixed."

But Rachel doesn't fit into any of these patterns. What does Rachel need? Surely not just an opportunity to lecture to me on the sanctity of marriage and the rules of proper behavior?

"Rachel, knock it off. We talk too much. You are enrolling in a class on relaxation training."

This is the college class taught by myself and my colleague, a rangy, funny woman, well liked by students. It's comfortable, easy and useful to people who need instruction in overcoming tension-related difficulties. We're popular teachers because our subject is 'feeling better'.

Recently, relaxation training has become trendy. Many members of the class are referred by doctors as adjunct treatment for migraine headaches, chronic back pain, asthma, ulcers or other somatic difficulties. Participants often lessen their reliance on pain killers, so enrolling in a class turns out to be inexpensive medicine.

Rachel is here and prepares to train herself to relax in this new setting. She is to lie quietly on a mat, encouraged by the company of others, while I direct her through guided imagery and progressive muscle relaxation exercises. Anything, but arguing over her rules for living. I'm tired of Rachel's current learning plateau. It's flat and far too verbal.

As the pace of modern life increases in our hot, overcrowded city, more and more citizens fall victim to the "hurry sickness." Their stress comes from internal or external events, pressures or feelings. A certain amount of stress is stimulating and exciting and life can be interesting when we are challenged to think creatively, to find solutions to problems. But too much stress crushes us.

Stress consists of an event, plus how we feel about it, how we interpret it and what we do to cope.

An example of group stress is our economic recession. When the bottom fell out of our economy, Texans were appalled to suffer stress in the pocketbook.

So students can test themselves Nora and I ask questions.

"Which of the following would you call stressful?

A.   Buying a wonderful new expensive home?

B.   Discovering that your smartest child is flunking his senior year in High School?

C.   Being asked to interview for the job you have wanted for years?

D.   Being audited?"

E.   Discovering the price of oil has skyrocketed overnight? Wow!

Our students answer that all five life events can be stressful. Life requires change. Anything causing us to adapt requires a great deal from our minds and bodies. The surprise is that positive and pleasurable events create as much inner consternation as painful and negative happenings. The amount of stress we feel depends on the amount of change required by us to cope. The amount of damage from stress reflects the effectiveness of our coping skills.

Nora, tall, easygoing, with slow talkin' concern for students, and I, the overenthusiastic psychotherapist, consider ourselves pleasant people. We think we are the last persons ever to be Stress Carriers. We take care not to trigger the phenomenon called down-shifting, the physiological response humans make to a perception of threat.

Human brains sensing danger activate at a primitive level. Early parts of the brain take over. At this point all human beings lose the ability to reason, think or remember and instead they slip immediately into the ancient fight/flight response.

Anxious or depressed people, referred into this class,

want to learn to be calm, relaxed and pleasure loving. So Nora and I tell silly jokes. We smile a lot, as sincerely as we can manage, five days a week for sixteen weeks at a crack.

Oh, oh, look over there.... Rachel is frozen in a sort of paralysis. In the dim light of the gym I can see her fingers and toes extended, her arms and legs straining open. There is an ugly, crucified look to her body. Her muscles are knotting, twisting. Other students are beginning to soften and slump, and as always someone snores softly.

I have been leading a guided imagery exercise. Today, it's a simple pleasant fantasy about a desert island, a place meant to be restful, comfortable and remote. Our students are to put away their awareness of responsibilities for a while and their reward will be a sense of relief, however temporary.

Ordinarily, I tiptoe in my tennis shoes about the gym. Part of my responsibility is lightly tapping anyone on the shoulder who is whistling, puffing or downright snoring. This is meant to be light trance, not "night-night."

"Turn over on your stomach," I often whisper.

But I am only aware of the rigid posture Rachel has assumed. In the faint light she looks like a stiffened corpse.

Eight

> "In fact they are mad people in full delirium, nevertheless, they take railway tickets, they dine and sleep in hotels, they speak to a great number of people. We are, it is true, sometimes told that they were thought a little odd, that they looked preoccupied and dreamy, but after all they are not recognized as mad people...".

Pierre Janet

*F*araway, *the voice retreats 'til she hears nothing. A mist falls and through it, a small girlchild lies alone on her back in a darkened tunnel. Through her bent knees, she can sometimes see the candle shining from the altar far away. She cannot move her feet. The witch has used magic powers and the girl is stuck, glued to the stony floor with blood. Her feet can never carry her out. Fear presses down upon her. She can't breathe! The heaviness on her chest grows as her body stiffens, grows colder. Finally she is dead. Her name is Peeper.*

Oh, no. What now? Rachel is cataleptic, stiff and cold to my touch. I hurry the class off the fantasy island, back to the fantasy mainland, then to the sweaty reality of our gymnasium. As quickly as I can, I make up a verbal invitation to the students.

"Everyone, now return to your everyday waking state. Remember to stretch, wiggle your fingers and toes. Go ahead, yawn. Now become alert."

I hope the brevity of the trip is not noticeable to everyone. Nora is looking at me with surprise. Everyone but Rachel responds to my suggestion "to come back to everyday awareness." Once more, the lights are turned on, gleaming, reflecting in the giant mirrors and the epoxied oaken floor. The sudden glare is stunning.

Class members smile woozily, put on their shoes and pick up their mats to stack them against the wall next to the red enamel doors marked Exit. Walking out into the daylight some students chatter, others are thoughtfully quiet, still responding to the pleasure of positive, light trance.

Now I can move close to Rachel to touch her. I want to question her softly, yet as firmly as I can, as she slowly, slowly opens her eyes, stares directly into mine and crushes my hand in her chilly grip. Her fingers feel bony and harsh.

"I could not stay! I went away. Relaxation is awful! I lost myself and went somewhere dark and cold. Help me."

Rachel's teeth are chattering and her skin has a blue tinge. Nora knows what is wrong.

"She's in shock."

Covered with a warm purple and red plaid blanket on the couch in the First Aid Office, Rachel seems to doze. Nora sits beside her looking through her First Aid manual. The Paramedics are on their way.

The child is waking with feelings of expectation and joy. Today is the day for the family outing to the seashore. New friends of Mommy and Daddy's are coming along. She doesn't like them, but she'll have fun playing in the water and building a sand castle. A whole day without work at home.. She dresses in a hurry so she can make sandwiches for Mommy and Daddy and stir together her first potato salad.

Mashed egg is hard to handle and smears easily the outside of the bowl. The girl wipes it off as Mommy and Daddy's friends arrive. They have brought no other little children. Too bad.

Mommy is having a well day! The child will have fun in the sunshine and enjoy a ride, sitting on Daddy's friend's lap near the window so she can see. The man's wife drives. She is a skinny lady and can fit into the front seat with Mommy who takes lots more room than her half. Daddy, the man and the little girl are back here together. Mommy's friend hugs tight, rubbing the child's arms and back. Sometimes he holds her knees in his sweaty hand. She can feel his breath puffing on the back of her neck and hear the wet noise his nose makes. He smells smoky and brown, like Mommy and Daddy.

Look at the maple trees, with dark green leaves and big brown branches, big enough for tree houses. Along the way are warehouses and sweat shops, where people work hard. Auntie spends long days in a sweat shop. I wish Auntie could come to the shore some day, but she doesn't like Mommy any more, since the accident.

Summer cottages appear, little white Cape Cod houses dotting the hills. There are fences around one or two of the houses, but mostly the yards run into one another. Friendly. Too bad Mommy hates Auntie. The daylight shines softly so that the sky looks like the inside of a seashell.

"When hurricanes come, these houses will not be wiped away. It will take too long for the wind to get through these round hills from the ocean. These little houses, like my dollhouse, will survive a long, long time. They will not die."

At the rocky beach the grownups choose a secluded spot on the wide open sand to set up green umbrellas and tables. Daddy brings new lawn chairs and two coolers of beer. The child carries the little yellow pail and shovel the man gave her as they got in the car. She tries hard to think he is nice.

"I wish he would find someone else to play with. Not me."

The day is calm. Tugs and trawlers hang against the blue ocean, like paper cutouts. Seagulls squawk and whirl in circles.

"The mommy and daddy seagulls are white. The baby seagulls are grey and their voices are peeping sounds rather than squawks."

The coarse grey sand feels warm, collapsing the foot prints the child leaves behind. She has to walk fast not to burn her skinny feet.

"Mommy isn't sick. Today she is 'social' and that means today she likes people."

79

The girl wanders to the water's edge where the waves splash over her hot feet. The water is cool on pink toes, turning the little wigglers red, then blue.

"*The sound of the waves, rolling in to shore, gives her a peaceful feeling inside. The waves are pretty to watch, with the sun shining through their tops where they curl into white. When she is a rich lady, she will live near this ocean in a pretty New England cottage with a slanted roof and she will paint nice pictures like the pictures on calendars. The pictures will be of pretty children and dogs and cats wearing clothes just like people, with hair ribbons. Every day will be clean and pretty like this.*

She loves the blues of the water. Most of all, though, she loves the clean, white clouds. Pretty, pretty. They float freely and lightly in the sky."

"*Beautiful, isn't it?*"

Daddy's friend comes up behind the child to put his arm around her waist. He squeezes hard. His hands are chilly. Black hairs spring out from the tops of them.

"*Yes, it is pretty.*"

"*I'll be taking you swimming after lunch while the grown-ups nap.*"

"*I don't know how to swim.*"

"*I'll teach you. It's easy to learn to swim.*"

"*I don't want to go in the deep water.*"

"*Oh, I'll hold you really tight. You'll be safe with me. I promise we won't go too far out. When the water reaches my waist I'll stop.*"

She looks closely at the man's waist to see how high it is. How different he looks from Daddy. Looking back at the rhythmic rise and fall of the waves, the girl thinks about the difference... This man has dark skin with a soft dimpled stomach hanging over his trunks. Daddy has no stomach. Below his waist Daddy is skinny. He is thin, hard and sharp.

The waves move forward, rolling, dropping down, down upon themselves. Back and forth, up and down go the waves. Back and forth like rhythm in music. The little girl's eyes see back into her head where the ugly pictures are.

Daddy stands in a circle with people dressed like him. He

holds a shining cup in his painted hands. Daddy's fingers are different colors, like rosy Easter eggs. When he drinks, red wetness dribbles out of his mouth and down his chin. Deep inside her the girl knows what he is drinking. Daddy stares darkly in his a long black dress. With a black cloth over his head, he is singing in the cellar. His voice echoes between the stone walls...

The bad picture dissolves quickly away. She is back looking at the shifting, sliding ocean and Daddy's friend's puffy body. He has been talking to her about swimming. This man's hair is like oil on a mudpuddle. He has muddy eyes, which slide rapidly from side to side in his round face. The smell from under his arms makes her back away.

She does not want to go with him. But Mommy will be very angry with her if she says no ,'cause the child knows she must please big people.

"I guess."

"Good, we have a date. Shall I walk you over to the blanket?"

Wavering over the blankets, unpacking the baskets, Mommy is unsteady on her large feet in the soft sand.

"Mommy is laughing. This kind of laugh is nice, not shrill, loud, hurtful or a croaking giggle that will not stop."

There is mother of pearl sunshine on the child's warm skin. It makes her safe. She runs to the picnic. Her uneasyness about the afternoon prods her, like a persistent vibration inside. Yet food tastes good. Hot dogs! Spicy, with flecks of grease bubbling through the skin. The narrow bun turns doughy in her damp hand. She squeezes it tight to hold in the mustard. She's usually not a hungry kind of girl.

"A very poor eater," Mommy says, explaining the girl's small size. At home anger sits at the table with complaint, sulleness. But today is different, warm and delicious, smelling of salty wieners, relish and beer."

"Can I sit with you?" The child moves over on the blanket to make room for Daddy's friend.

"Folks, I will entertain Rachel after lunch so you can rest. I really enjoy children."

"Oh, I imagine you know a great deal about kids. It's a

shame you don't have a houseful. Oh!, yes, I do know about you."

Mommy stares directly at the man, nodding. Her large mouth smiles a wide creamy grin. In the bright sunshine the child can see Mommy has put something greasy on her hair to hold it down. Thin and fine, at home Mommy's hair makes sparks in the dark like a cat's fur, flying up again on top as soon as it is combed. She wears it short , short in back. When Mommy and Daddy aren't fighting, Daddy shaves Mommy's neck for her.

With plastic forks everyone eats the crumbling green apple pie. Sand is in the plates now, speckling the lips of the feasters. A variety of faded, dingy crotcheted pillows is unpacked. Mommy and Daddy and the lady settle down to nap. Smiling, cuddling close, the ladies cover themselves with blankets. Daddy is smiling, too. He has not spoken since leaving home, but now he looks pleased. He may have been worrying about missing Mass today. There are many days in which he does not speak. Today he looks happy with the day Mommy has planned.

"Well, shall we begin our adventure?" The man extends his hand.

"We certainly are going to have a good time!"

Jerkily, together the man and the little girl walk to the water's edge. She cannot match his long steps. The girl is looking at his huge shadow and her small one. She feels herself in a dream, one she has dreamed many times. Daddy's friend begins running in circles in the water, splashing, inspiring the child to laugh and do the same.

Unexpectedly, Daddy's friend picks her up. He dunks the child head down. She gasps, swallowing a mixture of sand and sea water, choking. The man holds her close to his fat chest with his strong arms.

"Lets build a sand castle."

The man looks back towards the picnic site. All that can be seen are blankets moving over a tangle of bodies.

"We'll let your lunch settle before we swim." The child nods and crumples to the sand, still coughing. Time passes, while she tries to amuse the man. Used to playing alone, she watches his heavy hands carefully to see what he does to entertain himself. Scowling, he moves sand from one damp heap to another.

There should be doors and windows in the lumpy house he has made. The child adds a fancy front door with a shell knocker. Next, she wants a moat and a turret. It is to be a real castle, not just an ordinary house. The turret will have a flag from a piece of seaweed and... "

The man is impatient. He does not care about the castle.

"Now, Rachel, now. Time for your swim lesson. Come on, I'll race you to see who gets wet first!"

The girl hesitates for a moment, then runs into the water, yelling and splashing. Looming behind her, the man picks her up once more in his beefy arms. His fleshy stomach presses against her body in a sweaty caress.

"Quiet now." Daddy's friend begins to walk out into the ocean. As he holds her close, close, his hand slides inside the leg of her bathing suit.

"Please put me down."

The grinning man lowers her, slowly, into the top of a wave. The water is over her head.

"No, please don't. I'm afraid." Daddy's friend laughs.

"I'll hold you tight. Don't you worry, Sweetheart. Come, I'll show you how to float."

Lying in the water, the child's head rests on his arm. His immense right hand is under her buttocks. She is terrified, stiffening. Leaning against him she feels his hand pushing painfully between her legs. She twists in uncontrolled alarm and slips underwater. The man's hands grab her hair, jerking her up. Scanning the shore, he tucks the child firmly under one arm.

"Be quiet. Behave yourself, you hear me? Else I'm going to leave you here in deep water to drown, all alone. Understand?"

Rachel's teeth are chattering. Her body is numb. The sun is behind clouds. The cold ocean is not her friend. It is her enemy, a betrayer. She is cold, then warm between her legs, wetting herself. Mommy will be angry.

Daddy's friend's fat face glares at her. His hand is over her mouth . Two boys swim nearer, shouting laughingly to each *other, pushing an air mattress along the top of the waves. The child hears the man whisper slowly and carefully, lips pressed against her ear.*

"Not to tell. I do not wish to be cast out."

The man talks on and on, his fingers fiercely probing the child. Her other self already knows about the placebetween her legs.

"You are all right, safe, safe. Everything is going to be all right. Don't cry." The voice is familiar.

"All I want is to be out of the water." Closing her eyes, the child lets her "other me" take charge. This little girl is too small to take care of herself, but her other-me knows what to do.

"Let the man do what he wants. That's right. Or else Mother will say you are bad again, and you'll have to be cleansed in the cleansing ceremony. You don't want that, do you? I'll help you. I'll stay with you. I promise, I'll stay for awhile." As yet, the voice has no name.

The man brings the girl back to the shore. She knows she will never, never, never go into the ocean again. She will never swim.

When Daddy's friend puts the child down on the sand, her legs won't walk. He leaves her crumpled near the edge of the water, catching her breath. The salt water stings the scratches on her thighs, the soft tissue within her. She hears the voice, strong and sweet in her head.

"I'm holding you. Feel my arms around you now. You're safe with me."

Mommy is waddling toward the girl, her heavy body shoving her strange feet deep into the sand. Large footprints show her third toe is long and sharp like that of a giant bird. She smiles wide, wide, and winks at her daughter. She is not angry today.

"Have you two been having fun?"

The child cannot nod. She has never seen Mommy walk so far or smile so widely. Mommy pulls her up, panting, pushing the little girl to the pile of blankets. Heaving herself down, Mommy pants. Between gasps she murmurs to the man.

"No longer for sale. Important plans. Don't overstep.

Things other than your little appetites, you know."

Daddy's friend continues to grin. Finding a towel, the child winds it around her shoulders. Soon, the grown ups are wrapped in each other's arms again, eyes half closed. No one notices when the girl leaves.

Out of sight she squeezes her minute body between giant grainy boulders protruding onto the sand. No one is here, no people. She will have this cool, quiet, speckled temple all to herself. Burrowing into the sand, she curls herself into a fetal position.

Nine

*"The first exorcism I performed was very fright-
ening for me. When they brought the young man to
me, he was suffering greatly. He was foaming at
the mouth. He was grinding his teeth, He lunged
for me at one point. I held up my crucifix and
prayed. I felt spiritually more than physically att-
tacked. There's often this strong physical reaction
from the sufferer. We are dealing with incredible
forces and unpredictable reactions, and after all,
we're only poor human beings."*

Father Guglielmo Lauriola, *San Francisco*

Childhood depression has been recently ac-
knowledged by researchers and clinicians. Rachel must
have been one of those youngsters. Little children do not
know how to tell others they are sad, but they appear
disconsolate to observers, and have profound appetite
loss, fatigue and sleep disturbances. Passive, depressed
children think slowly and harbor thoughts of death and
suicide. With low self-esteem they withdraw socially.
The most seriously depressed preschoolers turn out to be
abused or neglected. In these studies, mothers of these
severely depressed children are also seriously disturbed.

After "The Day of the Stressful Stress Management
Class," as Nora calls it, all the month of March is a waste
of time, as far as any movement in Rachel's therapy is
concerned.

"I'm letting my school work go. I have no idea why I
can't function at home or at school. It has something to

do with therapy."

I have no doubt, this is the case. Rachel once organized her time around family and schooling. Now, her sense of time wraps around her therapeutic sessions. She cannot concentrate as usual, for something important is happening to her awareness. Waking up emotionally, the effort exhausts her.

"My husband is more and more doubtful about therapy, so you can understand why I don't want to make any changes that will upset him. Just stop my physical pain. Please! My husband tells me it is best to focus on my science classes. He insists I get my mind off this constant preoccupation with the past."

Spouses, who are deeply troubled themselves, cannot act effectively as therapists. Marriages are meant to be reciprocal partnerships. My client owes time and affection to her "loved one", but there is no loyalty of that kind due me. Our exchange is money, in return for time and my experience, training and careful attention.

Therapy is constantly surprising. For one thing, in order to heal, a depressed client must overcome her difficulty expressing anger. At the same time people who are chronically angry need to admit hurt feelings, insecurity or fear before their hostility can lessen.

Rachel continues to be mild, helpful, still largely unaware of the emotional swamp in which she lives. She is unfailingly polite with everyone else in her life, but she is making progress because she dares be a little rude to me.

Her nights are horrific, nightmare filled. Afraid to sleep, she senses violence may emerge within her if she relaxes. Sleep she must sometimes, in spite of the terror awaiting her.

Mommy hunkers down in the dark cellar, smoking. The child is afraid to look down the stairs, smelling the sweet odor rising up the decaying steps. Mommy and Daddy both smoke and smoke, lips clamped around cigarettes, white or brown. Sometimes, Mommy lights up while a smoking Camel burns away in the ashtray. Mommy leaves butts on the back of the toilet or soggy on the drain board. Waking in the morning, her coughing and choking scares Rachel. She knows her mother and father can burn up in bed. What will she do, if they catch on fire?

The house smells like old rope. The sweet odor hangs in the wall paper, in the rotting wood of the doors and windows.

Pictures flood Rachel's mind, overwhelming her body. Images connect themselves to her muscles, tangling around her bones, making them ache. They come unbidden, these horrible pictures, images of gore. Her chronic physical pain returns night after night. Sleep brings her new nightmares.

The aureate altar is covered with blood, spilling down upon the white silk cloth, where the butchered animal is lying, entrails exposed. All rites must be performed according to Lucifer's wishes.

The man stands with arms raised above his head. His knife drips blood, blending into the sleeves of his crimson gown. The entranced girl stands facing the altar, spellbound. Spellbound means bound by spells. The child knows.

Ten

"There is a tremendous pressure in society to find some evil subculture and to say 'Ah ha!' when there's something devilish afoot. It makes the world more understandable. After Matamoros, I was interviewed by a reporter from a television station. He needed some footage on why Satanists were going to be killing people in New York next, and I could tell I was disappointing him."

Marc Galanter, *Psychiatrist*

"Roberta, I cannot come to therapy today. I must write to you instead. I dreamed I saw Mother with a board in her hands. I still see it descending toward me. Even the knots and splinters are clear. I awoke knowing my skull may burst. My headache pain is a scream against the gaping, torn, upside down ceiling of my mind. The sense of my body whirls inside me, broken and searing. I feel my own teeth clench into the back of my skull. Why do they gnaw so? They are icy teeth. Now they become fiery flashes of purple and red. I dream Mother tears away at the same spot again and again. My eyes burst away, fire burns where they were once contained. The stabbing pain moves down my neck, screaming a chant. My ears reglue themselves, leap to the top of my skull to protect me. Mother wants my brain. The chanting increases. There is shrieking as a razor shaves away my scalp and at last I am still and quiet.

I dream again. I work in a factory and I am a cripple, broken bodied. My brain has been removed, like my heart, and yet I am not dead. Help me Roberta! I am so tired and hurt. I must rest, but I don't know how."

tired and hurt. I must rest, but I don't know how."

Today Roger uses his therapy session to recover from his most recent shock.

"These kids I'm trying to reach, do you know that some are as young as ten? They get their "weird stuff" from movies and books, but mostly from rock music. They've got street classifications: Punks, Suicidals, Skates, Pops, Hard Cores, Skin Heads, Politicals and the Occult. Bands like DOA, Dead on Arrival, GBH, Great Bodily Harm, TSOL, D.I., C2D, MIA."

"You're all worked up again."

"Heavy Metal has affected millions of kids! It's not a fad just for the obsessed. I'm not scared for the common Punk. I see them in their black nylon hose, torn fishnet stuff, with safety pins through their noses and white faces and I remember what its like to be young and rebellious. Hell, I had long hair in the '70's. I know all about being seen as sinister. Punk's part of Pop culture. I can get Dr. Martin boots through the Penney's catalogue if I want to! And spikes."

Pacing again, Roger is bellowing. He shouts so loudly, I hardly hear words. Something about the Suiciders. He's getting too high. Together we've only dealt with his depressive episodes. I'd hate to see him get hyped over his antisatanic mission, unable to bring himself down except through emotional collapse.

"Metal Heads, Head Bangers, Rebel Riders, Rivet Heads, Stoners, Rockers!" Roger is chanting," Death, Suicide, Drugs, Violence, Sex and Rock and Roll!"

Roger is not only high. He's compulsive, like the kids he's trying to help. Obsessed. It's frightening to see this degree of fervor in an emotionally fragile man.

"Judas Priest, Black Sabbath, Merciful Fate, Iron Maiden, Metallica, DIO, Grim Reaper, Slayer, Megadeth! AC/DC, WASP, SOD! Do you know what that stands for? Storm Troopers of Death! I suppose that's all right with you! Why should you care if Ozzie Ozbourne gets stinking rich singing 'Suicide is the Only Way Out?'"

"No, it's not all right with me. What do you want me

to do? Upset my own life? Look, I grew up loving the Blues. Despair music speaks to young people now, just as the Blues spoke to Black people in the South. Just as the Blues spoke to us when we were kids. Powerful music is about anger and hurt. Anger and hurt, Roger."

"No, this music is about hate. The Black Metal stuff. The Satan promoters. I hate them back."

Quieter, now, he's finally running down, ready to level.

"Listen, here's what I'm worked up about. I guess I'd better let you know. See if I'm crazy. I'll give you the short version. A couple of kids are into Junior satanism. They're playing a game, see? The boy's sister keeps winning, so the boy gets up early the next morning and hits her three times with an axe. She's still alive, so she tells her brother she's won!"

I stay quiet. I'm learning. In a few minutes Roger's shoulders shake. He holds his head on with both hands.

His sobs are male, hard and raw.

" ...not your kids, Roger. You have a sweet thoughtful boy and girl, nice normal kids. And they have a loving father as a guide. They're not going to get into that kind of trouble. No way are they 'Deep End' kids. You're a 'good enough' Dad. You care, you follow through. Your kids love you."

"Roberta, I don't want my kids to know about the Devil 'cause they'll look for him and find him.

"How do you know, Roger? Do you think that happened to you?"

It' s time for Roger to accept medication.

Eleven

"Satan has been the best friend the church has ever had, as he has kept it in business all these years!"- the Ninth Satanic Statement - is not limited just to the religious organization referred to as 'the church.' How convenient an enemy the Devil has been for the weak and insecure! Crusaders against the Devil maintained that Satan, even if accepted on an anthropomorphic basis, was neither so evil nor so dangerous that he could not be personally vanquished."

Anton La Vey

What do you think, Sam? Is fear of the Devil part of an emotional illness?

"Not necessarily. In kids it's just sloppy thinking. Many kids haven't been given sensible religious values to use and they have to confront the age old questions without help. Luckily, good parents feed in positive ideas and remind kids they're OK. They show them good things in life, to take the sunshine with the shit."

"But what about the Devil?"

"Which Devil? Are you talking about the Devil as a symbol, or a genuine force in the world? I guess it would be normal to believe in the Devil, if you were raised in Northern Ireland or some southern parts of the United States. In Spain belief in the Devil is held by around a third of the population. In spite of all the Catholics there, that's lower than the number of believers in this country. Politically, to Moslems Satan is important. The French and the Danes don't seem to take him seriously at all."

"Then what about people with personality disorders? Like cultists."

"Sure, cultists are extra dependent people, so they may need a Devil to keep them togather. Everybody seeks a self, an identity. While growing up, all individuals have to struggle against their dark side, their own impulses. Although most people are willing to take responsibility for their own nastiness, their greediness, or their vicious thoughts, some people will not accept their childishness. Why not blame the Devil? That's what he's for, isn't he? A convenience?"

There is a lot of talk about the Devil in our town. Even though we citizens of Texas are growing in psychological sophistication, most still feel more apprehension about psychotherapy than fundamentalist religion.

What do you therapists do, people ask? Ann Landers sends people into therapy, but she doesn't explain what happens in a therapist's office. Do you have to be crazy to go into therapy? Are sex therapists only interested in sex? What's a family therapist? What's the difference between a psychologist and a psychiatrist, other than about fifty dollars?

No, you don't have to be crazy. Most people come in because they sense they are missing something. Sex therapists are experts in relationships, not just genitals. Family therapists are trained in seeing a dysfunctional family as a system of interrelationships that need adjustment, so that individuals in the family can develop themselves. A psychologist studies how people think and feel. A psychiatrist does this too, along with going to medical school to become an M.D.

I know no one comes into therapy easily or comfortably. Clients want happiness or success, not to peer deeply into themselves. Their hesitancy reflects their fear of what they may find.

"If I look inside, I may see my demons," says a warm, sweet woman who becomes a friend. Her demons turn out to be only the discouragements of the child she once was, teased for being fat. Therapy reveals hidden parts of her personality and all her surprises are happy ones.

Almost at once, she releases more emotional energy into living fully, turning her life into a series of interesting undertakings. Her demons were her talents, unused and nagging her painfully. I'm glad she looked inside and I'm glad we have lunch together now. Her fear of the Devil has disappeared.

As a sex therapist, I treat victims of incest among my clients. I believe all therapists do, but some don't know it. That's highly possible, because many incest victims repress all memory of the incest. Loss of memory is a coping mechanism which allows an abused child to survive.

By controlling her thoughts and feelings, she can block out all recognition of sexual mistreatment. Because many adults are blocked, they cannot tell what happened to them as children. They truly do not know. If the abuse was cruel, violent or sadistic, repression is the main defense against the pain of recall. Recent psychiatric literature describes twelve women who suffered violent incestuous abuse for years. Nine of the twelve have been amnesic, remembering nothing, until they were in therapy in their thirties and forties.

Prosecution and conviction of incest offenders happens in only a few cases. It has been estimated that within the next ten years, twenty-eight million children will be sexually abused. Twenty five million will be girls. A full twenty-eight percent of one thousand, two hundred college age women have had sex with an adult before they turned thirteen.

Only six percent of those violations were reported. Half of children sexually abused are under the age of eleven. The American Psychology Association concludes that in cases of incest which involve young girls, twenty-five percent of the abusers are fathers, another twenty-five percent are stepfathers, and the remaining fifty percent involve adoptive fathers, grandfathers, brothers, uncles and cousins.

Rachel's therapy remains at a halt. She humors me by

coming, but just being here is not good enough. Rachel is refusing to put herself in any situation in which she might feel. She has agreed to keep a journal as part of her contract with me. I sometimes listen as she reads excerpts. So far, she has written only insignificant happenings with her daughters, snatches of trivia and everydayness. I'm bored again, a warning sign, and getting angry, which means I'm about to do something.

"Let's rest for a while, Rachel. Why don't we use this hour for quiet comfort. Count backward from ten to one. Now add feelings of calm and quiet. Inhale peace and exhale all blocks to your experience."

"I can't do that, Roberta. It would be such a waste of precious time. I need to talk to you about the girls. We must plan their future." But Rachel's eyes are closed.

"You're right, Rachel. This hour can be very important to us both."

Please read aloud to me from what you see on the last page of your journal. In a monotone Rachel reads to me from the blank page. And it is at that moment Rachel's therapy begins.

The child sits, listening to the laughter going on behind the closed parlor doors. Small for her age, she is emaciated. Long blonde hair accents the smallness of her pale oval face. Her expression is blank and only the rigid stance of her body betrays how frightened she is. The brown mahogany doors slide slowly open.

"Come here." The girl rises. Her face feels stiff as she walks into the parlor.

"You know what to do." Mother's voice is harsh.The girl begins to tremble. She cannot move. Mother grabs her by the arm, pushing her down violently onto the stained hardwood floor. She begins to undress the child. Mother tears at her undershirt, her ragged panties.

"I will not cry! I will not feel! Get Lilith! Get Lilith! I need Lilith, go away, Rachel!"

"I'm here."

Mother's friend is a giant. Tall, with dark slick hair, he is smiling, but not a nice smile. The girl has never seen hair so black. It is shiny, like shoe polish. The man's teeth are yellow and crooked, immense, exposed by his grin. From where she crouches, the child hears the air whistling into his wide nostrils. A scent of sweetness comes from his hair. The man is panting, as he moves his ample body toward her. She crawls away, but with a few steps he is holding tightly her shoulders, her neck. His hands are sweating and large. They can cover her body. The child cannot stop shaking as he moves his hands down and turns her toward him. She will be all right. Lilith will be here.

She is suffocating from the weight of his body against her. She knows she is going to be sick.

"Do it." She hears Mother whisper next to her ear.

"Put it in your mouth! You know what to do!"

The girl gags. She beats her ineffectual fists against the bulk of the man's stomach, fighting to get away.

"You little bitch! What do you think you are doing?" The child pulls away.

"Going to be sick."

The man slaps her face with the flat of his hand, then uses her mouth again. She vomits as he ejaculates. He strikes her again. Lilith does not feel the hurt.

"Go wash, you little fool." Mother's voice is fierce, low. Her friend cannot hear.

"You tell your father Bobby was here and I'll beat the shit out of you."

"I promise."

The child picks up her clothes to creep down the hall on the long journey to the bathroom. There , she dabs at herself with a grimy washcloth. Her body is icy. Red marks, from being hit, reflect in the cracked mirror. She will not look again.

"Set the table for supper!"Mother is saying goodbye to Bob.

The girl obeys Mother's orders. She listens idly to the silly laughter, as Mother's giggles come from the third floor stoop of the grey tenement building. This apartment is called a rabbit run, because each room opens upon the next. There are four rooms. Down the hall the old man and woman in the other half of the tenement share the speckled toilet.

Daddy makes money for the rent working on the fish pier. Whenhe comes home, shiny with scales, he stinks. When he leaves in the dark mornings, he stinks. The smell of fish is on his skin, his clothes, and on his breath, combined with a brown smoky odor. On the kitchen table he cuts the heads and tails off the fish he takes from a befouled bucket. Sometimes, the girl watches the sad eyes of the fish, sorry for them, hating the idea of murdering poor creatures.

Tonight she is unthinking, feeling nothing.

Mother holds her head high, giggling under her breath. She has dollar bills in her hand. Rolling them together, she puts them in her dress pocket.

Daddy is coughing, as he climbs the long flight of stairs. In a cloud of smoke, Camel cigarette in mouth, Daddy slouches through the outside door. Compared to neighbor men, Daddy is small. His mustache is black, like his thinning hair. He does not smile or talk , unless he is drunk. Then he does not stop talking. His hands are bony, with large knobby knuckles.

The child catches Daddy's smell, made up of smoke, fish, beer and the sweat of many days and nights. Standing beside him, Mother looms huge, her soft, fat body overwhelming Daddy's skinniness. From here Rachel can see Mother's profile. The bottoms of Mother's ears point upward and backward. Her odd soft ears join her head far below her jawline. Mother is special. Her ears and feet make her important to the others.

"Was he here? Tell me or I'll kill you!"

Daddy is brave, he has been drinking. He grabs the youngster's long hair, savagely pulling her head back. Mother stands in the doorway to the inner rooms. Her wide smile gives her a look of high excitement. A new battle is coming.

"No, nobody was here, Daddy!

"You're lying."

She can tell on Mother or lie. Either way she will be beaten. Either way no longer matters.

Mother, cheeks flushed, eyes shining, licks her lips with her heavy tongue. She glares down at the girl from the doorway. The child can see Mother's hand is clenched in her pocket.

It is time for the girl to die now. Tonight, when the parents are asleep will be the time. Peeper has reemerged and Peeper has decided.

Musing in my crowded office, I remind myself, crazy people do have children. That makes them crazy parents.

What could be more terrifying than a madwomen as a mother?

A father who believes himself Satan?

Twelve

*"'...A Black Mass is like a Catholic Mass, except things
are done backwards and chants are said in reverse. This
shows you how to use a living altar..A human altar. A
woman. You get a woman to take off her clothes and
you stick candles in her openings'*

*"Yeah? That's heavy shit, man,' Ricky was im-
pressed. 'I'll take it.*

"Say You Love Satan," **David St. Clair**

Roger insists on talking all about the book I
lent him. Roger is writing a book himself, and he is also
back on lithium. It's too soon to notice major changes, but
he seems much calmer.

"Like this one, my book is a real shocker."

I need to look through my paperback again, to remember the details. Ricky Kasso is the name of the boy
who wields a murder knife in this true story. Ricky heard
about Le Vey's 'Satan's Bible' from a clerk in an occult
book store:

The kid listened with fascination as the book seller told
him what was described inside the wrapper. Power.
Spells and other important stuff, like candle burning.
There was instruction on chants and incantations. The
most important part was direction on how to do it right.

Then the clerk came to the Black Mass.

Ricky scowled. He had no idea of what the man was
talking about. But he soon learned this was not something for the 'Velcro heads'. This was something for him.

Ricky spent his time at his parent's vacation home in

the woods, smoking marijuana and reading his precious book. Closing his eyes, he would make pictures from the text. They were images far removed from his young real life with his Christian parents and their ideas of morality. If this book is telling the truth, he thought, then nothing was impossible. He would have power over himself and over others.

He didn't have to put up with this little, boring life and the trivial beliefs his parents had.

Satan was the way. He had the answers Ricky needed to get what he must have.

Maybe Jesus was enough for his Mom and Dad, and they might just die and go to Heaven and that stuff, but what about right now. Being fourteen required a lot of power, like getting yourself on the football team. That wasn't the kind of thing Jesus was about to help you with. Or rock music or a chemical high. No fun with the Lord.

Ricky changed, became cocky. In his last year of Junior High he walked and talked with assurance.

Music was his overwhelming interest, his friends thought, and his favorite group was Black Sabbath, with Ozzy Osbourne.

Ozzy was everything. And Satan. Ricky couldn't stop talking about how Ozzy bit the head off a chicken, and how Satan gave him, Ricky, devil power.

St. Clair's book goes on to tell of the night when Ricky stabs another teenage boy to death in a satanic ritual, then screams at the dying youth, "Say you love Satan!"

Ricky and his young followers buried the mutilated body in a shallow grave in the woods that night, where their bonfire ceremony had been held.

Days later, in his cell, jailed as the prime suspect, Ricky hanged himself.

Today, Roger has bought his own copy and, as he hands mine back to me, he is crying. He remembers when he prayed to the Devil for himself.

"I was a thirteen year old. Tried making my pact with the evil forces. My mom died anyway. She had ovarian cancer."

Roger never knew Ricky Kasso, but suffers for him. And for those evil-thinking, angry, drugged out, crazy kids he is coming to know and love.

Like the Man of Sorrows, Roger is acquainted with despair. He has slid into the depressed phase of his illness.

Thirteen

"The figure of Satan, too, has undergone a curious development, from the time of his first undistin-
guished appearance in the Old Testament texts, to
his heyday in Christianity...The devil remains as an
appendix to psychology. It is a psychological rule
that when an archetype has lost its metaphysical
hypostasis, it becomes identified with the conscious mind of an individual, which it influences
and refashions in its own form."

Carl Jung, *Psychology and Religion*

Mother, Daddy and the child sit down to supper.
Tasteless spare ribs, boiled, run together with pale, canned
green beans . It's a change from the usual yellow-fatted, boiled
chicken or the fried fish, complete with heads and tails. As usual, the girl does not eat. She hunches on her chair, until time to
be sent away to do the dishes.

Lilith does not allow her to feel pain. Tonight, Peeper will
end the struggle. She has died before and knows how.

In bed the child hears Mommy and Daddy in the next bedroom, making noises. She closes her eyes and thinks about
Grandpa. She remembers him hugging her. He smells good,
like washing machine soap. She helps him with his canaries.
With their loud chirping, they are fun. Cheerful. The girl can
watch them launch their yellow bodies from perch to perch.

The dusty smell of feathers lets her know she is in his safe
and life-filled apartment. Grandpa lives on the floor below her
rabbbit-run, and he invites her to come see him whenever she
likes. When she spends the night with Grandpa, she sleeps in
the same room with the canaries, who have their little heads
under their wings. In the morning they sing her awake. Soft to
the touch and tame, the canaries let her hold them. They trust

*her with their tiny bodies. She can feel their hearts beating.
She longs for Grandpa to hold her, as she held the canaries.*

*"Make the cold go away." Now the girl sees herself sitting
next to Grandpa at the dinner table. It is a Sunday. She dips
her biscuit carefully into chicken gravy, imitating the old man.
Next to Grandpa's elbow , she learns about dunking, happiness and love.*

*Then the bad pictures come, as they always do. They scare
her so much , she wets the bed again. Mother will punish her if
she finds out, maybe cleanse her. In the worst picture Grandpa
is hanging in the air. The rope around his neck is up high. She
doesn't understand why he won't wake up.*

*"Come down. Come down. You need to fix the sore place on
your head."*

Fourteen

" He is the enemy number one, the tempter par excellence....He is the secret enemy that sows errors and misfortunes in human history...the treacherous and cunning enchanter who finds his way into us by way of the senses..."

Pope VI, *November 15, 1972*

Rachel, perfect student, wife and mother, is failing in school. She initiates a new attempt to leave therapy.

"I can't study. Therefore, I must drop out of school or out of therapy." she states firmly. I can tell she has rehearsed her speech.

"School is important, Roberta. I'm sure you can do a great deal for me in the future, perhaps. I want you to understand what I'm saying. Recently, I have decided, I too, want to become a professional woman. I will be a therapist myself. I know school is necessary to get the correct credentials, so for now, I will focus on my studies. Don't you agree I'm making the correct choice?"

"I do not."

Of course Rachel avoids reexperiencing old pain. Humans do not often voluntarily opt for severe suffering. I don't. Rachel continues on with her reasons for stopping therapy now. This much resistance may mean Rachel and I are finally getting somewhere, but I must wait for Rachel to be willing to help herself.

Therapeutic change cannot always be clearly observed. Sometimes, a person's "crisis resolution" creates the kind of drama we see in movies or read in novels.

People sob out their conflict and feel immediate relief. Others experience their own powerful anger. They go on to rage, then grief and finally forgive themselves. Across the hall from my office is a bathroom, a required necessity for a psychotherapist's office. Sometimes, doing emotional "work," highly emotional clients develop sudden stomach aches or a terrible need to empty bowels or bladder. Therapy is humanizing. But more often, changes occur in miniature steps, too small to be seen by themselves. Rachel does not know how far she has come, even though her daughters tell her she is changing.

"You're listening to us, Mom."

Rachel is more sensitive, a warmer, calmer person. Still, she scolds herself for doing poorly at school.

Tonight, I am to meet "the Girls." This evening is a fall dusky beauty with a blazing, purple-pink sunset and warm winds rattling the palms. The green of the lawn looks chocolate brown.

In my white tile hallway the girls line up politely, red haired stairsteps. Each gives me an obligatory kiss, keeping their eyes on Mama to make sure they do everything right. As they troop out the door in a line of ruffles, starch and clean white stockings, I sympathize with them. They are so crisply curled and painfully clean.

The box they bring to me makes a liquid sound. They have found it on the porch. My name is on it.

Unwrapped, the little girls and I can see the restaurant sized fruit jar the box concealed holds something round, half floating, pink on top and dark below.

It takes the strong light of the front hall to identify it as the severed head of a black cat. Its crumpled ears flatten against the bottom of the jar.

Fifteen

"... the passionate attraction to all that is dead, decayed, putrid, sickly; it is the passion to transform that which is alive into something unalive; to destroy for the sake of destruction..."

Erich Fromm

Sam chuckles. He reads aloud to me from Ambrose Bierce's Devil's Dictionary.

"Being as an archangel, Satan made himself multifariously objectionable and finally was expelled from Heaven. Halfway down in his descent he paused, bent his head in thought a moment and at last went back.

'There is one favor I should like to ask', said he.'Name it.'

'Man, I understand, is about to be created. He will need laws.'

'What, Wretch! You his appointed adversary, charged from the dawn of eternity with hatred of his soul - you ask for the right to make his laws?'

'Pardon; what I have to ask is that he be permitted to make them himself.' It was so ordered."

"I don't get it," I say honestly. Sam looks at me with disgust.

"Human beings are willful."

"That's why Rachel is so difficult for me, Sam. She's extraordinaryly willful, makes her own laws. Now she insists on being completely in charge of her own therapy and she doesn't choose well."

"Rachel, Rachel. Always Rachel. I was reading great literature. Of course, she's stubborn. She's inordinately afraid of being out of control."

Sam picks up his hat and stomps away. I can hear his cowboy boots, slapping their way to the garage. So I do have Rachel on my mind. She has wasted two more weeks of therapy. Most clients who are giving up therapy simply stay away. Or call on the phone to say, "I've quit."

Today, she shows up right on time, fiercely insisting I must not expect her to continue. On a hunch I ask her to relax, while she explains just once more. I promise I will not argue with her. I know the child Rachel once was is still alive inside her, no matter how matronly the rest of her personality has become. I can help, if I can only reach that little girl.

Rachel refuses the couch. "I will lie on the carpet. I prefer not to lie on the couch."

She glances briefly at me, surprised, as I sit down on the floor beside her. I sprawl easily in my jeans. Today, Rachel is dressed in pants and tennis shoes, something I have never seen her wear before. Where are the ruffled dresses? The severe necklines?

Rachel lies back on the rug, talking about giving up therapy. As she stares at the ceiling, her hands begin to tremble slightly. Fiercely her fingers twist together. Her jaw tightens.

I speak slowly and quietly to her, inviting her into a relaxed state. Suddenly Rachel's whole face and body changes. Her nose becomes sharp, pale. As I watch, suddenly alarmed, Rachel becomes rigid. Rachel's nose is "sharper than a pin."

I'm quoting Shakespeare in my own head. Stop it, Doctor. This is no time to ramble in your mind about Falstaff's death. Stop ruminating, Roberta. Pay attention, stay present and don't be afraid. You're her therapist. This is your job. Don't shy away."

As all color fades from Rachel's face, her chin looks

long and narrow. Now her body arches backward, stiffly, vibrating with tension. A seizure? Grand Mal? No, it appears to be a profound trance state. Grown-up Rachel is reaching back into her life.

"Relax in any way that is best for you, Rachel," I drone on. "Remember I am here in this room with you. You may remember anything that is beneficial to you. If your unconscious chooses to protect you from anything you do not wish to remember, that will also be to your benefit.

Concentrate on your breathing, now, taking long, slow, easy breaths, breathing in relaxation, breathing out tension and concern, just letting go. You may wish to relax even more and if this is so, you may count backwards from ten to one."

Rachel moans. She gasps for breath, then screams.

"No! No! No! please! no! no! no! please! please!"

Her legs move apart, toes pointing outward, arms stretched along the floor, straining, spread-eagled. Her position is sexual, violent, tortured. Immediately I think of bondage.

For more than an hour Rachel is rigid, moaning, whispering, murmuring. I sit quietly beside her, reminding her she can choose to come back and regain her present sense of physical reality in this room. Where is Rachel?

She has descended into terror. Will she ever comprehend? She knows nothing, feels everything.

Sixteen

"Rachel's story is polymorphous perversity".

Sam

*T*he girl is playing quietly in the attic on the splintery floor when she hears heavy footsteps coming upstairs. The stair is creaking from the enormous weight of the woman's body. Will it be Mommy or Mother, panting, forcing her awkward body upward? The child can see the woman's head appear at the head of the stairs. And there is Grandpa with her! The little girl almost jumps up from behind the many wooden crates. She has been secretly playing in the doll house Grandpa made just for her. It has been hidden here. Mother will not let her keep it downstairs.

"The doll house is in storage," Mother proclaims. Mother musn't find her. It is bad to play upstairs.

Grandpa isn't yelling like Mother. With his quiet voice he tries to calm her. He calls Mother, Iris.

"You and your companions have done a lot of damage, Iris. You must behave from now on. It is my duty to see that you do." His voice sounds sad and kind.

Mother becomes wild, "crazy." The girl knows that word. Daddy yells it at Iris when they fight with cooking pots and kitchen knives. That's the word Daddy shouted, when Mother hit him with the iron.

Mother stumbles to Grandpa's workbench full of carpentry tools. She picks up a hammer. The crunching sound the girl will always hear in her dreams. Grandpa falls down on the floor. Red eyed, wild, Mother turns her evil, bad person face in the direction of the wall of wooden boxes. Her eyes are like the fish eyes downstairs on the table, staring wide.

"I musn't make a sound. I musn't breathe."

The child crouches deeper, close to her doll house, behind the wooden crates.

This is where Mother sees her.

Seventeen

*"Since I have started studying the uncon-
scious I have become so interesting to myself.*

*But these two discoveries- that the life of our
sexual instincts cannot be wholly tamed, and that
mental processes are in themselves unconscious
and only reach the ego and come under its control
through incomplete and untrustworthy perceptions-
these two discoveries amount to a statement that
the ego is not master in its own house."*

Sigmund Freud
The Origins of Psychoanalysis
A Difficulty in the Path of Psychoanalysis

"**I**s that what you psychoanalysts believe, Sam?
I just can't see how an archaic way of looking at humans
can be useful in Rachel's treatment. She thrives on therapy with a Feminist perspective. As a woman she deserves
a feeling of self-worth. Why can't she develop self-
esteem, even after growing up female in this masculi-
nized culture?"

Sam is half seduced into a male/female confrontation.
Sometimes he and I choose verbal substitutes for sweaty
wrestling matches on the floor. Although that's been
known to happen too, with delightful results. This time
he ignores my invitation to fight.

"Kiddo, psychoanalysts have never agreed about cases
like Rachel's. Are you surprised? Why should we get
along inside our club any better than you do with members of your Feminist troops? I remember when your
camp split in two. One group brayed after Gloria Steinam
and another after Bette Friedan. And what about Kate

Millett? You have your iconoclasts. So do we.

I believe mild dingbats go crazy, when their normal sexual maturation is upset fairly late in their lives. Loonier crazies, like Rachel, are stuck at earlier stages of childish psychosexual unfolding. I believe her severe form of personality distortion has its origin in infancy. Anxiety is crippling her, but I certainly don't believe it comes from anything like repressed sexual appetite. Quite the opposite. The early Freud probably wouldn't have believed that either. When he became old, he seems to have decided anxiety was a direct consequence of sexual repression, but he may have just been losing his own libido by then.

Still, I think you deliberately misunderstand Freud just to argue with me about Rachel. I want to remind you that all behavior is dynamic, defensive and purposeful. You must focus on Rachel's behavior. You can't just poke her with a pin and watch her, while her pent up emotional balloon collapses.

Hypnotherapy isn't at all enough by itself. The howling and screaming you allow Rachel is far off the mark. You don't have to humiliate her for hours to cure her. Catharsis, my foot! She is a hysteric, and she's entertaining both of you with her drama.

And now, you seem to view the defense of your errors in therapy as a moral question. That allows you to climb on your high horse and talk down to me. In spite of your shrill Feminist objections, I will go on using what I know. And I will insist on change in my clients, even if you don't, using the terms anal, oral, phallic and genital, when they suit my needs. Here's an example, Roberta."

Sam smiles. He is over his mad.

"Thirty years ago, the chairman of my dissertation committee was an "anal retentive" fellow. He was clearly, absolutely, full-of-shit."

"Sam, stop it. I label you a teeth-grinding combination of erudite white-haired therapist and dirty mouth."

"And you're a Rosy-breasted Bed Thrasher. I fascinate you, correct? I am scatological, whenever you need it.

Soon, I'll have you moaning, 'talk dirty to me, Sam'. Why, haven't you ever heard of someone who is anal 'explosive?'"

"Enough of this. I'm not trying to be ribald. I'm trying to talk to you about Rachel, Sam."

"That's what I thought. I suggest some behavioral techniques, along with your hypnotherapy and emotional support. And do not fall for her dramatic attempts to manipulate you. Now, I want you to notice I'm walking out the door. You can come with me, if you do not talk about Rachel."

Sam's squeezes my hand. He's training me out of obsessiveness. Shall I pout, or give in to my grown-up playmate and my own happiness?

I want to thank Sam for humanizing me, but I stop myself. After all, I have my pride.

"Wait for me, I have to put on my shoes!"

Notes:

Rachel and I are working in still another session: She squirms on the blue carpet of the guest room, remembering:

Grandpa is lying on his stomach on the floor. Mother moves heavily toward the trembling child. The gigantic woman looks like a red, lumpy balloon, too full of air. The whites of her tiny eyes are pink, bulging behind hilly cheeks.

"You have to help me. Get a chair!" Mother speaks in English, instead of her usual French.

Lilith, not Rachel, runs to the kitchen below. She finds a stool she can lift and grapples it back up the stair. The long legs bang on every step.

"Bring a rope!"

Under Grandpa's work table, Lilith finds the rope Grandpa uses to tie shut his crates.

High on the step ladder, Lilith slides the rope over one of the rafters. Mother makes the knots.

Mother drags Grandpa by the rope around his neck. The girl cannot see what is next, but she can hear Mother grunting from the weight.

113

"You won't tell. Do you hear me, you little bitch? I'll kill you first."

Lilith glares into Mother's eyes, refusing to speak, but Rachel shrieks in terror.

"I won't tell. I promise, I won't tell, Mommy! But this gigantic panting woman is not Mommy.

It is the Mother , who is merciless. She picks up a board in her heavy hands and swings it in an arc. There is a hollow echoing sound in the child's head. The echo goes on for a long time. Rachel goes to sleep.

"Rachel, your memories are useful. Experiencing them heals you. I'll stay right beside you as long as you need me. No, I'm not Lilith. I'm Roberta. I promise I won't leave you. Learn what you need to know. Remember about Grandpa and how he fell down. Remember how you went to sleep in the attic."

When she wakes up, the child can't see.

"Help me, Grandpa. Please, where are you?" Hands stroke the child. A voice explains, she is in a hospital.

"Have you ever been in a hospital before, Rachel?" The voice is a woman's. The girl shrinks from the touch of the soft hands.

"Why is everything dark?" The girl tries to move, but she hurts all over. The ache is enough to make her sick at her stomach again.

"Please help me, Lilith." The woman is a nurse.

"There's a lady coming, who wants to talk with you. She wants to find out how you got hurt. Can you talk to her right now? Do you feel well enough?"

Something is terribly wrong. The girl hears a door opening. The nurse says Hello. There are light, hesitant footsteps coming towards her bed.

"I don't like this place! Let me out!" the child cries out.

Stiff with fear, the girl feels caged.

"Take me out of here. I want to leave. I want my Grandpa!"

Her body is icy. The nurse covers her with a blanket and holds her hand. The other lady talks to the girl , softly.

*"How did your head and your poor little body get hurt,
Honey?"*

"Be quiet, Rachel, don't tell." Lilith tightens Rachel's jaw.
She can feel her chin moving forward, as if a small but firm
hand tugs it outward.

"I don't know. I can't remember. Where's my Mommy? "

"What can't you tell?" More footsteps come into the room.

*"This is the doctor who takes care of you. He bandaged your
head and your chest, and took good care of your eyes."* It
sounds as if the nurse is singing far away. A new voice
booms.

"I'm Dr. Whitmore." His voice, too, is low in pitch, not a
shrieky voice. What is she trying to think about? Her head
won't work. Is it one of Mommy's voices that screeches?

"How are you feeling?"

"I want Grandpa to take me home now." There is silence.
The other lady is near the bed again, stroking the child's hand.

"Do you know why you are here?"

This lady smells like rubbing alcohol. It is a clean smell.
Perhaps it is the sheets. The girl's thoughts won't talk straight
in her head.

"No." The lady speaks softly, singing to her from some other
room, still holding her twisting hand.

"I want Grandpa, please."

*"Dear, your Grandpa's dead. You had your accident right
after you found him."*

*"Dead? No! no! no! no! He's not, he's not. Get my
Grandpa, now! I want Grandpa."*

"Lilith, I need you; please save me". The girl knows what
dead means .Blood and hurt. In the ground forever and ever.
She can't have Grandpa's hugs. No more hugs, no more hugs,
no more safety.

Lilith is here.

"I'll take care of you, always."

The child feels the pain for a minute, then falls asleep.

In her jeans and running shoes, my client sprawls on
the floor, listening to me read. She has turned her back
to the picture she hates, but she can tolerate being in the

same room with it, if only for a short time. This is progress. In my old red leather chair I'm reading, aloud, the notes from the long ago consultation between a doctor and Rachel's mother. I have just received these spotty copies of the decaying papers, saved for years in some official basement level. I imagine in most places hospital records are now on microfilm.

"According to his notes, the doctor tells your mother you are responding well to medication. Your repair surgeries appear to be healing successfully, but you have become hysterical, when told about your Grandfather's death. You tear at your bandages, out of control. Suddenly, you stop your struggle, smile and close your eyes. It says here, that the nurses stand looking at you, puzzled, before they move on to their other responsibilities.

When they mention your odd behavior to your doctor he speaks to your mother about it. Your mother is, of course, upset. She claims the hospital staff is encouraging your craziness.

She did not choose to bring that girl here, he says. Meddling neighbors had no business in her attic, mother says. They found the child where her grandfather had left her, beaten. There was an obvious reason he hanged himself. Everyone knows, she told me, he was a child molester. Now, she will take care of her little girl herself. She will take the child home at once. Mother claims we are after her money, and so she has called her 'personal physician". Together, they will take the girl "where she belongs.'

Then, Mother screams that her child tells lies, makes up things, 'she's a sly one, living in a fantasy world. Rachel is crazy. From what my father did to her. Ask her doctor.'"

It appears Dr. Whitmore is suspicious of Mother's story and her manner.

He sends you home, Rachel, but here, in his hard-to-read M.D. handwriting he suggests the authorities keep an eye on your mother.

She gets back at him, though. She never pays your

116

bill."

Rachel is silent for a long time. I pull myself out of the warm chair to poke her in the ribs. "Response?"

"I guess they forgot what he said about Mother. No one helped me."

The child Rachel awakes. Her nurse asks if she wants to eat. Lilith is still asleep.

"Lets play a game." The good smelling nurse cranks up the bed. "I'll feed you a spoonful of your supper, and you guess what it is. All right?"

The child tastes the spoonful of vegetables and guesses it is peas. They taste good and she remembers she ishungry.

"Good girl! Now, I'll surprise you. You'll not guess this spoonful." The spoon holds something smooth and warm, a little salty. It smells like butter.

"Mashed potatoes!"

"I can't fool you."

Rachel's noise has wakened Lilith. She is angry.

"Watch out, she's trying to get you to tell."

"I'm not hungry, anymore," the patient tells her nurse. "Go away." Lilith closes her eyes, pretending to be asleep.

Peeper is born at the moment Rachel sees Grandpa hanging. The Peeper part needs her Grandpa, choosing to die with Grandpa. Since her life is only a few hours long, in unconscious reasoning, she is allowed to come back whenever Rachel feels overwhelming despair. Lilith and Rachel cannot always tolerate existence.

Then, dead Peeper resurrects in Rachel's brain.

Eighteen

"It is possible that in certain cases the evil spirit goes so far as to exercise his influence not only on material things but even on man's body, so that one can speak of 'diabolical possession.'"

John Paul II, *August 13, 1986*

"**R**achel has four little girls, who need her to love them and treat them fairly. How will she give love, when she never knew it as a child? She can't learn mothering from books, although she tries with her whole heart. Nevertheless, she is stuck. We're at another impasse Sam, and I give up."

"Keep using what works. For you, it seems to be the hypnotherapy and confronting her crazy ideas. You women are courageous. What's the trouble, Siggy? Too much suffering for you?" Sam waits for me to calm myself.

"Sweetie, remember Rachel is learning about love. From you."

I struggle with the lump in my throat. Sam is giving me credit. The lump grows so big I squeak when I try to talk around it. Finally, it melts and runs down my face as salt water.

"Thanks, Sam, you're being very kind. That's the trouble. I can't let her down, but I can't bring myself to hurt her any more. She's not allowed to tell me what happened to her. She's had a merciful loss of memory in her brain, but her body remembers and shows me something terrible. And I get scared."

Notes:
"Rachel, deepen your trance by counting slowly backwards from ten to one, slowing your breathing. That's right. Remember, you are safe in this office and I am right beside you. You can come back any time you wish. Whenever you choose, remember we are together. I wonder what you will choose to remember today?...Your breathing is slow, easy. Your cheeks a healthy pink, and your face is relaxed. If you go back to an earlier time in your life, and you want to take my image with you, please do so. I will go with you."

There is a squawk as Mother kills the chicken in the cellar. I wait to be called.

"I'm here. Don't be frightened. You will be all right. I won't let it hurt," Lillith reminds the child.

Still her legs shake, her body is rigid. Preparing herself for the coming ordeal, she hears Mother thumping up the stairs. Every muscle in her childish body readies.

"Rachel, time for church." Leading the way to the cellar Mother gestures the child to follow. Mechanically, awkwardly, the girl does so.

The smell here is sharp, chemical acidity and something rotting away in the dark behind the mottled cellar walls. Tiny specks of phosphorescence glow from the damp stone , where the whitewash flakes away in peeling patches.

"Take off your clothes. You know the rules." Mother pours the blood into a goblet.

"Lilith, help me drink. You have to help me, please."

"Drink, you little slut." Mother holds the golden goblet against the child's rigid lips. The woman's shadow wavers, enormous, on the wall.

"Say the words, Cunt! Do you need to be told? "

"I take this into my body. This, in the name of Beelzebub."

"Drink, imp of Satan! I'll smack your ass if you puke!"

As she swallows thick warmth, the loathsome smell over-

whelms the girl. The taste is sour, musty. Her stomach jumps and quivers. A slimy lump forms in her throat. She keeps down the clotting liquid. Inside her throat feels sticky, thick.

The Mother scoops more blood from a canning jar with her huge hand. Her nails are yellow and curved without the scarlet polish she wears at night. She rubs red fluid over the girl's stiff body.

The smell is obscene. The child gags, as titanic Mother pushes her down to the mold and dust of the filthy floor. Taking the rope from the table, the hulking woman ties the girl to the stakes imbedded in the floor. The child is spread-eagled.

"Please, don't hurt me, Mother. I'll be good !"

Mother's swollen fingers squeeze the tongs they have taken from the table. She begins to sing raucously, excitedly, leaning over her daughter. Joyously, her furrowed tongue extends through her song.

"I will fix you. You are an imp! Imp! Child of Satan!"

The girl hears a scream. A tearing pain twists inside her, as moisture runs between her legs, then puddles in the dust. Her shaking stops, when her body arches backward.

Lilith is angry. This has gone too far. She will be in charge now. The pain stops.

"You damn pig!," Mother screams, and stamps her strange feet. Shaking her unwieldy fist, she unties the child's hands. Purple red rings circle the girl's wrists, stinging.

"Clean up your mess. You are vile, an evil child of Satan!"

Mother clambers up the stairs, swaying heavily.

Each week Mommy or the Mother emerges further from the Rachel's memories. The giantess is a ghost from a living nightmare, a storybook witch. Her distorted beliefs in her own evil lead to outbreaks of ritualistic cruelty.

"Do you suppose Mother is a genuine freak, Sam? An aberration?"

"Maybe. There are humans whose development is severely impaired, of course. Their brains, neurology and their bodies are all out of balance. These folks are unique accidents of biology. Someone like that can't fit into ordinary society. Mother sounds as if she has no regulatory control over herself.

That makes her a monster. It would be as if she exists in her own universe. Aware of only herself, she would have no compunction about hurting anyone else. She would feel no remorse, show no sympathy. If Rachel's description is accurate, Mother is ruled only by impulse with a broken brain, developed improperly, incapable of holding back her thunderous rage."

Rachel is in session, discussing her marriage. Lately she has been uneasy about her husband's habitual 'nights out.'

"I know he deserves time away from me and the girls, yet..." suddenly she slumps in her chair.

Pictures from far away form in my head. I see another child, someone I have never known, but a child to whom I feel close. The little girl holds a long, silver knife over her head, as she faces the altar. Beside her, Beelzebub nods in readiness. Devoid of feeling, the girl waits obediently. The knife she holds is magic. The black cat lies tied on the altar. It cries out to the child.

Rachel's awareness is far away. Can she hear me? I speak into her ear, tap her shoulders, grasp her cold, tight hands. She will not return as yet.

"I am your friend," mews the cat, "I keep your feet warm. I rub against your legs when you are cold." At the cat's entreaty, shrill choking sounds push themselves out of the girl's throat to join the plea of the cat.

"Rachel, come back now to be with me. You're screaming, Rachel."

The child does as she is told. The poor kitty's blood drips into the white cloth. Its bulging eyes look for the girl. Shiny entrails ooze outward, through the slash in grey fur. The cat continues to cry. The heads of the celebrants remain bowed,

121

even when Beelzebub is angry with the child. She has been bad and has made an unforgivable mistake.

Mother knows what to do about the girl. She must be punished. Locked away in the dark with the dying kitty, the child atones for her disobediance. The child is never again to scream.

She must be prepared for the ritual killings to come.

Nineteen

"Sadistic sexual fantasies are likely to have been present in childhood. The age of onset of sadistic activities is also variable, but is commonly by early adulthood. The condition is usually chronic in its extreme form. When Sexual Sadism is practiced with nonconsenting partners, the activity is likely to be repeated until the individual is apprehended."

Diagnostic and Statistical Manual III

Deaths, subject to medical and legal investigation, vary from town to town. In some places, high suicide rates reflect a higher number of autopsies. Authorities are often quick to agree with relatives that a death is a "suicide." Whether a suicide is even recorded, depends on sex, age and social class. Vaguely defined "accidents" often imply suicide. One method of getting information about a mysterious death is a psychological autopsy, in which researchers examine psychiatric and medical records and interview survivors to judge the intentions of the deceased.

Since he was an unimportant person, this was not done for Rachel's Grandpa.

Rachel is rocking back and forth, still sitting on the floor in my overcrowded office, her arms locked tight around her knees. She is sobbing, looking and sounding young, telling me about the newspaper in her hometown.

"It's still publishing in a rickety building, crowded between the sea wall and the post office." The copy of a clipping from the weekly came through the mail today.

Again and again I read the account to Rachel.

"Man Found Hanged, Suicide Ruled"

"A 53-year-old citizen of our town was found hanged this morning, and a man collapsed dead on the floor of the Mission last night. Found hanged was Jules Jaque Borchet. Examiner, Frank Borlial said death was due to strangulation by hanging, and pronounced it suicide. Succumbing at the Mission was an unknown man of undetermined age."

"I didn't make it up. About Grandpa. I'm not crazy." Filled with relief, Rachel weeps on and on.

I have to talk something out with Sam.

"By now, of course, I'm fascinated by the similarities between mental illness, witchcraft and devil worship. In New England possession didn't seem to be generated by the traumas of infancy or early childhoods. Instead, demonic 'possession' was caused by Puritan society itself.

Rather than a sign of mental breakdown, possession was an attempt to maintain mental stability in a place where people absolutely believed in a Devil. Think of the tremendous cultural pressure to go along with imaginative people who responded to those pressures by becoming 'possessed' themselves. The most interesting thing is that most of them lived in the households of ministers or other godly parents."

"What, Roberta? Are you talking to me?"

Twenty

"Some individuals with the disorder may for many years engage in sadistic acts without a need to increase their potential for inflicting serious physical damage. Others, however, either because of an increased need or a diminished capacity for restraint, increase the severity of the sadistic acts over time or during periods of stress. When the disorder is severe, these individuals may rape, torture, or kill their victims. Although brutality commonly occurs in the families of individuals with this disorder, there is no information on whether Sexual Sadism is more common in family members."

Diagnostic and Statistical Manual III

Since I became Dr. Richards, I've learned more than I want to know about survivors of incest. For almost twenty years evidence has been collected that child abuse is more frequent and more damaging than we like to believe. In the past we protected family privacy at all costs and could not see how adults displayed confusing symptoms to us because they had been abused as children. By now I am unshockable, but more and more angry.

One of my clients is a charming, vivacious writer who grew up in a house of prostitution. Her Mom was one of the whores. When little Carol was five, her mother trained her carefully in oral sex, to provide something special for customers. Years later, Carol's nights continue to be filled with night terrors. Her bad dreams forced her into therapy.

"I must frighten away my Boogy Men." I play good

125

mother to her for a time. We do a lot of crying together, but laugh some, too. Powerfully attached to me, Carol works well. Eventually, she cures herself of bulimia and codeine addiction. Now, she enjoys her marriage and her four year old boy. On her way to recovery she gives up dependence on me. We are friends.

I develop my self confidence as a therapist with Carol. Because of her, I trust my intuition as much as my training. I do know what I am doing. Sometimes.

A victim of multiple sclerosis , an entertaining young lady, comes to see me weekly. She is confined to a wheelchair, but the chair isn't her presenting problem. Tormented by memories of forcible rape, she comes to therapy. Like most other victims, she blames herself.

Now, she accepts the truth.

"I was raped, because I couldn't protect myself from my brother-in-law, not because I was bad. I have worked my way through all the rage, grief and mourning that once filled me with unexpressable anxiety. I'm well."

With her newly released energy, she is a diligent student and a witty, popular young woman. Boyfriends wheel her chair to interesting places on campus: the Little Theater or to the gym, to support her team. Her sorority sisters fight to see who gets to go with her to the Dean of Women's scholarship teas. This woman's greatest need was not to walk, but to overcome her deeply imbedded self-disgust.

Twenty to thirty per cent of adult women and ten per cent of adult men have had some sexual association with a much older person during adolescence or in childhood. We think that about twenty five per cent of sexually abused children are under the age of five years old.

The Harvard Mental Health Letter of May, 1993, tells that in 1989 one thousand two hundred children died from abuse by beating, shooting, stabbing, burning, strangling or shaking. Of course, many deaths and sexual onslaughts are unreported.

Today a shy appearing, but unusually beautiful girl

comes to my office. She has pleading, gray eyes and wispy, blond hair.

"I don't understand why so many boys pursue me. Why me?" During her many sexual encounters, she grows numb. Afterwards, when she can feel again, she is appallingly angry with herself for "being cheap" and sick at heart.

"I'm out of control, Dr. Richards." It's true. She's compulsive, likely a sex addict. In therapy, she can remember, clearly, how old she was when she first became a sex partner to her father.

Lately, this lovely girl fully understands she was introduced to sex far too early and by the wrong person. Dad used her body in an affectionate and loving way, as he introduced her to his favorite positions. Of course, she was grateful for his attention. She felt loved and appreciated by Daddy as she grew up. Now, she is utterly confused. What should she feel? Today, she looks for love, through sex with boys she barely knows and does not like. That allows her to fail and to punish herself for being so available.

In the hospital on antidepressants, she is safely off the sex market for a while. Because she had arranged to shoot herself and missed, she had to "be put away," she says. Clearly, she is a danger to herself. I'll visit her again tomorrow, and we'll talk about her future.

In a way, she is like my first client, Billie. When Billie was a little girl, she was trained to be a hooker. Her place of employment was the back seat of her father's taxi, in which she wore a shorty nightgown and pigtails. Billie had three personalities, with separate names and identities. I taught her Transactional Analysis, about the Parent, Adult, and Child Ego States.

"How many 'I's do you have, Billie? Sometimes you're critical of others. Sometimes you help people. Sometimes you solve problems, and sometimes you don't know how. You are three people and so is everyone else I know. The taught-part of you is the Parent, and the sensible data-processing part of you is your Adult.Your

Child is your feeling self. You're functioning just the way your brain says you're supposed to. The trouble is, you're scared of the personalities inside you.

But I'm not afraid. I'll help you watch out for your Critical Parent. It's just memorized recordings of your Mom and Dad's behavior, when you were growing up. Because your parents didn't know how to be kind, their messages are screwing you up. Your internalized Parent is just plain mean. That's why you pick on yourself.

But I won't let you hurt you. Soon you will stop being hateful to yourself. You feel cruel, now, because that's how you were treated when you were small. I believe you, when you say you hated the way your parents acted, but without retraining, you'll imitate them. This is your big chance to be different."

The "people" within her immediately lost their ability to dominate Billie's life. Their identities melted away, and their names were forgotten.

"It's perfectly all right with me that my people are brain functions," she crowed, "But I really did believe three different women inhabited my body. That's how I felt."

Billie became more rational. She tested reality. Then she discovered reasoning, which her parents had never demonstrated. Her friends still call her "Dip stick" and "Air head," but Billie is no longer frenetic. She has grown up, but not lost her childlike charm. She's as funny as ever. When I run into her, now, she likes to remind me that I should have given her a group rate for our first therapy session. She enjoys a red hot marriage to a man who loves her dearly. He is sexually excited when she tells him about her past. Billie is wholeheartedly whorish with him, to his continuous delight.

Notes:

Rachel writes in her journal, still unsure who "the girl" is.

The girl reads Black Beauty again and again, lost in her fantasy world with a happy ending for the abused. Her Daddy will be home soon. She hopes Mommy and Daddy won't fight.

Last time, when Mommy threw the iron at Daddy, she cut his head. Daddy drew a butcher knife.

"I'm going to kill you this time," he screamed. The neighbors came upstairs, then. The police came, too.

Sam insists I am too involved with Rachel.

"You're tired, preoccupied. And you're unavailable to me." I agree. I often think, talk and act with Rachel in mind. But Sam has pointed my behavior out to me one too many times. He can't tell me what to do! Even though, sometimes, he does make me think.

He doesn't believe that long repressed memories, emerging in Rachel, after all these years, can be accurate. Should I be more skeptical of her awful stories? No controlled studies of memories like this have been made. I don't want to be overreacting to my own ignorance.

It is crucial to Rachel that I believe her. But, what if she is responding to my subtle suggestions and keeping me going with more and more gruesome details? I would feel like the fool Sam suggests I am. I try to decide if I am listening to true repressed memories or fabricated ones. With reassurance, clarification and gentle confrontation, I try to reach to the end of Rachel's pain. Her outpouring of suffering continues.

I'm making a training video for psychotherapists in other parts of the country to view and critique. These clinicians live and practice far away from our cowboy style and are interested in "brief therapy" methods for adult victims of child sexual abuse. My women actresses will play themselves. They have volunteered to help, pleased with their recovery from nightmares, bouts of depression and psychosomatic illnesses.

I wonder about Rachel. Would she learn from other women, who have had painful experiences with early sexuality? She is a long way from recovered, but wants to take part. She betrays no conscious awareness of the depth of her abuse.

I introduce the insistent Rachel to women, who have

worked steadfastly, to overcome childhood traumas. Rachel wants nothing to do with them. Superior and righteous, she sees herself as much older, an all-knowing mother figure.

Of course, I should have known. Her self image is strong and flawless, a someone who needs no assistance. After all, she has her perfect marriage and her perfect family.

"I'm also doing exceptionally well in school," she says, as she introduces herself. None of us know we are in the company of Lilith.

Twenty One

"Keep still! Don't say anything! Don't touch me!"
Frau Emmy

Sigmund Freud *in Breuer & Freud, 1893-1895.*

"**R**elax, Rachel, and notice your breathing, easy and deep..."

As she walks into the kitchen, the girl hears a growl. In the middle of the room a gigantic German Shepherd, brown and black, snarls, showing yellow teeth bared.

"Isn't he appealing? We are great friends. He is a gift from admirers. This fine creature will stay with us now for a while." Although her laugh is musical and merry, this fat woman giggles too long. She is Mother.

"Mephisto is to be trained to be my familiar."

Again Mother chortles as if she cannot stop. Urged forward the dog jumps against the child, knocking her backward. His eager dew claws stab and rake. His drool is sticky. As it smears her dress and hands she reexperiences a familiar nausea. Afraid to vomit, she is even more afraid of the huge animal. The child steadies herself. Mother's shrill cackle is a high pitched sound of triumph.

"Rachel, you will take him out every night. I'll watch you from the kitchen window to see you do the job right!"

Mother shuts the dog in the bathroom, as the child lays out the supper of canned sardines and cold potatoes. After the girl washes the greasy supper dishes in the cracked sink , the Mother puts the dog on a new leather leash.

"It is time. Doggie is to be taken out."

On the far side of the street from the tenement, Mephisto pulls the child across a field through the tall, stiff, half-frozen grass. The ground is rutted and uneven. In her outsized shoes, the girl trips.

"Please dog, hurry. Go to the bathroom!"

She hates this snuffling, lunging beast. Mephisto, sensing she is afraid of him, tugs harder on the leash, running ahead. The girl panics, afraid the dog will get away.

Glancing backward, she thinks she can see Mother's face in the window, watching. The child must not lose the dog! She nearly falls again, as she tightens her grip on the leash, but the dog is far stronger and more agile than the child. Excited Mephisto lurches ahead. Losing her hold on the leash , the girl stumbles over the frozen clods of earth and sprawls to the hard ground. The child's bony knees bleed, only a little, in the icy cold. Mother opens the window and screams for the girl to catch her pet.. The child runs as fast as she can, but it is no use. There is no way her thin legs can catch up with the huge beast.

"You fool, you stupid ass!" Mother slowly staggers across the street, nightclothes flopping around her. The girl is filled with wonder. The Mother has left the tenement, and it is daytime.

"You'll pay for this!" Mother calls to Mephisto. Obediently, head down, tail wagging, he slinks to her. The dog and Mother understand each other well. The gigantic woman reaches down to pet Mephisto, giving him the affection for which the child, watching them, yearns.

Something gives way inside ,and the girl knows Mommy loves the dog, and does not love her. Mommy has never petted the child in this way or talked to her in the crooning, soothing voice she uses now. The child hates the dog, more than she has ever hated anything. She cannot control him. He is stronger and heavier than she and loved. Her body shakes in despair.

"Sam, help me, listen and don't insult me. Today, in trance, Rachel had a tantrum. She's filled with rage. I guess that's inevitable, but I'm confused. There are too many directions for me to approach Rachel's story, and I can't get a focus. She's got me deeply interested in the rankest superstition and folklore, demonology, witchcraft, child abuse, pedophilia, battering, sexual torture, murder, family curses, group pathology, schizophrenia, and multiple personality. And now you can add satanism."

"You forgot to mention plain old psychopathology, Roberta. Her mother, I mean, not your perpetual client. Do make some kind of diagnostic decision about Rachel and, then, forget about her for a while. Diagnose her mother too, her father and her neighbors. But be scientific and brief, for God's sake! You can always change Rachel's diagnosis later, if you need to, but right now center yourself, Kid."

"You may call me Doctor, Sam. You're not my supervisor now. And you didn't quit, I fired you. Well, at least I let you go, after I passed my Boards. I'm trying to be ethical and clear and I have no help. I can't just tack on a diagnosis that doesn't convince me. Most everything in the D.S.M. III-R fits Rachel, sometimes, but only for a few minutes. Then something new arises. Right now, I'm sure she has a personality disorder and not a clear cut psychosis."

"What about borderline?"

"Possibly. I guess... a child, threatened as Rachel was, would learn to shift rapidly between states of psychosis and neurosis. She might try to be crazy, to keep contact with someone else, someone important to her, some one really crazy, like her Mommy. Or, maybe her shifting states represent a woman who can no longer hold back terrible memories."

I'm getting ready to protect myself from Sam's skepticism again. Today, I believe Rachel's recollections are accurate recollections, not bizarre fantasies from a mind fine-tuned to exaggeration. I take a stand. Rachel is telling the truth and the truth, itself, is unbelievable. I am actually dealing with satanism, torture and human sacrifice.

Here in my office Rachel goes back, time and again, to the East Coast fishing village of her childhood's suffering. Her Memory Lane is strewn with broken glass.

"Relax, Rachel. Just breathe quietly. Pay attention to each breath. Take yourself back. Retrieve memories useful to you."

I sit next to Rachel, wondering if I have any idea what is really going on. Sam says I will know a client is borderline when I say to myself, "Oh, shit. Here she is again." He claims I will be angry even before that person enters the room, because I'll remember what happened last time.

"Borderline" means the therapist will be frustrated.

Strangers will feel gigantic pity for this client and will not be able to understand my resentment. They may soon learn that she will have an insatiable need for attention at any cost, and feel entitled to anything she wants, just because she wants it. Requiring extra time, care and excessive consideration, including special attention, she will have an exquisite awareness of any rejection, which she will exercise whenever I make a mistake or lose my focus for a moment.

A borderline client will not tolerate confrontation. My interpretations will be twisted into something I do not mean. Chronically complaining of feelings of boredom and emptiness, this person will consistently piss me off by splitting the transference to me, her caretaker, in two.

I will ricochet between my own pity and annoyance. This will be the sort of hurting human who insists on extra sessions during a crisis, but forgets to keep appointments as soon as the intensity lessens.

She will always be in love or just over it. The moment romance cools, she will be overwhelmed with disgust for the person who was recently adored. Everyone lets a borderline down, usually one person at a time. I will, too. The borderline will be the woman who threatens suicide by saying, "I just want to go to sleep forever."

When hospitalized, she will tell the Chief of Staff, "I don't know how Dr. Richards could have misunderstood me so completely. I just wanted her to understand I was feeling tired."

This sort of client intuitively pits people against each other, then watches the fighting from the sidelines. Having done this since she was in her terrible twos, she will be an expert. Way back then, her parents were divided over how to handle her. Stuck in her development, the borderline client is unhappy.

Sam gives me his stock lecture about how to work with a borderline client.

"Let me remind you of three defensive rules. First, beware of the rescue fantasy in the client's mind. You are supposed to have grown beyond her own rescue fantasy, which involves feelings of omnipotence (I can help anybody). Next, all information will come in tiny pieces, never as a whole story. Don't expect much. Lastly, you are apt to end up with egg on your face, no matter how well you do. Your chief function will be to clarify, clarify, clarify. Plan carefully, stay concrete, use a contract, and work closely with someone else, with whom you can communicate well, like me. If you and your colleague can't talk honestly, you both will be manipulated into taking opposing sides. Remember the caretaker is never supposed to feel successful. That's the secret game."

I feel disloyal to Rachel when I listen like this. But Sam and I do seem "split" over Rachel. To me that just means I don't agree with him.

"Sam, listen, just for a minute. Rachel can't be a textbook borderline because she is coming around. Isn't she? So she does a little excessive clinging and kicks me away too hard sometimes. But, like Jimmy Carter used to say, 'in my heart...' I know she is getting well. She does far more than her fifty percent of the therapeutic work."

Rachel is lying quietly on my rug, pale, and breathing deeply to calm herself. I believe she is genuine in what she says. But, as she searches her past, month after long month, can I go on investing myself to this extent?

Will I end up disappointed, played with, angry and worn out? My efforts wasted? Having seduced myself into believing Rachel's fantasies?

Sam thinks so.

Twenty Two

"Obsessive Compulsive Disorder. The essential features are recurrent obsessions or compulsions. Obsessions are recurrent, persistent ideas, thoughts, images, or impulses that are ego-dystonic, that is, they are not experienced as voluntarily produced, but rather as thoughts that invade consciousness and are experienced as senseless and repugnant."

Diagnostic and Statistical Manual III

This year , maybe Mommy will be pleased with the girl. Maybe this year, somehow, the child can make Mommy happy.

Genetics, social conditions or family dynamics set the scene for childhood depression, but stress is the immediate cause. Immune system changes relate directly to mood changes. When a child is depressed, the natural killer (NK) cells become less active. These are the master regulators of the immune system. In depression, white blood cells do not multiply normally. Are immune responses the cause of mood changes? Vice versa? No one knows as yet. It may be, that children train themselves to be unwell.

A severe childhood condition associated with depression is called "failure to thrive." Depressed children do not grow normally, nor develop physically in the sequence we expect of them. Misfortune can trigger depression in one vulnerable child, anxiety in another, or acute schizophrenia in a child who is genetically susceptible to that disease.

In therapy adult clients usually blame their depression on their long-ago parents, whom, they believe, damaged their self-esteem. "Bad parents" are remembered as cold and unloving.

"My parents didn't love me." Most depressed people believe they were actually rejected by their parents. Do they report this because they are depressed, or are they depressed as a result of their treatment during formative years? I listen and ask questions. At some point in therapy, most clients cheer up. Their parents weren't "so bad, after all."

"Mom did the best she could."

But Rachel's story is different. As she becomes stronger and clearer, her parents grow more monstrous, vicious. I wonder how Rachel protected her sanity at all, living in a crazy house. Was her life there all suffering?

Or does she remember only pain because she is a severely depressed adult?

Rachel's Journal:

The Christian martyrs are all dead. They got hurt on a rack and a wheel. One martyr was skinned alive to get to be a saint. Maybe studying torture like that makes nuns mean. The saint stories may be too much for the Sisters, the girl reasons. They become brutal. Nuns believe in banging knuckles up against the blackboard. Each has a belt, cut into tails for striking children's hands.

The English, spoken in this Catholic school, is almost incomprehensible to the child. At home, she speaks little or not at all, "like Daddy when he is angry or drunk." Words the girl learned out of books she is afraid to pronounce, so she is quiet. She is familiar with Mother's French derivative "swear" words, oaths and slang names for genitals, but that language is not appropriate for school , she is certain.

Someday, when she is a lady, the child will speak elegantly in good American. Not moving, the child makes herself invisible, secretly thankful she is small, unlike the girl who sits at the desk next to her. That is the girl with the big breasts. It is immoral to have large titties in the fourth grade in a "good girls" school. The child keeps her head turned away in disgust from her overly developed neighbor.

There are few windows in this musty red and black brick building with the iron fence. The school is two stories all, like a fortress. Inside, large crosses hang from the Sisters' waists, as they move from child to child, directing and correcting. No one questions their authority. Being correct is important.

One schoolroom Sister is a frightening variation on Mommy, Mother and Iris. She has a big, big face, scowls, and unfailingly knows what must be done immediately. The girl likes the nun who passes out the bags of broken Hosts for sale. This sister has a sweet face. She says "hello" to the child when she opens the Rectory door. The girl wants to say "hello" back to her, but is too shy. She thinks a lot about "hello" and what it means. Little else enters her awareness.

Mother has had a fight with the school. The Sisters are angry, because the girl comes to school so infrequently. Perhaps they have asked why. The girl will go to public school and be demoted. It has been decided. It doesn't matter. Nothing matters. Nothing, but "hello," has mattered for a long time.

"Rachel, you've been in touch with scenes of pain and humiliation you experienced as a child. You've been brave. But there must be positive things to remember, too. Everyone has some good times to remember. As you take yourself back this time, find what you did to have fun.What did you do to make your life better? Find a good time."

In public school the child looks forward to each day, feeling safe, away from home. She learns about animals and people, geography, weather and the pyramids. Her teacher says she is "a good listener." There is an important change in her world. Her teacher likes her. The girl has fallen in love with a woman who is healthy, humorous, and forgiving.

On a special Wednesday, the child discovers she can read far beyond her age group. Through books, she discovers the world , like the posters in the library say she can. Books are impor-

139

tant.

Reading carefully, the little girl tries on other people's lives. Intellectually, she is off and running.

"Find a good time," echoes in her dream.

The girl is the quietest child in her sunny school room, maybe in the whole school. Usually, no one but the teacher notices she is here.Learning to write from her ink well, she successfully makes a whole row of R's and is pleased. The girl does not smear her letters.

"Felicitous," she says to herself. Doing things neatly is important.

Twenty Three

*M*other sends the girl to the store, across the street and down the block. The child is afraid, for Mother says the store lady is a witch.

"A feeble, foolish old crone! Old and foolish, foolish and old, old, old!. Soon to be cold, no one will scold. Too bold, old, soon cold," Mother sings happily. Her laugh can be heard all the way down the stairs to the chilly sidewalk. Mother must be right. The girl remembers the witchlike, uneven strands of long gray-black and white hair, which hang down the store lady's back. Her nose looks pointed, all right. It sticks out, far ahead of her skinny body. The little bell on the Store Witch's door jingles when a customer comes into the tiny space where the merchandise is kept. Then the old woman knows it is time to come out from behind the curtains of the back room.

"Hello, Rachel," the old lady's voice rasps, "How are you today?" The child wishes hard the witch didn't know her.

"Fine, thank you"

"What can I get for you, Dear? Bread? Milk?"

"My Mommy needs..." with her hand Rachel makes the sign she has been taught.

"The scowl on the witch's face makes deep wrinkles, as she

141

hands Rachel something lumpy and light, wrapped in paper. The Store Witch does not ask for money.

"Oh, your Mommy, your Mommy! She gets what she wants. Who knows, with that one." She gives the girl a tiny smile and a whispery pat on the shoulder. The old lady's hands are dry like the scratchy grass stalks in the field across the street.

"Would you like a piece of licorice, Rachel?"

"Oh, yes, thank you." If she is a witch, maybe she's a nice witch. The child makes the good taste last all the way home. The sweet syrup slides down her throat, the black lump sticks to her teeth.

Mother is mixing awful smelling stuff, talking loudly in a singsong voice. She stares at her daughter, as if she does not remember her. As the girl hands over the crumpled paper package, Mother becomes alert. Behind her puffy eyelids, her tiny eyes fix on the child. She concentrates her stare, weaving in place, like a snake hypnotizing a songbird.

"How is the health of the witch of the grocery store?"

"All right." Mother grins. She shakes her head, then adds a piece of twisted hair to her boiling potion.

The girl is not told when the store witch dies. On an icy day she discovers the little store boarded up. A neighbor says the old lady was dead for a long time before she was found, washed up on the icy shoreline. She had walked into the river up over her head.

The child is thoughtful. She holds a private memorial service in her room for the old lady. In love with beautiful words from books, the child chants her favorites. Words create a soothing sensation in her thin body. Chanting is important. The girl comforts herself with the loveliness of language.

"Luminous, devotion, chastity," she murmurs, "sunrise." Enchantment and beauty touch her ugly room.

"Affection, engaged, filial, pristine, and pure. Cleanliness. Adoration. How sad it is no one cared about the lonely old store licorice witch lady."

Twenty Four

"302.10 Zoophilia
The essential feature is the use of animals as a repeatedly preferred or exclusive method of achieving sexual excitement. The animal may be the object of intercourse or may be trained to sexually excite the human partner by licking or rubbing."

Diagnostic and Statistical Manual III

"**R**achel," I say, "the last time you 'went back,' you were able to have a good feeling. You liked what you were learning in school when you made beautiful letters. You experienced enjoyment. Enjoyment is a feeling, Rachel. You do feel. Allowing yourself to feel means you are growing in courage. So, pay attention to your breathing, and relax. Breathe in bravery and breathe out fear. Breathe out all blocks to this experience."

At the tenement, the kitchen is the only comfortable room. It is warmed by a Humphrey heater. The child chooses to dress herself in the cold bedroom. She must be away from the Mother. This dark,, cheerless morning, she readies herself for school, unable to button her ill-fitting plaid dress. Her fingers are chilled. Her clothes, discards of mother's, are always hugely too big and fasted together with safety pins..

"Come straight home. I have plans for you," Mother growls.

The "good" part of the child Rachel will not think what "after school" may mean. Her "bad" part, strong, willful Lilith, says Rachel had better prepare herself.

The school bell rings to signal time to go home. Lilith re-

143

minds Rachel she is to "take over." Mechanically, the girls now rigid bod jolts along the weather scarred sidewalk toward home. Lilith becomes visible. She has a jutting jaw, clenched teeth and a scowl. Her eyes are smoky and fierce. Though Lilith is strong, it is Rachel compulsiveness that is forcing them back to the tenement..

As Rachel is tiny, meek and quiet, Lilith is tall and powerful, ready to take on any adversary. Lilith saunters insolently, sometimes, to feel her strength. Rachel walks hesitantly, so no one can see or hear her. Climbing the steep, worn stairs, the girl hears the the dog's barking, as the sharp sound bounces off the peeling waterstained walls. When Mother opens the door, Mephisto leaps on Lilith. Mother giggles with pleasure. Snickering, Mother watches the girl, she thinks is Rachel, run into the bathroom, slamming the door.

"Come out of there, Imp! I'm holding our doggie."

"No, I'm not coming out." Lilith's fury thickens her voice.

"Unlock that goddamn door." The child peeks through a crack. Mother's right hand holds the dog's collar. Her other hand clutches a blanket, which the dog sniffs wildly, wheeling in a tight circle on his back legs.

"We are going to the cellar!" Then Mother recites words the girl knows by heart. The sounds vibrate deep in her bones. The bad dream into which she falls is a familiar one. Rachel opens the bathroom door. The Mother sings, as she pushes the girl toward the steps. Her voice is a squeal of joy, then a demented mutter.

The cellar is raw and damp. Mother drops the blanket on the dirt floor. The dog circles the blanket, his nose buried in its folds. He is panting.

"Take off your clothes!" Mother's voice sounds like those of the men on the wharf.

"No!" Lilith fights to the outside of the body and backs into the dark cellar corner.

"I won't! I won't!"

The dog snarls, panting with excitement, as Lilith shouts. Mother murmurs to the dog, stroking his giant body.

"We're going to play a game. We'll practice for the future.

We'll practice evil, evil practice. We're going to have fun. Mephisto fun!"

"Rachel, on the blanket, now!"

Mother grabs the child's arm, bending it backward, easily forcing the girl to the floor. With one large hand she rips away the child's panties. Lilith's head snaps hard against the dirt. From where she lies, stunned, the child can see Mother, massaging the dog's large private part, pulling away the hairy foreskin, rubbing the shiny pink membrane beneath. Mother wheezes and cackles. This laugh is strident, penetrating. Lilith struggles, but she is tied.

The dog is pushed down upon her. Undulating his massive body ponderously, his toenails tear the skin on the girl's thin, straining legs, hands and arms. Hot saliva from his open mouth pours down on her face and neck. She looks up to see his tongue flopping with his rhythm . His eyes are pale yellow. Mother leans against a post, a cigarette in her mouth, watching, her stubby fingers deep inside her body.

"Get him off!" Lilith demands. Mother chants ecstatically, as she probes herself. On a box next to her burns a black candle.

The girl wakes in the icy cellar, lying on the shredded blanket, sticky, in a tangle of crumpled clothing. The candle has burned away. She is sobbing,

"I want my Mommy," cries Rachel.

"I do have feelings, Roberta. I am sick, angry, weary and profoundly sad. There is no other girl here. There is only me, Rachel.

This happened to me," Rachel 2 says. Grown up Rachel opens her eyes.

Twenty Five

"What amazes me is the number of people who are really quite outside even fundamentalist religions, but who believe in the devil, just as part of the atmosphere. That may be partly because the evidence of the devil is more dramatic than the evidence of a benign counterposing force, call it God or whatever you will. As Milton pointed out, the devil is more interesting."

Reverend William P. Nye
Pastor, All Souls Universalist Church, Brooklyn

In the popular press a domestic aggressor is a wife beater, a man who attacks his woman and sometimes his children. But therapists know, women are not passive victims of family violence. There is evidence that female violence in marriage is as common as male violence. Wives hit husbands, just as husbands hit wives, and are as likely to begin the fight. Wives kill their husbands as often as husbands kill their wives. Of course, when physically matched, men are usually stronger and can inflict greater damage on a spouse than a woman.

Most assaults are only hair grabbing, pushing, slapping, but women do kick, bite and hit with fists more often than men. They threaten to use knives or guns.

Men beat women more often than women beat men, true. But when all cases of domestic violence are added up, men are injured more often and more seriously than women, since women tend to attack with weapons.

Police tell me, men hesitate to tell anyone they have been abused by their wives. Men stay in abusive homes for the same reasons women do: economics, habit and inability to cope with new situations. Some of them stay to protect their children, but Rachel's father had no intention of protecting her. But neither, would he allow her to be killed. She was useful.

Notes:
"Mother is muscular, powerful and vengeful. Daddy carries the scars of her physically-established right to be boss," says Rachel, remembering. In her log she writes her discoveries.

"Rachel does things to please Mommy, bad things. She wants Mommy to love her, even though she knows she should say "no" to Mommy, like Lilith does. Lilith scolds Rachel when she gives in to the demands of Mommy, Mother or the Witch. Lilith hates the Mother and stands up to her. She dares the Mother to make her cry or to feel the pain.

But Rachel knows she will do anything for Mommy, Mother or the Witch. Any of them. That's because she is afraid of the demons. Lilith hasn't lived with Mommy and Daddy as long as Rachel. Lilith appeared in the ocean, when the man gave Rachel her swimming lesson.

It is because Rachel has lived with Mommy and Daddy so long, that she knows the truth. She is possessed by evil spirits, and the Devil himself has commanded her strict obedience. Of course Rachel 1 complies."

Sam can see when I have Rachel on my mind.
"You're right. She can't manage her own anxiety," he says. "She can only let her terror show to you, out of all the people in the world. She's phobic, afraid of dogs, the dark, water, cats and men with dark eyes. But being afraid of things doesn't drain off all her panic. It doesn't keep her from being tortured every minute by anxiety.

Of course she's extremely controlled, as you say. When normal people are anxious, they worry about being embarrassed, humiliated or punished for being bad.

When Rachel is anxious, she is afraid she's going to fly apart, die or explode into pieces."
"That's right, Sam. Exactly as she describes herself."

147

"You allow her to regress, and she does in spades. That's not how one treats borderlines. But Rachel gets better. You're evidently doing the right thing. Keep going."

"Rachel is terrified, Sam. She can't turn off her frightening memories, and she is angry, rageful, and repressed, all at the same time. She is being downright aggressive. That nice lady is a real bitch!"

"Hurray! There's hope for her yet! How do you expect her to act, now that she is awake?"

"But she's self-destructive. She was about to drown herself in the irrigation ditch. I think, I just talked her out of it."

"Good for you, too. That's exactly the right thing to do. Talk her out of it this week and next week and the next and the next. She has a desperate need for reassurance. Your interest in her defends her against her gigantic anxieties, her psychotic fantasies."

"I keep telling you. These are not fantasies, Sam! They are memories of terrible events, and sadistic satanists fascinated with sexual torture. They excused it as religious ritual."

Sam admires objectivity. Stories of witchcraft or satanism leave him cold. Inattentive. Mental states, on the other hand, interest him immensely.

"I know that you are in this one for the long haul. I'm just sorry you got so involved, Doctor. I had other plans for you in this decade."

"Why didn't she try to save herself? Why did she return home, over and over, to be tortured?"

He smiles lasciviously, handing me a book marked with paper clips.

"I think you ought to read it, now. Its a novel. A love and adventure story and has no redeeming social value."

"Are you still playing supervisor and mental-illness-coach with me?" Sam pats me on the head with an exaggerated gesture. He leads me to my office and pushes me through the door, which he closes behind me. Inside, I feel relief that I have strong guidance, as I stumble through Rachel's dark wood. Maybe I will take my mind of this case for a while.

The door opens once more. A manly hand appears holding a cup of fresh coffee from whole roasted beans, hand ground. With it is a note, saying my next appointment has been cancelled. The coffee is dark with a hint of mint. The aroma is wonderful.

Of children labeled borderline studied at the Massachusetts Mental Health Center, ten were physically abused and twenty-two were raised in violent or chronically upset homes. Parents encouraged bizarre behavior.

One of the boys had his head shaved by his mother and slept in her bed so he could watch her sexual encounters. A little girl was believed to be a witch by her family. Consequently, her mother tried to pull out her daughter's tongue. At the insistence of his Mom, a ten year old boy wore girl's clothing to school. At home, the same Mommy took her son to bed, where she encouraged him to bite her. She playfully bit him back.

Mothers are overrepresented in this literature of craziness. I don't like that. What a bum rap! Are we back to the schizophregenic-mother theory in just another form? Or the frozen womb notion?

Sam believes that is so, because the word "Mother" stands for home. That's why it turns up as all important so often.

Rachel grew up in one of those crazy-making homes with little chance to test reality. Violence was both threatened and real, combined with powerful early sexual stimulation. Treatment like that can keep any child from developing an inner self. Such a child has no sense of security or built-in ability to connect with other human beings.

Individual psychotherapy is absolutely necessary for this kind of damaged individual, although difficult for therapists. The emotional shifts in the client are severe and confusing. Drug therapy is often appropriate. A therapist should expect panic and attempts to escape or shut down. Forbidden feelings and fantasies are always close to the surface.The therapist must to be loyal, sincerely interested, consistent, patient and non-punishing. Trust means everything.

"Oh, no. The therapist must be perfect. Impossible! I didn't know this treatment was going to be for life. Rachel and I have now gone through her childhood and early adolescence together and   there is more to come. No wonder Sam believes I've left him for a woman."

Daddy is yelling at Iris again. I am exhausted. My head aches unbearably. I musn't sleep. My nightmares are filled with illusions, lies, time distortion, killings, rituals, eeriness and black anger. I am trapped in my broken body, and I am doomed. I disgust myself. I am crazy. Crazy. I mustn't get close to anyone. I might slip and tell, and if I do everyone will know, I do evil.

I must go to church. Concealed in a stately polished pew I may find rest in a dream of death. I dress and leave the rickety tenement house without Mommy or Daddy seeing me. Walking along the ocean front under the giant maples, I breath the salty air and the cool fog. I have no shadow. The hollow sound of a fog horn warns the ships to beware of rocks. Bumpy pink cobblestones on the old streets are slippery and black with rotting leaves. The door of the church is gigantic, but I can open it by pushing with my whole body. Entering the quiet seclusion of the grey granite church , I look around. I am alone.

"Dear God, I pray you to make me dead "right now." Peeper slips to the cold floor.

"I am so dirty. So very dirty, dirty, dirty." At that moment a priest visiting the nave of the church, might look through the dozens of candles burning as votive offerings, to see a little girl kneeling on bony knees.

"I am Peeper. I plead with you, God, let me die and stay dead."

The miracle of the church is the emergence of Lilith once more. Rachel's gift from God is courage.

It is starting to snow when Rachel leaves the church for home, still alive.

Recently, public concern has led to the overreporting of suspected child abuse. Often a child is too young to testify. Since sexual abuse of extremely young children rarely involves penetration of orifices, it is difficult to find physical evidence. Very young children cannot describe their experiences accurately. Five to thirty percent of cases are unsubstantiated allegations made by the malicious, who have misinterpreted physical symptoms or behavior. Well-meaning persons make mistakes, too. Unfounded allegations arise in divorce cases. Children, who listen to their parent's worries about each other's behavior, doubt their own perceptions.

Once in a while, a child makes a false accusation, but unlike Freud, experts now believe it is rare when a child fantasizes about sex with an adult. How can any of us know for sure?

Another therapy session: Rachel tells me what she sees, hears, and, nowadays, what she feels.

The broken, dark green shades are drawn to keep out the sunshine. Daddy has left for the day. Mommy is back in bed. The rooms are crowded with litter. Crumpled bills and filled ashtrays are heaped together on the kitchen table. Toast crusts scatter along the floor. Remnants of pizzas crumble , slowly, in the bathroom down the hall. The table next to the television holds Mommy's drying Hostess cream filled cupcakes, Camel cigarette butts and Fig Newtons.

Nibbling and smoking, she watches her programs. When she is not in bed, her place is in the faded overstuffed chair. Even in winter, she wears her semitransparent nylon nightgowns, displaying huge, sagging breasts. Her belly hangs around her hips. Mommy's shoulders and skeletal frame are gigantically out of proportion to her height. Pungent, her odor is a combination of raspberries and ozone, tuna fish, archaic sweat and flowery perfume. Stuffed animals are arranged in cozy heaps, piled around her bed.

There is no designated place for anything. When I clean house, Mother grows angry. When I do not clean house ,

151

Mother grows angry. Today, propped against a stained cup of cold coffee, there is a note scrawled across an unpaid bill.

"Clean the house. Feeling like shit." I can hear Mother's raucous voice screaming aloud in my head. To make the noise stop, I put my hands over my ears.

The *"good"* child in me, created by the ceremonial tortures, begins by cleaning up the filth in the soiled kitchen, scrubbing and scraping the linoleum. With a basket of wet wash I drag myself to the cramped third floor porch , to hang clothes on the line.

Downstairs, Mother lumbers out of the bedroom, her eyes bright, vitreous. She is breathing fast, panting and coughing.

"I forgot to give you your medicine, Rachel." With her rolling walk she swaggers to the cupboard, and takes out a bottle of thick brown liquid.

"No! Not that bad stuff! It gives me awful tummy aches. I won't take it anymore," shouts Lilith.

"You'll take your medicine now or else, Rachel." Mother pours the malodorous liquid into a bent and rusty tablespoon.

"You must be cleansed, cleansed, sends, cleansed, friends, ends, mends, cleansed, rends, bends, tends, cleansed."

When I hear the rhyming, the good child alter in me , Rachel 1, obeys. I take the medicine over Lilith's objections. Hurrying, I finish my chores before my stomach starts to hurt. Then I know I will have to stay in the bathroom.

"Mommy says the medicine will make the bad in me go away, so I'll always be good. It never works. I always do bad things."

My middle starts to spasm. I must not cry with the cramps which burn and twist through me. I must not cry. I don't hurt.

"There is no pain." Lilith whispers to me, as I run into the bathroom.

Peeper sits contemplating death, holding the butcher knife. She stares down at its sharp edge.There are tiny nicks along it, from the struggles of the dying fish. The knife remembers the killings it has done. Just one more. Peeper knows dying brings release from the nightmare in which she exists. She has died before, in church and in the tunnel.

Rachel's Journal:

Again, I can't sleep. I lie quietly in my bed until Mommy and Daddy are asleep, then get my pad and pen. Lying on the floor, I write a story. This time it is a mystery about a haunted cave.. Day or night, when Mommy cannot see me, I read. At night, I write.

Mommy hates me "wasting time." At home, I hide my books and all my writings, so Mommy will not tear them up again or burn them. My story of a butterfly has won a contest, but Mommy refused to allow me to travel to Boston to receive my prize.

"I do not want you to get involved with the wrong kind of people, Rachel."

This is the year I have my first friend, my teacher. She says I have talent.

"Can you stay after school to help grade papers?" asks Mrs. Bouchard.

I know Mother will be mad, but I decide to take the risk. I hate home. I like being needed, it makes me feel respectable. The problem is that sometimes the teacher asks me personal questions.

"Do you eat breakfast?" or "How did you hurt yourself, Rachel?"

I must be careful what I say. I did not tell the policeman, the one who asked questions about Mommy.

Tonight,I write my happy family story. The floor grows cold in the late hours of the night. I wrap myself in a ragged out-grown, transparent nightgown. Yesterday, I washed out Mommy's sour smell and hung this nightie on the fire escape until it dried.

My spindly feet sink into scratchy woolen socks. Under my blanket tent, I practice good penmanship.

"Once, long, long ago, in a far off land, there was a happy family. The mother loved her daughter and the father was known, far and wide, for being a kind man. The family members wore beautiful, warm clothes. Their home was always

*clean, cozy and warm, with many enveloping, feather comfort-
ers of cream colored satin, and several soft, luxurious beds."*
    Someday, I'll have lots of friends and write a real book.

    *Mommy is yelling. Daddy does not yell, although he is an-
gry. Policemen are here. Questions and more questions.*
    "Is this jail?"
    "This is a hearing."
    *I know what to say. I have been asked before. This time I am
in a big room. A nice lady is with me. The lady is pretty and
talks in a soft comfortable voice.*
    "Would you like a soda?"
    "No, thank you," Mommy is out of sight somewhere.
    *"Is it time to start?" The people stand up when an old man
walks into the room.*
    *"You have to tell the truth," he says.Where are Mommy and
Daddy? I hear my name. The lady walks me to the chair at the
table.*
    "Sit down here. Are you frightened?"
    *"I don't want to go to jail. I have to go to school." I hear the
old man's loud voice as he asks my name.*
    *"Where do you live? Is this woman your mother? Is this
man your father?"*
    "Yes,"
    "Does your Mother?...
    "No," Lilith replies,"no."
    The lawyer for the State looks across the table at me.
Lilith convinces him she has no idea what he is talking about.
    *A voice in my head rattles my skull. I know nothing. I nev-
er did see anything.*

    *I walk home from school alone, hunched over. I have no
friends among the children because I am different. If I found a
kid friend, I could never bring her home. No one must see or
know what happens there. What if I brought someone home
and Mommy, no... Mother didn't like them? Who knows what
terrible things could happen. If I'm like Mother, I might make
evil things happen, too.*
    I have Lilith to help when things get really bad. Lilith will

always take care of me. Lilith is getting stronger each day, more powerful. She is not like kids in school either. They are silly and play. Lilith does not play.

We dream of running far away. Just Lilith and me, hiding in the trunk of my teacher's car. Maybe she would like the two of us to live with her. I will be good and Lilith will be brave. I promise to cook, clean and whatever else needs doing. Lilith will protect the three of us.

"Roberta, I can tell you what it was like for me. I'm there." Rachel speaks deliberately, clearly, eyes half-closed.

"My shabby clothes embarrass me. They keep me out of activities based on popularity. I still wear the discarded see-through blouses of my mother's and her awkward cotton skirts, three sizes too large for me. My brown lace-up shoes are scuffed and run down at the heels. Other girls wear loafers with bright copper pennies. I have no poodle skirt, no pleated plaids. When choosing up sides, other kids taunt me for my clumsiness. Most often, I am ignored. Inside, I am dead."

"We are the chosen, the chosen." The words repeat themselves in my head. I have to shake myself or pull my hair to make the words stop. When the voices quiet, I can concentrate.

"If I am good, Roberta, I won't have to be cleansed and miss school. Already two years behind the other children I am always the oldest and the smallest child in the class.

When Mommy is sick I have to miss school to take care of her and that is often.

I am tired, yet once again I am hopeful. Does Mommy seem better? Am I silly to wish so? Hope chains me to this place."

'Teachers are crazy,' Mother says.

She explodes in rage, pounds the table and stamps her feet. Is Mommy sick again?

Away from home I am..... is the word happy? My classroom is bright. Sunshine makes the desk tops look as if they are made of glass. As much as I love this room,

155

I hate anything involving contact with other children. Hate and love are feelings. I know I'm not good enough for the other children. I strongly prefer the background where I'll be unobserved. My desk is in the back of the room, where I can secretly watch my teacher. Her voice is soothing and she is small, with a pretty smile and masses of tiny wrinkles like cross hatching lines on an etching.

Black curls touch her shoulders, and she has just enough gray hairs for subtle shading, like a portrait done in the colored chalk we used for art last week. My teacher is beautiful, kind and good, I know.

If only I could live here with the smell of books and library paste. Today's assignment is written on the board. I will be learning. A smile tips up the corners of my mouth. I am home."

Trying to help Rachel I have only this guide to go by:

"Diagnostic criteria for Multiple Personality: A.The existence within the individual of two or more distinct personalities, each of which is dominant at a particular time. B.The personality that is dominant at any particular time determines the individual's behavior. C. Each individual personality is complex and integrated with its own unique behavior patterns and social relationships.Child Abuse and other forms of severe emotional trauma in childhood may be predisposing factors."
Diagnostic and Statistical Manual III

Multiple personality is an exotic label most therapists have hesitated to use. It still thrills us, as it did eighty years ago, when Morton Prince first described it.

There are few subjects as controversial, unless it is how to stop the spread of AIDS, whether we should circumcise boy babies, or whether satanic abuse stories are rooted in fact. Recently, multiple personality has been reported more and more often in professional literature and there are a variety of sensational novels about unfortunate people with sixty, eighty or more persons inside them.

Is this a fad, a passing interest or an actual increase? The number of reported cases is increasing dramatically every day. Still most therapists say they have never encountered a case of multiple personality in all their years of practice. A small number of clinicians do almost all the reporting of this strange disorder and I haven't wanted to be one. Are these particular therapists extra alert diagnosticians? Or do they choose the diagnosis of multiple personality, because the idea is intriguing to them personally? Do they somehow "bring out" multiplicity?

It's strange how the goals of any therapist and needs of the client can come together. Dramatically their imaginations combine. The phenomenon of transference allows a therapist to encourage and reward certain behaviors. Naturally, other behaviors are discouraged by disinterest. This may encourage what may be only a dramatic urge to develop into a separate identity in the client, as if another person is sharing the client's body and brain.

Here is a classic example. A client is ashamed of herself. Secretly, she feels she has been "too easy" with several men. However, she is being pressured by each man to continue to go to bed with him. This popular lady's therapist worries that his client will pick up transmissible sexual diseases.

With that concern, the therapist reinforces his client's guilt. Now the client develops, what is called, an 'ego alien' feeling. She feels "bad" about what she has been enjoying, a sensation strange and uncomfortable. It does not seem "part of" her, although her shame has been there all along. Before, she only experienced emotions that were "liberated, wild and free." Now she feels like two people. She is whore and madonna, the saint and sinner, moral maiden and promiscuous woman. Is she two personalities? No, only a conflicted person.

But Rachel is different. Her body develops symptoms, she hears voices, images intrude on her thoughts, many thoughts are interrupted or just taken away and peculiar behavior seems forced on her body. Her hallucinations are not psychosis. They are memories.

All the physical symptoms Rachel endures sound like Sybil. Her depression, inability to sleep and self mutilation can be understood as outcomes of sexual abuse. She has shouldered the blame, as children do for the sins perpetrated on them.

"I'm bad. Nothing is enough to cleanse my badness. I'm dirty," someone inside her repeats. Even the hostile alters are acting out of this feeling of badness. Yet we know it was not Rachel the child who was bad.

But maybe multiple personality is too fancy a diagnosis for my friend, Rachel. Or Rachel's mother. I'm unsure how developed each personality in Rachel may be. And of course, I've never had a chance to observe Mommy, Mother, Iris and the Witch.

"Stop picking on me, Sam!"

"You are unconsciously telegraphing Rachel that she can be a more interesting client, if she has more than one personality. Of course, she, like other hysterics is always self-dramatizing. Now, she's affected by your developing interest in multiple personality. It's her way of attracting attention from you, while avoiding personal responsibility for her life."

Sam is wrong. He's like the False Memory Syndrome Foundation people, who think we have made all this up, or the Fundamentalist Christians who say that acknowledging satanic abuse means God isn't in charge of the universe.

He thinks he's "scientific," and perhaps will never be convinced Rachel has the credentials to join the roster of true multiples.

Sam has strong doubts about the existence of systematic satanic abuse and he embodies the ideological idea that Multiple Personality Disorder can't exist, which is some of the bad medicine that exists in traditional psychiatry. Maybe I'm able to accept the idea of mutiplicity because of the Woman's Movement. We, women, have opened up the question of incest. We're honest about how many of us have been sexually abused.

There may be more cases of satanic child abuse than we ever want to know. Opinions are only opinions.

Devout believers in satanic ritual abuse envision a world wide conspiracy that is headed by important people in high places. Extreme skeptics say that cruel and inhuman practices cannot be real, forgetting both the Spanish Inquisition and the Holocaust.

But, what I am struggling with are not just women's issues. The new diagnosis of Post Traumatic Stress Disorder came out of the Viet Nam War. If so many of our strong and healthy young men were completely undone by periodic stress, shock and fear, there is more about trauma we need to learn as soon as we can. Get the old biases out of the way! Inner Child work has become popular, a mass appeal item. There clearly is an anti - psychiatry revolution going on "right here in River City".

Of course, I am uncertain. But for the first time I'm backed up by the new diagnostic manual. Before there was only Sybil and Eve. Am I one of those therapists who becomes too...interested? Have I exaggerated Rachel's history, because now "it's in the book?"

I don't want to become polarized about "truth" in this argument. It 's not my business to come to a conclusion. I don't have expertise in evidence collection. All I must develop is some calm and sensible understanding of multiplicity and the phenomenon of satanic abuse. For that I need to learn about the psychology of destructive cults and the torment they are said to inflict. Rachel can teach me, if I will listen and learn. Sam can keep me centered. I don't have to know anything for sure.

Rachel is terrified. Her fear springs from her perilous urge to be physically violent. She feels compelled to attack her children. Only with the greatest self control, can she force herself to leave the room rather than batter her redhaired daughters. Her fists ache to strike out. She hears herself screaming at the girls, her ears echoing with Mother's obscenities. In Rachel's brain resounds a grisly voice with a familiar rasp. The worst has happened and the curse has taken over. Rachel has become the hated one. Mother.

Sam will not agree with me philosophically, but he is standing by, in the next room, in case I need him. I am ready to entice that hostile alter to come out. But rather than Mother-in-Rachel, whom I dread, I meet Peeper.

She introduces herself through a charcoal drawing. On a gravestone in a bleak, grey and white cemetery her name is carved. Dates of her birth and demise are carefully inscribed on the black and smeary image of a mossy stone. A bare tree with dead branches stands to one side. Peeper has made this picture for me to tell me where she and other children died.

I inquire of Rachel about the picture she has just drawn. Her shaking hands still hold the black stump of a charcoal drawing stick. The fingers of her right hand are smeared with charcoal dust. Rachel looks puzzled, then frightened. She has no comprehension of the drawing. It has drawn its own bleak images.

This one of Rachel's little alters did not live to grow up, yet strangely, at times, in order to live, Rachel becomes Peeper. And Peeper is dead.

Lilith draws pictures for me too, first a huge dog face with long teeth and glowing eyes. Drool drips from the lolling tongue. In other scenes there are stick figures with penises that are not twigs, but giant organs, sketched to look like cobras about to strike. Their hoods are red with blood. Another picture is a ring of witches, exciting themselves with huge dildos, and next is a cermonial scene of costumed figures, kneeling around a disembodied human head on a stake.

I review my clinical notes once more, years worth of wonder and speculation. There was so much to learn and few sources of help. I can make a list of what I didn't know back then. It's long:

I needed to learn about dissociation disorders and how to take semistructured clinical interviews for persons suspected of being multiples. I would find and appreciate the work of Kluft, Braun, Putnam, Ross and others, and learn to say "MPD." Little by little, I would seek out other clinicians, who had bumped into this hidden disorder, and were able to think and write about it.

I would learn others felt disoriented, confused and blocked when confronted with so many symptoms. Their multiples had blackouts and time loss, like mine, unremembered places they had been, strange things they had done, great changes in talents and abilities. Their life histories were made up of disjointed pieces and their identities got mixed up by other people, their own children, and especially by their therapists.

I needed to know, then, that multiples are in trance most of the time. Enthrallment occurs, which means being completely absorbed in something so that nothing else seems to exist. That's a part of being so hypnotizable. Spontaneous regression is part of their picture, and clients truly believe they "get little." Negative hallucinations are mental abilities that make things disappear from their awareness, just as if they aren't there. This can affect seeing or hearing, which is blocked out, just as the perception of pain is made to just "go away." When I tape recorded Lilith, the earlier Rachel and little Peeper, they could only hear themselves and not each other .

"I don't hear anyone else, so what's the problem?"

Trance logic was a term I desperately needed to know about when Rachel and I started exploring. That is the absolute acceptance by the client of strange contrary beliefs and thoroughly illogical ideas. For instance, the hostile alters in Rachel would not accept the idea that they inhabited the same body with the others, that if the body died they would also die.

"That's her body, not mine."

In trance logic, self-mutilation has to do with safety. Cutting oneself lets something out and reduces tension,

or punishes the " bad" child, who was the person origi-
nally victimized. Burning oneself purifies the part of the
body that was made impure. Drinking something caustic, like lye, will make clean the little throat subjected to
oral rape. A person, who is a multiple, experiences a
world inside filled with people who feel real, and there
is no overcrowding.

So Peeper can be a dead alter that reappears occasionally. The internal children know grown up words, and
alters that lived long ago understand what is happening
right now.

Imagery assaults multiples, they relive shocking trauma, and terrible flashbacks are going to occur, through
spontaneous self hypnosis with or without a therapist.
Nightmares will be constant and terrifying. Panic, anxiety attacks and phobias are to be expected, since constant
reminders of abuse are seen, heard or felt by the victim.
Or even imagined.

When the alters began to emerge from Rachel, they
did not come out through a sort of revolving door. Instead, there was often overlapping, confusion, noise and
quarrelsome interference, until we all learned how to
work together.

98% of MPD clients have a history of severe, repetitive
abuse, beginning before the age of five. Most of them
will have amnesia for childhood.

Rachel is sitting in my office. I tell her she must make
an appointment with a psychiatrist to find out about
medication. The doctor's name is Dr. Fielding. I have
every reason to believe Rachel is more suicidal than ever.

Upset, Rachel wants her own doctor, me, to perform a
miracle. She expects me to make her well, at once. She
has ulcers, colitis, severe muscle spasms and is anorex-
tic/bulimic. The last condition is a secret, Rachel thinks.

She seems convinced I have not guessed, even though
we have talked about it in trance very directly and Rachel's body can only be, sometimes,m described as "skeletal." When she is not having blinding headaches, she is

frightened by her lack of sleep.

"Why do I need to see a psychiatrist? You want me to take pills! You know that if I have too many pills, I will use them to commit suicide. I will."

Rachel uses her most powerful threat. I do not answer, but she can see that I am angry. I can feel my frown. Rachel waits for my argument. Instead, I open the door and gesture her out of my office. Furious, Rachel takes her books and walks down the hall, aware of her posture. She hold herself erect. "Walk proud," I whisper.

Rachel's Journal:

Roberta's words made me stubborn. Pills, drugs. She doesn't understand! Drugs make terrible, awful things happen to me. Never again. I must be in total control at all times. I remember, I know why.

Mommy takes pills. Mommy smokes. Mommy drinks. Mother makes me take medicine and drink from a golden cup. Then I do "bad" things. Medicine brings so much pain and shame, that long ago I begged for death. I had to stop what medicine does. I want to turn around, to see if Dr. Richards is watching me walk haughtily away, but I don't. What if she is not looking after me? How I hate my own dependency. I want to "get well." But I want to do it my own way. I have to. I hate Dr. Richards. I hate Roberta!

This evening Dr. Fielding calls me.

"Dr. Richards tells me she believes you are suicidal. She wants me to make an appointment with you."

"I'm entirely too busy just now, Doctor. May I call you back?"

How dare she do this to me! Only crazy people see a psychiatrist. I'm not crazy! When I do not return his call, Dr. Fielding calls me again. It is a Saturday night. His voice is patient. Holding the phone, I feel cornered. I deny I am suicidal. Lilith does her "I'm as well as can be" act. She is cool and poised.

On Sunday, Dr. Fielding calls to see if I am still alive.

"Of course, I am fine." Lilith is convincing. I need no

163

intervention from Dr. Fielding, Lilith has decided.

For three weeks I go into the bathroom every twenty minutes from colitis. I eat Tagamets for ulcer pain, have nightmares about murder, blood and pain, lose sleep, and massage my neck until my hands are tired. I struggle to relieve the muscle spasms and fantasize about killing myself. After twenty-one days, I acknowledge I am desperate. I must crawl back on my emotional knees. Dr. Richards has not called me. How she will be grieving over me, when I walk into her office.

Instead, she is talking to another client on the phone. She waves, pointing to a chair and the steaming pot in the corner. Of course, I can't put hot coffee into my suffering stomach. I wait. The discussion from this end of the phone conversation sounds like it may be about suicide. Dr. Richards talks for a long time, before she hangs up. She looks at me, waiting for me to speak. The silence is a long one.

"I will do whatever you think I need to do," I say.

Notes:
Rachel looks haggard. Her skin is yellow and dry and she has khaki circles under her eyes. I phone Dr. Fielding to make an appointment.

Lilith keeps Rachel's first visit with her new psychiatrist.

"His office is dark," she tells me. "His blinds are shut. The room and the man are both claustrophobic. Even his desk is ugly. It's precise, neat and ominous."

Dr. Fielding himself, "is a little short guy, not what I expected. Although his accent is Indian, not German, he is anything but fatherly. He is a dark-eyed lady's man with a gigolo mustache. However, he behaves like a psychiatrist. He sits with a pencil and pad in his lap."

Lilith laughs with scorn.

'Tell me about yourself, Rachel? Why are you here?,' he said."

'I am remembering painful experiences from my past and Dr. Richards thinks I may be suicidal. However, she is incorrect. I am coping nicely. I just need something to help me sleep'.

'All right, I will give you something for rest and I will see you again next week.'

"Shit! I thought I was never going to have to see this creepy pro again! He's not going to get anything out of me!"

"Thank you, doctor, I'll see you next week."

Planning never to go back, it is the next day before she realizes the doctor will not refill her prescription without a return visit. Lilith is irked.

Notes: 1988, Women's Support Group:

"Rachel," my client says to herself, "make yourself go into the house. You are a grown woman and have no reason to be afraid."

Through the window, I can see Rachel hiding behind the steering wheel, parked as far away from the street light as the street will allow her. Instead of walking briskly in, to become a member of the women's therapy group, she crouches in front of my office in the moon-wash of this fall evening. She breathes slowly and exhales carefully, so the piccolo scream that occasionally steams out of her mouth won't burst out now, unbidden. She readies herself. Each time she comes to this house for therapy, she debates whether to come in or to run away.

Now she is "in group." Will she be accepted, humiliated or hurt? Debased? Something huge and hulking in her brain stops her thinking, or smears her vision. Numbness moves through her body, when she must deal with new experiences.

"This is how I was as a youngster. Terrified. Hunching. Those same feelings are here again," Rachel is able to tell me.

"That may be true, but you also have had years of practice in keeping yourself going, anyway." From individual therapy Rachel has learned a great deal about herself, but she believes she has far, far to go. Discouraged, she scoldsherself fiercely, harshly.

"Stupid! Fool." Tonight she stops herself just in time, unwilling to slip into a litany of verbal self abuse that will end up with the word "Imp." At the sound of that word Rachel always hates herself. This particular internal cruelty, a compulsive ritual, must stop! With a mental shove she moves herself out of her old car and stiffly walks through rust and green foliage to the front door.

Her quaking hand on the handle of my front door appears pale and bluish to her in the moonlight. It is thin, transparent.

"I must eat more."

This is a thought. Rachel knows the difference between a thought and a feeling. Feeling words are 'mad, happy, sad, hurt'. She practices feeling feelings and naming them. She can put into words what she is experiencing. That's why she can be in group.

"You are ready," I insist.

"But what if I am not!," she tells herself. Deep inside her, pink and painful, Rachel believes, is buried the evil, dirty, used self which will never be comfortable with women who are clean.

"All together" is what they are. "Decent," she says.

What will her companions in group say, if they find out who the real Rachel is, and what she has done? Rachel truly believes she and they are world's apart. The differences between them might as well be written on a sign around her neck, spelling out "Beware!" "Evil!" "Used!" "Dirty!"

Can she risk being judged and rejected? The deep voice in Rachel's head is Lilith.

"You are not a quitter!"

Lilith pushes Rachel into my group room, an enclosure she expects will be filled with mental and emotional strain. Rachel knows, intellectually, it is only my living room. But, for her, anguish leans against the walls, or lies, languorously along the black piano, ready to leap.Rachel has walked past this room a hundred times on the way to the office. She knows this setting is arranged to suggest safety. There is a fire in the fireplace, with chairs in a semi-circle around the warmth of the flames. Four women are already here. She names them: "Worldly", "Well-educated", "Successful" and "Dressed Beautifully." The last four of the eight group members file in, smiling and self assured. Rachel watches, judges and labels.

Jo is "aggressive", because she talks and laughs, Rachel explains to me, later in our individual session. Jo speaks about sex, boldly, as if it is an everyday thing. Clearly, she is bragging! Her tales are ribald, dirty stories murmured behind her hand as if to a friend.

"That's not open... authentic behavior. I think you must put a stop to it, right now!" Rachel is now telling me how to run group.

"Since it troubles you, Rachel, why not say something to her about it, yourself?"

"But you're the leader, Roberta, it's not my place to make trouble."

Besides group, Rachel comes more often now, for sessions as well. In deep trance a kind of suffering stupor, Rachel relives, over and over, terrifying scenes from childhood. At last, she accepts that she is very ill, not simply physically. This realization may allow her to get well. Again and again, she surrenders herself to pain and terror, reexperiencing the shock and horror of a cruelly molested child. Rachel approaches her torture systematically, bravely. Dare I say, ritualistically? Little by little, session by session, the impact of these gruesome scenes lessens. I no longer have doubts about her diagnosis. I just don't know what to do about it.

Rachel tells me about her strong interest in Lydia. She is fascinated with her, even more than with the other group members, learning new words and behaviors from her. Lydia is sometimes self-assured and poised, but she says she is a 'basket-case.' That's a term Rachel wants to remember as she has already learned 'falling apart' and 'all together'.

"'All together', is how these women are, and I'm not, " she says.

Very tall, with short blond hair and a husky voice, Lydia is seeing a psychiatrist for medication. He is the same Dr. Fielding I forced Rachel to see. But this glamorous woman likes him. Her group time is spent talking about his large, dark eyes and provocative, therapeutic methods.

"Can it be that Lydia has a childish, clinging self?" Rachel wants to know. "She is a clever woman, but always ruminating about a man." Not yet out of a marriage mess in which she entangles herself, Lydia is attempting to catch still another male to confuse. She shares her plan to find a man with group.

I call her a "man junkie." Rachel is shocked. How mean I am! Calling names. Everyone else laughs, including Lydia.

The self-proclaimed scholar, Ginny, is working on a book about therapy. She is "just here to learn." Rachel knows better. So does every other member of the group. We are very smart about each other, just blind to ourselves. Rachel begins to see us all more clearly.

A dark haired, "heavy" participant aims to become "hellishly" slim without dealing with her "past", her habits, her children, her parents, her relationship with her husband, her job, or with us. She has a crush on a colleague at work and intends to attract him with her future svelte figure.

"Man junkie," Rachel whispers, sqeakily. No one laughs or notices Rachel has spoken. I'm glad she made her try. Now Rachel has something else to think over.

"Speak up, Rachel."

Roxanne is tall and dark, and full of hatred for her mother. She is having an affair with a married businessman, whom she flies to meet for weekends in Hawaii. Her travel money is almost gone. What to do? Her confidences are steamy, passionate retrospectives.

"I might as well be in Hugh Hefner's mansion, talking about sex, sex, sex," Rachel complains to me. In group we hear how Jo's most recent romantic encounter was on a commercial air flight.

"Right there. I didn't have a stitch on underneath, " she chortles.

"Unlike me", Rachel says later, "these women are not 'nervous.' They must know what they are doing...yet, somehow I guess that is not true. Perhaps they are not in control."

Rachel learns how often she projects her own ideas on other people. Control is her fiercest desire, not theirs. In this group we have both "over" and "out of control" issues.

"A need for too much-control is your constant struggle, Rachel. They just want what they want."

"Oh. I see," she says. But she doesn't. In tears, Rachel tells me her discovery.

"During group, I discovered I have no identity. Those other women know their pasts and who they are. I know only my name, but not why I am here."

In the world of female seduction we have an expert in this very group. Her name is Lana. Sultry, she has a wide white toothed smile. Her swept back hair is a daring bottle-blond. All at once, Rachel displays a love for a worldly look. Lana has been color-draped and wears becoming purples, scarlets and hot pinks with lipsticks to match.

So does Rachel now, while hanging on every word of Lana's descriptions, wanting to be "just like her." She makes Lana into her "big sister."

"She will teach me to be sensual. Unlike me, Lana is a real woman."

"Oh, how is that? Tell me." Rachel can't come up with an answer.

Since Lana's husband "travels", and is obsessed with his business, Lana thinks of him as much older than herself, although he is only a year her senior. He constantly scolds Lana, as if she were a child. Lana laughs like Jo, as she recounts her sexual exploits with young men, boys or old lechers. But she is emotionally moved only by one man, one who is cruel to her, a male tease. Lana takes foolish risks with him and others. I point out that several times she has endangered herself, abandoned by a stranger in a motel with no money or a way home.

"Perhaps I don't want to be just like her, after all," Rachel decides.

Tonight in group, Lana works on her relationship with her father. She discovers she has married Dad. By now this surprises no one in this semi-circle around the fire.

"I thought that the first time you described Fred," Lydia shouts out. Rachel would have said so first, before Lydia , but she wasn't sure enough. She's getting faster, though, at knowing what is going on inside someone else. Rachel, herself, is the one who is difficult to read, keeping herself blank.

Lana cries. She begs her absent "father-in-her-head" to love her. She pounds pillows and pleads with an empty chair. There is no answer.

"Daddy, Daddy, please notice me. Please love me!" We cheer Lana on, weeping with her. In front of each of us, Lana becomes a little child, speaking in a piping voice. She looks shyly from under her eye lashes.

"I love you, Daddy. Please love me back." There is no answer from the woman who role plays Daddy. Her silence reflects the reality of Lana's relationship.The next week Lana separates her illusion of Father from her real life "Fred." At last she accepts the hated truth. They are not the same man. Lana will never get the love, acceptance and approval from her long-ago father for which she has longed. The best she can do is Fred. She has been a Cinderella, waiting for the Prince.

"While waiting for your Prince to come, enjoy the frog," I quote Ric Masten.

Lana knows, now, she married Fred to serve as Prince-substitute.

"Take him or leave him," the group choruses. Lana takes him.

The next week she is radiant. She and Fred are going to Italy together. Together, they experience wonderful loving encounters. Her life is pulsing with excitement,170 and Lana has fallen in love with her grown children, as well as with her same old husband.

"I had decided she was so...cheap, but..." Rachel wonders out loud.

"She was lonely, Rachel. You know what that's like."

"I can't wait to show my kids my new self," Lana crows.

"At last I am a wife and a mother!" Her devotion is genuine. The group is shocked.

Rachel is tormented with more flashbacks from her recent work. She may need antidepressant medication, but hostile Lilith will not cooperate with the confused psychiatrist to whom I referred Rachel. In group, now, we are forced to listen to a running account of Lilith's clashes with him. Dr. Fielding calls her behavior, "acting out."

Describing her dreadful first appointment with Dr. Fielding, Lilith, who has obviously joined Rachel in group, makes herself heard. Repeatedly.

"So, 'tell me your latest dream,' the doctor says. I comply. He interprets," Lilith is explaining, loudly.

"'Sexual elements'," he says.

"Boy, do I straighten him out. YOU are WRONG!," I say.

"You aren't listening. You haven't heard all the parts of my dream. You have completely misconstrued what I've been telling you. Dr. Richards says you have to work on the whole dream at once, then break it up into elements. She does it that way."

Dr. Fielding is not at all upset. He does not argue. Looking, unblinkingly, at the woman he believes is Rachel, he holds his neutral expression, remaining impassive, as he has been trained. Lilith lets her fury out to us, week after week, deeply insulted. Appearing to us as Rachel, she continues to complain about the serene psychiatrist. The group tires of her whining, bored with her long, enduring outrage.

"An asshole!" Lilith goes on,"Wasting my money at

seventy some dollars an hour! Ten dollars a minute!"

Lydia decides to feel hurt for the well meaning doctor.

"That's not the way I see him at all. He's so sweet and handsome, and he cares about you, Rachel, honestly. I just know he doesn't really think about the money." Lydia is going to cry.

"Bullshit, Lydia!" It's therapeutic for Lilith to take out Rachel's anger on kindly, puzzled Dr. Fielding, even on poor, misguided Lydia, but I, too, am weary of her animosity. Here she goes, once more, repeating each one of her major complaints.

"He is mismanaging my case!"

"What do you think, Group? Does what Rachel is saying sound like displaced anger?"

"Can we get on to something else, Rachel?" Lydia makes a try. Although, Lilith is still talking, I shout out impatiently, "Who's next? Does anyone have anything new to report?"

As she joined the group, Rachel's once shy over politeness impressed the ladies. Now, Lilith's vicious manner and language astound, then bore the members of the "Wednesday Night Laboratory in Human Behavior."

"What makes me so damn mad is that I can't forget the day I told him my dream," Lilith goes on, not hearing me." He interpreted it all wrong, all wrong! He put in some sexual thing! I told him he had left out half. He violated me. Paying him all that damn money, I should have an accurate interpretation of my whole fucking dream! If he can't get his shit together, how can he help me?"

The group follows me, as I stand and move to the kitchen table. I close the sliding door. In this cramped space we will continue, without Lilith.

The next week, we find Lilith has fired Dr. Fielding, without telling him. That is, she never goes back. Feeling triumphant, Rachel does without medication.

"I'll show him!"

I'm relieved Rachel can tolerate her own anger and can

function without medication, always a controversial issue, especially with multiples. And without guilt. She skips her chance to obsess about what a rude, bad child she has been to innocent Dr. Fielding. At the same time, she practices anger at someone fairly safe. That's a good idea, even though her real reasons are out of her awareness. What a brat she is!

Sam laughs when I tell him. "You have unleashed a Rachel-Monster into the street. She's running amok."

"I'm afraid Lilith is doing Rachel's emotional work for her."

"Why not? She always has. That's what she's for." Why is Sam defending my client from me, now? I expect him to be on my side.

Rachel learns to care deeply for each of the delightful, interesting, defective women in group. Their outside polish does not reflect the tormenting inner games they play. They are flawed, but so am I, and so is Rachel. And love is where you find it. "Fake it 'til you make it," becomes Rachel's principal motto. By now she trusts her air of competence to get her through encounters with people and crises, like job interviews.

But she doesn't do well carrying on a marriage and being a mother. Something is terribly wrong at home. "Who do I want to be right now? Which of my behaviors is appropriate?" she must ask herself, as she breathes deeply. Then she fakes it. At home she is often wrong.

"Peeper believes suffering is forever and, only death can end it. Lilith is convinced my struggle for survival is constant and will go on through all time. As Rachel I know anything is manageable, in the 'now.' I can handle the present moment," she explains. Rachel has learned something important.

"In a little while, what is happening now will change. Change can be trusted," she tells herself, twenty times a day. Her amnesic barriers are falling away, so she tells Peeper and Lilith too, but they don't get it.

"Or they won't listen to me when I'm strong."

Many times Rachel runs away from her feelings, afraid

to get close to people and touch personalities for long.

Of course, she's terrified any closeness will lead to pain.

"Sometimes, in group, I can stay present, emotionally close, for a whole minute or two, " she says

."Other times I just slip away into the past. I may drop in, but don't count on me to stay.

You have to understand and let me come and go."

Twenty Six

"Diagnostic criteria for Sexual Sadism:

On a nonconsenting partner, the individual has repeatedly intentionally inflicted psychological or physical suffering in order to produce sexual excitement.

Sexual Sadism may, in extremely rare instances, be associated with Pedophilia, in which case both diagnoses are warranted."

Diagnostic and Statistical Manual III

I appreciate the recent supportive information available to me in new books. Now Sam is not my only colleague, although he's still my closest and most doubting. Courageous writers are tackling the subject of child abuse as a reality. They are my compadres, although they don't know me, they are patting me on the back, just where I need it. "...it's imperative that you be willing to hear and believe the worst, no matter how disturbing."

I'm rereading Ellen Bass and Laura Davis, from their book "The Courage to Heal". I may not keep their big white paper back under my pillow, but, certainly, I will have it close at hand. At the same time I know that this book might cause a lot of trouble. Its advice is aimed at people experiencing post traumatic stress. Its use certainly does heighten the pressure of suggestion clients feel when it lists ways children are incested, then goes on to state that if a person is unable to remember any specific instance of abuse, but still had a feeling that something abusive happened, chances are that it is true.

I wonder about the danger of creating false memories,

175

when I read the advice that belief that one was abused doesn't require the sort of evidence that is acceptable in a law court. Sometimes, the authors state that the truth of abuse begins with a little feeling, and it is acceptable to assume the validity of that feeling. If one has symptoms and believes in past abuse, then one has probably discovered an actual fact.

I don't know. That has not been my experience with Rachel. I see danger in these assumptions. Bringing false charges against families can cause the greatest pain imaginable. I wouldn't want to encourage that. But it's true that the first real information is usually a feeling. How confusing.

Here is the part I am looking for. The authors understand victims of abuse often hurt themselves physically, cutting or burning themselves to inflict injury. Survivors are programed to hurt themselves, because as children they were indoctrinated into pain. As grownups, they simply continue these behaviors, never knowing they have choice. Mutilation provides a powerful feeling of letting go that many survivors desire. It may seem to them to be extreme self control or a punishment, a way to get out anger, or even just an opportunity to feel.

Rachel is cutting herself again, carving lines in the skin of her thighs and hips.

"I am tired, Roberta. I've recreated the feeling of 'tired, so tired,' and I don't know how to let it go."

"Work, Rachel, work now."

I've been sick. My fever is gone, but I want to sleep. Peeper whispers quietly to me , almost all the time.

"No more bad dreams. No more sick Mommy to care for. No more Mother to do awful things to me that hurt so bad. No more Witch.

It is time for me to go through with Peeper's secret plan. I know Mother will always win, if Lilith fights with her. Daddy will hurt me , if Mommy wants him to. Daddy is evil, and does bad things to me. Am I dreaming? I am so confused and

176

alone and dirty. I am used. I am not like the clean, little girls at school. Tonight, while Mommy and Daddy drink , Peeper will do it. Then there will be no more bad dreams and no more pain.

Once more, Peeper leans against the wall, sitting on the bathroom floor, rubbing the razor lightly back and forth, over her wrist. She is far away, at peace, as if coming to her real home. This is the feeling she has when she rests her back against the pew in the church, after Mother has hurt Rachel.

"Do it! Do it! Rachel," the voice inside my head screams. The inflection is Mother's.

Still Peeper's body rests quietly. She is always a quiet child. Ever since she died. The razor goes back and forth a little deeper each time, making no sound. A trickle of blood runs onto the worn linoleum floor. I can see those red drops from far away. Who is the "I" who sees?

Now Lilith is shouting, furious..

"No, don't give up. No! It's my body." Thoughts rocket back and forth inside Rachel's head. "I am evil. Satan lives inside me. I am bad, dirty." The razor quakes in my hand.

"I want to die."

"No! No!." Lilith is insistent. Her voice is loud. She outshouts Peeper, who is now only a childish murmur.

"You'll lose if you give in. But you can win! You can stay alive and win!"

The razor suddenly is sharp and as cold as a hailstone. I am too tired to make a decision.

"Why can't you leave me alone, Lilith? Go away! Don't you know I can't win? That woman and the man always win. Go away! Let me alone! Can I stand one more day? I hate me, I hate me, I hate me, I hate me. Please let me die!"

I am afraid to stand up. I may see myself in the mirror. Will I have his horns? Do other people see Satan in my face? Mother does. Lilith swells like a balloon. She breathes in, deeply, fully.

"No matter how bad it gets, I'm not a quitter ," she says, "I won't give up. Someday, I'll win."

Lilith drops the razor into the trash, washes her hands and stands, avoiding the mirror for Rachel's sake. In the chilly bed-

room she winds herself deep into the covers to read the next chapter of "Black Beauty."

It is September and time again for school to start. I am only a little taller than last year, with many hours of reading behind me. I dream of books and beautiful, complex words.

Sometimes, I use lovely combinations of nouns and verbs and adjectives to write letters to my teacher, which I hide.

The walk to my house from school is always a crucial period. It gives Lilith time to come. Lilith knows how to prepare herself for her enemy. As she climbs the stairs, she gets ready.

Cheerfulness is not allowed at home. Mother will be angry and will not let me go back to school, if I betray myself and show happiness. The smell is there even before the door opens. Mother has been in the cellar, killing chickens.

"There you are. I've been waiting for you." Mother's voice is a bark. Her body stance is masculine, her hair and walk those of a massive man. Shaved close, the back of her head exposes her muscled shoulders and short neck. Her chin rests almost upon her fleshy chest. Like a wrestler, she is stocky, compact and powerful. Today, she waddles restlessly back and forth, twitching with implosive energy. The instruments are lying on the table.

"Drink this. Now!"

"No!" Lilith finds her voice.

"No, I won't." This time the spell is broken! The chant does not subdue Rachel for Lilith runs. And for the first time I, Rachel, run with her. Where? Where is my sanctuary? At the church , we can be safe for a while.

We must run quickly, quickly, rushing through the narrow leafy streets, dodging around corners, unable to pay attention to oncoming traffic. Under stumbling feet, red and yellow swatches of broken leaves crunch and scatter. We hear the sound of my gasping breath and the staggered pounding of the heart. We have to slow to a walk.

The grassy lawn slopes wetly away from where the people lie buried under lumpy old oak trees. The stones are gray granite. There are wilted flowers, yellow, pink or red carnations on some of the headstones,ß small and grand. The sky is gray over the corn field, which stretches away on the other side of the church. The rows of old stocks can be seen from the tall windows. The dead people of the town are planted in rows in the cemetery, like the corn in the field.

Inside the dark building now, we lean against the heavy carved doors, catching breath and stilling our selves. The church is empty and quiet. Three beautiful words,"Solitude, Peace and Sanctuary, "are repeated in the air above us.

Lilith hates Mother. To think these words is a sin, but the Mother makes life ugly. Lilith has moved far beyond depression, beyond rage. Only Rachel is still trying to understand.

"Mother is crazy, Rachel."

"Mother never does things to me in front of Daddy, does she, Lilith? I don't think Daddy knows about Mother. Does he? Sometimes Mother and he exchange special looks and he goes back to another Mass. He is gone for a long time.Then she ...hurts me. I hope Daddy doesn't know. If he does , it means he hates me too."

"He hates you, Rachel. Sometimes you know that."

Here, in this calm spot Lilith can reason about Rachel's mother and father. Rachel, too, tries to think about Mommy and Daddy. But it is too hard.

"Each time," Lilith tells me,"after the police officers have been called and have given up trying to make sense of the family fight, they leave Mommy and Daddy alone with you. Then Mommy and Daddy say everything is 'just fine.'

They pretend nothing has happened. That's one of the crazy-making games your Mother and Father like to play."

I didn't know that.

Here everything is so quiet and comfortable. I hug myself tightly.I have been quiet a long, long time, unaware of night-time creeping across the sky, outside the window.

It is dark, as I find my way by street light, hastened along by my anxiety and my orders from inside. I must go back for whatever is meant to be. I can hear my footsteps, muffled by the leaves decaying in mud puddles.

The moon is dime shaped, moving sideways, through silver, grey and black clouds. I do not understand that I am a part of Rachel, created by abuse, created to allow the pain to happen.

Lilith screams at me."You are making a dangerous mistake! Why are you always a fool? Do you want to be killed?" I hear her but, as good Rachel, I have to go home. Yes, it is true I may die at the hands of the Mother. I will be doing my duty.

Mommy is Mother. She is waiting for me, her eyes wild, popping, red from rage and gin. And Rachel has betrayed Lilith again.To the cellar. Mother's teeth are clenched.

"No, no, I'll be good. I promise. Please, no. Rachel repeats the pleas she has always pled. She has no control over her voice or the words, going through the begging ritual, dreamily, knowing each step in the cruel game, yet unable to stop.

Lilith disobeys Mother, but I, Rachel, cannot. I descend the stairs, just as I returned home, directed by an inner compulsion forged in childhood. Stuporously conditioned to accept pain and to blame myself for it, I once again risk torture.

The Mommy ,Rachel loved, was sickly and weak. A fat tired woman. She needed her, needed her, needed her, from the time Ishe was a tiny girl.

Where is sick Mommy? This Mother person is someone who cannot hear Rachel; at all, the monstrous side of the once weak woman called Mommy.

Halfway down the steep wooden stairs Mother picks Rachel up by her arm, dragging her down the last of the steps. Lifting her body is easy for the woman. She is strong like Iris whom Rachel has seen throw Daddy across a room.When angry the Mother has torn the door from the kitchen hallway, the window from the wall.

The grey stone wall sweats from the frigid air outside. There are no windows here. Wrathfully, without unbuttoning the ragged dress, Mother strips the child. Torn clothing is thrown aside.

Once more, Mother uses the stakes embedded in the dirt floor to tie the girl's arms. Weighting her with her bull-like body, Mother spreads her legs in a wide V and ties them.

Struggling,the girl can't reach anything sharp to defend herself. More instruments are on this cellar table, but they are beyond her grasp.

The girl fighting off Mother is Lilith. The girl lying on the cold ground cannot resist. She hears the throaty, reassuring *voice of Lilith telling her, once more, she need not feel the pain.*

Mother rubs chicken blood over the skinny body. She is moaning. Her figure hulks over the shiny implements lined up on a ragged towel.

She chooses a long thin something, then bends over , where the girl flounders in her bonds. The cotton swab, with the caustic solution Mother pushes into her vagina.

"I must take out the evil. There's so much evil , evil , evil, in you."

Singing loudly she inserts the tongs in place of the swab, far up through the pink of the child's labia. Warm blood dribbles down her legs, puddling on the pitted, crusty soil.

Now, brave Lilith lies on the chill , uneven floor in the little girl's place, cruelly tied to the wooden stakes. Someone else hysterically screams for forgiveness from the beast who bore her. Someone is mad with pain, a crazy child, unable to save herself. It is not Lilith. She would never beg.

In the dark and cold, Mother has left her alone in the murk, spread eagled for how many hours I can never recall. Rachel slipped away from consciousness long before.

"Roberta, I think that is when mother took... her...me... to the bad doctor again"

"Take your time, Rachel. Lean your head back and just talk to me.

The next day and the next and the next, I am ill. My fever climbs. Is it infection? I have to miss school. I can't walk or void. Now I cannot make my memory work either. It is broken. Bad dreams run through my sleep.

A severe vaginal infection is diagnosed, by the strange, old man who comes to my room. He is visiting Mommy. I must take medicine from his medical bag. Luckily, I have survived another 'accident.

Let me think a little while, Roberta. This part comes to me slowly.

Weeks pass. I am back at school, weak and confused. I have lost time, again, and can't remember. The phrase,'I musn't tell,' plays in my head, like music. Whatever it is about, I mustn't even tell myself. My mind melts.It runs out upon the ground, like red drops, puddling. Any effort to remember is tremendous. Thinking and remembering is too big a job for a little girl like me.

I lose myself in stories. Reading is the only wellness. The school library is sacred, and its priestess is the librarian. My teacher friend lends me her special books. I read with reverence and gratitude. Books save me from things too big and terrible to understand."

In the daytime Rachel is Black Beauty. Over and over, she reads about herself as a horse, who is without a home or love, sick from mistreatment. Like Beauty, she perseveres. At night Rachel reads and rereads "Little Women." The closeness of the family heals her. There is love and sharing.

Some day, she plans to have daughters of her own, lovely little women of whom she can be proud. She will be Marmie, kind and sensitive, knowing just what to do to ensure a good life for her daughters.

"Let me tell you about Christmastime, Roberta. I've just now remembered...and I'm so frightened."

It's winter and Christmas is near. I embroider a bureau scarf for my teacher, careful to make tiny stitches. I want to give it to her on the last day of school, before Christmas. I hate vacations, hate them, hate them, hate them!

At home, there will be the holiday ritual that always has to be completed in a particular order, an exact sequence. Unless Mother forgets this year.

Because it is Christmas, Mother will make me empty every cupboard and wash each one down. Then I must wash every cup, bowl and dish in order, one at a time.

Mother counts each piece of cracked china, over and over, writing figures on slips of paper, which she tucks away in cracks in the wall or in stacks behind the bedroom door.

Walls are to be scrubbed, the floors washed and waxed, and windows and storm doors cleaned, until all smears are gone. This tenement is old and rickety. The paint has peeled away. My work is futile.

When she is not counting dishes, Mother stays in bed watching television, favoring Kukla, Fran and Ollie, soap operas and game shows.

When she remembers me and my task, she comes out to inspect, count, criticize or threaten.

Mommy does not ordinarily notice her surroundings, but on days like this, when she is the Mother at Christmas, the house has to be approved. In this Mother mood she is never satisfied. I dream of a school which lasts the whole year long, with no breaks.

Now it is two days before Christmas. My gift is ready. Each stitch is in place to create pink roses and a lacy butterfly on the white linen of the scarf.

I have managed to keep the cloth clean, and it is still crisply white. I can hardly wait to give it to my teacher. I know she will appreciate my painstaking, devoted handiwork.

In my passage home from school the snow is crisp and clean and white like the scarf. In reverie I ponder its whiteness, knowing white stands for purity.

I am not pure, but evil and soiled. I must be vigilant not to dirty the snow. I move carefully, not to spoil any more whiteness than necessary.

Mother is crouched against the wall in the corner, smoking and scowling, murmuring to herself. She has put out the ironing board and on it the rusty iron is heating. The room is filled with tension. Mother does not seem to see me, as I tiptoe by and I close the door to my room behind me as tightly as I can.

This precious door has had one hinge broken as long as I can remember. Yet, it means safety. Mother cannot see me and will not become enraged, as she so often does in the kitchen. I put my books away in order, so I can find them even in the dim light I will later use. I sit on

183

the lumpy bed.

Suddenly, the door pushes open. The hot iron is in Mother's chunky hand. She scream,"You'll burn! You'll burn in the fires of Hell!"

Grabbing my hands in one of hers, she holds my quaking fingers against the bed as she burns them

"Evil. Your very soul is black!" Pulling down my panties with one massive hand, Mother rests the now smoking iron on my vagina.

In therapy more months go by. Laboriously putting together her stomach-turning puzzle, Rachel remembers bits and pieces of the cruelty that dominated her young life. She understands clearly the shifting aspects of her birth mother.

"I know you want me to stay in the 'here and now'. You always do, and you want me to begin to relate to my future. But my there and then is always in my here and now.

Which mother shall I work on today? The Mommy? The Mother? The Witch? Iris?

I do know they are like different people, inhabiting the same body. During Satanic rituals, this woman was the Witch, obeying Lucifer's commands. When I suffered her wrath, her hands were Moter's.

The person I loved and longed for was 'Mommy' who was well on rare 'good days' and needy on others. When I was little I believed with my whole heart, Mommy was never cruel to me like Mother or the Witch were. But she was often indifferent.

Iris was Daddy's wife, irate, passionate, out-of-control, the woman I thought might kill Daddy. She had no interest or relationship to me.

When I came home from school, I never knew which personality would be there."

"How do you feel about that?"

"Don't start with me, Roberta. You don't need all the therapy razzle dazzle to get me to talk. Just shut up and let me tell you."

Twenty Seven

"What is MPD? MPD is a little girl imagining that the abuse is happening to someone else...the imagining is so intense, subjectively compelling, and adaptive, that the abused child experiences dissociated aspects of herself as other people. It is this core characteristic of MPD that makes it a treatable disorder, because the imagining can be unlearned, and the past confronted and mastered.""

Colin Ross
Multiple Personality Disorder

Accidents, so many accidents.

" Mommy has an explanation for me. 'You are a clumsy, silly, clumsy, silly girl. We can't trust you.'

I don't know how they happen to me. How or why? I wake up and find that I have hurt myself again. My hands are burned and blistered. Embarrassed, I can't wear my clothes. What have I done? Why can't I remember?

Peeper knows. 'Crazy, because you're crazy, crazy!'

I remember going through the forbidding kitchen into my room and then, nothing. Unable to walk, I cannot go to school and will miss giving my teacher her gift. My anger towards myself is enormous, black like a hurricane cloud, moving slowly within me. The tip of the cloud reaches down into my throat, swelling my Adam's apple tight and sore. Shame. I can't do anything right. Mommy is correct. Over and over, she tells me I am stupid, clumsy. Mother screams that I am an imp because I am bad, and now I am stupid, too, because I can't think. Time slips out of my head into my pockets and is gone. When I remember to look at a clock or a calendar, I feel surprise stirring me that time passes at all.

It is too hard to pay attention for more than a few seconds to anything except stories.

'Stop, stop staring', Mother shouts. I am just being here. My hands are blistered and oozing, and I am ashamed about my bottom. Mommy put some medicine on it, but it hurts me more. I want to be alone.

My gift for teacher was just another 'silly Rachel' thing. I am clumsy and foolish. From now on I will keep to myself. I won't chase teachers for love any more. No more hurting inside my skin, just hurting outside.

'You are too tired. Give up.' Peeper comes again to advise me.

Why are people afraid of dying? Death to Peeper is a soft cool linen sheet, wrapped tightly around her, pinioning her arms from reaching out futilely, keeping her quiet, holding her back, away from loss, fear or punishment. I hate me. I have no reason to live, so I repeat the magical ritual that comes from wishing herself dead.

Over and over. This time Peeper may be free to die and kill Rachel to help her. The house is quiet. Once more, she goes to the kitchen for Mother's butcher knife. The bottom of the kitchen drawer is speckled with the droppings of the roaches. Where is the big knife? The sharpest one?

As before, Peeper shuts the bathroom door, testing the knife on her finger. It is sharp enough. Blood runs down from a small cut. But it is difficult for Peeper to hold the knife with Rachel's hands. The crusty streaked scabs take a long time to heal.

'I will do the cutting,' Peeper offers.

Lilith pushes Peeper's pale hand away."

Notes:

A therapy session: Rachel teaches me more about dissociative disease.

Christmas and New Year's traumas are behind her in actuality, but today they are happening in her head repeating, repeating. Perhaps she can talk them out.

"My hands are healed enough to do schoolwork. I know the routine, but something is gone, lost. I cannot retrieve what school meant to me.

With a pale, frightened face and wicked eyes, I seem to live outside myself, observing and watching. My inside grows numb. I become transparent, as if people can walk right through me. No one seems to notice, I am no longer here."

Twenty Eight

"I don't want it back. Don't look for it. It has the 'Mark of the Beast' on it."

Donald Eugene Maurice,31, after he walked into the woodshop at Appalachian State University in Boone, N.C., on Friday night and calmly used a power saw to cut off his right hand because it had the 'Mark of the Beast.'Maurice, who had a Satanic emblem tattooed on the hand, was listed in serious, but stable condition Saturday."

National press release

Some days, I think of Sam as an old, grey beard with years of musing about people and their fantasies behind him. Other times, Sam is my playmate, stimulating and lively. I ruminate out loud, warming him up to talk to me

"Do you know why I love you, fellow? You are long-winded, Sam, but never boring. Now about Rachel."

He and I are in a corner at a party, bored with other people. We avoid the glances of other guests eager to involve us in television football. I don't know if Sam will bite this time. Will he talk shop? Sam doesn't often resist, except if the topic is Rachel. He speaks at great length, sometimes, out of his Freudian training, of course, to which I invariably take exception. I know chances are good he will then provoke me into barely disguised rage.

Arguing with Sam is fun.

"All mothers pretend to be a good mothers," he is fond of saying, "And all children need to see Mother as good. In classic psychoanalysis this is done by dividing up Mother and splitting her into good and bad. Unfortunately, your Rachel split herself, as well."

"Roberta, you've convinced me Rachel is both bad, powerful Lilith, and good, accommodating Rachel, still waiting around to get the mothering she needs. The good little Rachel part refuses to grow up, until she gets mothered. Rachel's Bad Mother is cruel, and doesn't care for Rachel. But Rachel's Bad Mother is only temporary.

Good mother is real, also permanent, and Rachel waits for her to come back. Year after year, she believes the actual woman she experienced in daily life is not really Mother. Good Mother, Mommy, will appear, and she will be radiant and total, whole and perfect. She will love Rachel back to health.

So, if Rachel stays childish, she will always be a prisoner of this illusion. You are not helping her deal with reality.

It's highly unlikely, you know, that Rachel's earthly mother is actually the monster you both believe her to be. When you listen to Rachel's fear filled narratives about mother, you reinforce her infantile fantasy and her exaggerations. You've encouraged her added craziness about multiple personality, satanic worship, torture, sacrifices ... sadism."

"Have not!"

"Have too," Sam says, as he laughs at me.

"I have my own healthy skepticism about all this, Sam. And Rachel is no child."

"She is when she is hypnotized, Sweetie."

Twenty Nine

"Therapists working with their first case of two may get into trouble because of insufficient limit setting. To some extent this is unavoidable, because the patients are so interesting and needy. I doubt that there is a single MPD therapist in North American who hasn't gotten overinvolved in some way or other at some point. Its easy to spot overinvolvement with hindsight, but not so easy when the patient is hurting badly and in crisis. Criticism of insufficient limit setting and difficult to deliver diplomatically."

Colin Ross
Multiple Personality Disorder

"It sickens me", Sam says, "to think that the ability to give birth, to nurture and to nurse babies was perverted into some kind of belief in witches. I suspect some poor women believed they actually carried and suckled demons instead of children. Do you suppose that sick notion began because of birth deformities? There have always been biological accidents all through human history."

" I don't know. But what if some child's mother is a witch? I mean evil or cruel, refusing to take personal responsibility for anything. A mother who projects her own 'evil' onto the baby. What child is strong enough to hate her mother? Growing up she turns her anger against herself. A little girl cannot say 'Mommy is cruel, wrong, bad, sick, or crazy'. Instead she will say,'I've got to be the one who is bad, wrong, sick, or crazy.' Sam, what about a child molested sexually or demonically bat-

191

sexually or demonically battered by her mother? O.K.,what happens to a Rachel?"

Through chips and onion dip, Sam tries to enunciate without much success.

"I canth... guess. I'm certainly familiar with the trage- dy of battered children, you know, and most aware of their intense need for ideal mothers. It hurts me to hear about it. For instance, a little boy client of mine is abused physically and sexually by his Mom. He goes to live with an affectionate foster mother.

Of course, you know already it doesn't work. The boy prefers to go back to his original Mom. That bitch makes me think of Harlow's wire monkey surrogate mothers, scratchy, sharp and hollow. No matter how much her lit- tle boy wants her to stop beating and abusing him, even more, he longs for his Someday-Good-Mother."

I feel a wave of empathy for Sam. He loves his dam- aged kids.

"You know, Sam, it's not what you say that makes me mad. It's how you say it."

"That's trite. Are you having authority figure problems again, Doctor Baby? How about salsa, chips and a change of subject?"

"There, you're doing it again! For God's sake, don't pa- tronize me." I take a breath, unwilling to stop. The inter- esting part of what he will say might be next.

"Just one more thing. Listen. Clearly, from her descrip- tion Rachel's mother is a multiple, just like Rachel. She has three or more personalities. As you know, multiplici- ty runs in families."

"I don't know."

I was also ready to tell him how our Rachel became the Child Bride of the Devil and some kind of cult Priest- ess, but I shouldn't have paused. I've lost the rhythm. Sam is not interested.

"More chips," he says, looking away across the room. Over his shoulder he throws me a conversational crumb.

"I believe if any child promises Mother to pretend everything is always just fine when it is terrible, that child can be stuck forever in denial.

And when that child grows up she can come to you, Roberta, and you can be stuck forever with her therapy. An exciting story and drama. Double impasse.

Now, more chips. Talk theory to your hostess. She has to be polite to you. I don't."

Sam stands. I watch him move toward the knot of beery enthusiasts around the television. He'll even watch football to avoid talking about Rachel.

Thirty

"The Devil made me do it.".

Flip Wilson, *Comedian*

In group, week after week, now that Lilith has re-
treated, Rachel shares only one association. She continues to hate the purposely distorted picture of the mother
and child on my office wall, the room she can't tolerate
because the painting hangs there.

"I hate it. It's hideous. Hate is a feeling. I am feeling,"
she says. Visualizing the freakish mother and the twisted
little child in the picture down the hall, she twitches, as if
emotion simmers in her blood. If so, it bubbles powerfully, boiling its way upward through her.

"Tonight I cannot pay attention to you, Group. I can
only feel."

I can see her agony. Her lips and throat are losing control. Someone in group is talking about daily troubles, a
power struggle with an adolescent son, but Rachel cannot wait her turn. She is shouting.

"That picture in your office is a lie. Mothers don't hold
children on their laps!" The woman, talking about her beloved and disappointing offspring, looks startled and
stares at Rachel.

"Go on, Rachel," I say. Here it comes, I tell myself.

"Mothers debase children behind doors."

Then the scream comes. It is the shriek that is highest, shrillest instrumental voice in an orchestra. A long time later it seems, Rachel's screech turns to strangled sobs. When she can speak, she tells us the truth about the parlor. We women sit on the floor by the fireplace. Rachel asks me to hold her hand. She is cold.

"My voice is Rachel's," she says,"Rachel's foot twitches and shakes. Rachel's skin blanches, and I can see goose bumps on my skin. Rachel's breath comes in great gusts and tiny squeaks. So, I know that I am Rachel, I am Rachel 2, who does not believe."

"I am also little Rachel. I go back... there. I sit listening to the laughter that is going on behind the closed parlor doors, waiting to be summoned. The double doors open.

'Come here.' I rise slowly, as if in a trance.

'You know what to do.' I begin to tremble. I cannot move.'"

More than three hours have passed in this living room. Rachel lies next to the burned out fire. The logs in the fireplace are black. Crumpled paper napkins and stacks of coffee cups lie about on the carpet. Wilted and bent, women are huddled into nests made of blankets and afghans. They rest their heads on pillows or on their arms. In my state of exhausted reverie these women look like a nineteenth century painting of beautiful wives and mothers in a sultan's seraglio. This evening began with Rachel's thoughts about a painting, didn't it?

I ask Rachel to look around the faces of the group. These faces look weary and sad, but I want her to see them, clearly. They have not abandoned her. Her friends are crying .... for her. I invite each woman to whisper a message in Rachel's ear. This communication is to be private and absolutely honest. She self-consciously accepts each friend's touch, knowing it is positive and loving.

She believes they care for her. They believe she has courage and are proud of her.

Rachel changes, growing stronger, clearer, warmer.

In following weeks these close companions assist Rachel to unravel, further, the twisted threads of her life.

The false pageants and charades satanists arranged for her and the other children were pretenses. As were many ceremonies and tests.

Rachel was half drowned, caged, shut in a coffin with rats, cold and alone for days, starved and beaten. The group listens to the cruel lies, she was made to believe.

Little Rachel was "given an operation" in which a "magic bomb" had been sewn inside her. It would explode and kill her and anyone she cared about if she broke her silence. That her parents were her perpetrators was hard for her friends to believe, but they swallowed their shock and listened.

They and I learned that ritual abuse within families was particularly destructive, because of the continual presence of the parent pain givers. This ongoing kind of abuse also included the extended family, which was the cult. Children were raised to perform a given role within the" family" and made to feel they were part of the cruelest acts, as perpetrators themselves.

Rachel would not tell it all and had a special request. There were things she had done and seen that she believed the Group could not bear to hear. "After all," she said to me, "they are in therapy. "

I absolutely agreed, thinking that perhaps all of us might need to be protected from this kind of horror. I would appreciate some shielding myself. But it is my job to learn all I can about Rachel, and that means I must know about the sacrifices.

The killing of a human, or an animal in its place, was an attempt to set up communication with the Devil. Rachel was forced to participate in the killing of babies, children and adults in ritual settings. In bloody ceremonies, staged, or perhaps all too real, she was to receive magical strength. The drinking of blood, and the cannibalism of victim's bodies invested her with the spiritual powers of the sacrifice.

Of course I listened, and of course, I internally questioned the validity of what I was hearing. From where came the victims? Where are their remains? How can it be that there is no evidence available to the police? Rachel assures me that the victims come from the cult itself, including the babies, which were often aborted for sacrifice.

In therapy Group, sandwiched between tears, groans of fear and disgust, Rachel has the first fun she has ever had. The members talk and talk. First there is the embarrassment of remembering foibles and misunderstandings. Then, hilarious exaggerated discussions of human behavior, especially about sex, continue, week after week.

"Talking about sex is funny. Sometimes."

Rachel can laugh. Sometimes. But when the topic of sexual abuse comes up, she notices our newest member appears to be as uncomfortable as she is. Writhing in her chair, this new member stares at images reflected in the window beside her. When questioned, she balks. Now she is not coming to group. We continue without her for a few weeks, and I will not tell the group why she is not here, maintaining confidentiality. Rachel pretends to understand that, but she must know more about that troubled woman. She cannot stop thinking about her missing companion, the sister she never had. Rachel finds a way to telephone her, and forces herself to tell her ' new sister' that she has described to the Group some of her own sexual abuse.

"Can we work together?," she says. "I believe I know what you are feeling."

"Oh, yes!, yes! I want to talk," her hoped-for companion agrees. But she never returns.

Contrite and ashamed, Rachel believes she made a mistake, reaching out too far, too fast. The important thing, I remind myself, is that she is able to relate to someone else, not just to herself. Her world is enlarging, with her growing awareness. She does care for the welfare of others. Rachel has fought her way out of the tiny cell called "me."

The changed Rachel first sees Mimi in my waiting room. Grayly withdrawn, the angry Mimi carefully sits turned to the wall. Her leg and foot jiggle rhythmically, as she stares at the carpet.

"Hi," Rachel says, brightly. Mimi refuses to acknowledge her presence. Rachel tries again to relate to someone who may humiliate her. She will take a chance and hazard her shaky self esteem to open herself to someone in pain. When Mimi leaves my office, her white dress reflects the moonlight, and Rachel waits outside in the dark. She makes a gigantic effort to talk to this girl, and at a loss for something to offer, Rachel asks Mimi to visit her at school.

She does, following Rachel all day from class to class. Mimi frowns from morning light to dusk. This girl complains about cafeteria food, the teacher's clothes and the old cars the faculty members drive. The littered rest rooms disgust her. "Crowded and too hot," is her assessment of the library, Rachel has learned to love. Like a bad tempered pet dog, Mimi snaps at Rachel's heels.

"I need to remember Mimi is a 'depressive,'" Rachel tells me.

Finally, Mimi connects her now with her past life, which she loathes. Remembering the pain and embarrassment she felt as a child, she recognizes how the shadow of too-early sex smudged her life.

Her abuser was her uncle, mother's big brother. Young Mimi twisted this experience around her chronic feelings of despair. She tied a hard knot.

"I was so excited about entering Junior High, I walked all the way to his house to tell him about my new school. He asked me in. He was drunk and I shouldn't have gone. It's my fault."

Talking, talking, talking does not help Mimi, as it has helped Rachel. Instead, Mimi buys a giant bottle of aspirin. Even trying hard, she cannot swallow them all, and because she vomits too many tablets onto the floor, the dose is not lethal. Mimi's mother finds her, cleans her up, orders Mimi's stomach pumped, and scolds her daughter fiercely. The scolding is meant to cheer up Mimi, and to prove her mother cares. On anti-depressant medication Mimi feels somewhat better, but still drops out of high school. Sliding downward, steadily, into her illness, she commits herself to a county hospital.

Rachel has seen Mimi out on a pass, heavily drugged, her face swollen into a yellowish full moon. A dirty tan, her once bright blue eyes are empty. She is fat and has nothing to say to Rachel. How can it be that Rachel is getting "well" and "she is not?"

"She is younger than I am and has been loved and cared for as a child! I, on the other hand, with my history have no right to be well."

I ask how Rachel feels about what has happened to Mimi.

"Feel! Feel! Feel! Roberta, I have a feeling word for how it is to see her like that. Bad!"

I must teach Rachel about survivor guilt.

Is Sam going to move away with his sideways shuffle again, looking annoyed, if I talk about Rachel? My heart is pounding with my need to tell him. Just in case, I raise my voice

"We're not talking textbook, here, Doctor! I'm serious. This stuff is true. Rachel's history is filled with torture, mutilation, ritual cruelty, and witchcraft. Devil worship. Think murder! Think satanism! You are not believing me."

"You're upset." Sam uses active listening techniques, when I get on the topic of Rachel. Inside, I suspect he is far away in his head. Cleaning the garage. Figuring his income tax. Writing a bibliography.

"I'm stunned, Sam. I need you to listen to me. Right now! I've run into a genuine introject. Remember the video I'm making? The one about the effects of child abuse on adults? I'm using Rachel as one of the actresses as a mandatory-volunteer, in other words, I required her participation."

I've got to sit down, catch my breath and calm my voice.

"Rachel carries out her part with a certain dispatch. She's not excited to be on camera, but she's fairly composed and delivers her lines well. She's satisfactory as an actress. Somewhat wooden.Well, very wooden. But, Sam, the whole video is amateur, of course, and I know it won't go ringing down the halls of time or make me rich or famous," my voice climbs higher again, "But, here's the part I need to tell you, Sam. I'm scared."

"You're scared." Sam is good at paraphrasing. I look to make sure he is sincere.

"I'm listening, Babe." He means it.

"All right. Picture this. We performers are excited, about to watch ourselves on the monitor. Here's Rachel, she sees herself on screen. All at once, she stands straight up and staggers out of the room. I follow her and find her in the bathroom, gagging. Shaking with cold, she is terribly, wrenchingly, sick at her stomach."

"I have seen myself for the first time", she says. Only Sam, what she saw was in the form of a devil."

"You mean literally?"

"Yes, honest to God, Sam. I mean actually, literally, correctly. In her mind, her body image manifested itself as an imp from hell, clearly, precisely and malignantly. 'I'm sick,' she says, 'I know the real me.' To be honest, Sam, I have been aware she avoids mirrors, but I forgot. I think I have made a tragic blunder."

Comforting me with his warm, tweedy arm, Sam's voice is soothing. I hope he knows what I am doing. I don't.

"You've sure got a live one, Doc. No wonder hypnotherapy is so effective with her," he reminds me,"Rachel has been in trance since she was a tiny kid, even in her everyday waking state. I guess two hundred years ago, we would say she has a witch's curse on her."

" Is he just distracting me? If he is, it's working. I'm interested."

"Yes, really, Sweetie. Of course. Witches are real to battered children. Fairy stories were once used to warn kids, there are terrible beings out there. Be careful, children! Look out for the evil people."

I am to learn more about the noxious spell controlling my most complicated client. This morning the phone rings, near my old leather chair. Can this be Rachel shrieking?

"Come to the Westside college women's locker room, Roberta! Quickly!" Rachel is hiding, in torment.

"You have to help me. I can't stand it!" Gasping for breath, her voice is frighteningly childlike.

She's regressed again, I warn myself, as I drive as fast as I dare, frightened and angry at the interruption. Sam will have to cancel my next appointment for me. Rachel, I think to myself, I do have other clients. How many times have I said this to myself, yet I would never hesitate when the person in trouble is Rachel. We owe each other. We learn from one another, and there is no more precious gift than learning.

Where can I park this car? The student lot is full. I'll use the handicapped slot and explain later, if I get caught. Aren't I assisting a handicapped person? Isn't a history of torture a handicap? With gooseflesh poking up on my arms, I hurry through the battered doors marked Women. Huddled against the yellow metal lockers in the hot, smelly room, Rachel is scratching, twisting and moaning.

"Look! Look at me, Roberta." She drops hard onto the concrete floor. Pulling up her dress and taking down her underpants, Rachel spreads her thighs with both hands.

Swollen purple and crimson scratches lace around Rachel's vagina and down her legs. Rosy welts rise up from her whitened flesh. Twisting patterns trace along Rachel's skin, strung together in long, red convoluted trails. These are not hives. The eruptions are long and thin, not round. These are the marks of fingernails.

"Help me. Help me!" Rachel's breath hisses with her pain.

"They hurt, they sting! Make them go away!"

"How did these marks get on you? Did you hurt your-self?"

"I don't know! I don't know! I was ready to tell you something. Someone in my head screamed a warning not to tell. Then, suddenly, I couldn't stand the heat, the burning, down there. I bent over and stared at myself and saw scratches appearing, streaking from my... pri-vate places down my legs. Now, I can't remember what I wanted to tell you. Oh, Roberta. I can't believe I let you look."

That's the old Rachel. Embarrassed. Using a words like "private places." Immediately she moans louder, ashamed, yet desperate in her pain.

"You've got to help me." I speak as soothingly as I know how, assuring Rachel her manifestation is under-standable.

"It simply means," I improvise, "your therapy is work-ing again. Eventually you will be free from the pain of the past. I'm certain this symptom, this sign, will go away. It will leave you when the message from your body is fully registered on your consciousness. There is value in what is happening. These marks have meaning."

I attempt to speak to Rachel's unconscious, wanting to suggest the message of the welts is being received.

"Soon these marks will disappear. They will have com-pleted their mission."

I don't know if she believes what I am saying, but I desperately want to help. I'm battling something inside Rachel, impishly evil, cruel and perverse. Struggling to retain my composure, I keep my voice steady, although I'm badly frightened. I try to sound neutral, almost disin-terested. Rachel quiets. Her pain lessens. She can rest here on a bench, before her next class.

I realize how upset I am, when I can't remember where I parked the car. Then, stumbling upon it, I have to drive deliberately and slowly, concentrating, to avoid an accident. All this hideousness is getting to me, but I can't stop being involved. Listening is hard, and looking even harder.

Back home, I shrill shakily to Sam.

"It was stigmata, I know it was. Awful! Like medieval saints bleeding from their eyes and the palms of their hands. On Good Friday or something."

I'm not at all sure what I am talking about.

"Rachel's body must remember her abuse. Of that I'm certain. Rachel's skin reenacts the gruesomeness of her violations. Graphically. I have been shown a map of her past. Something keeps her from using words to tell me about it. She is not even allowed to know what happened to her, but part of her remembers having been beaten and raped. Pinched and scratched."

Sam pats me in the way I used to call patronizing before I needed it.

"Those are statues that weep, Sweetie. You're right, though, about bleeding palms. What was it, a Virgin exhibited, can you remember? Something dramatic in the area of hysterical signs. I'll look it up. You did the right thing, you know, comforting her, and downplaying your own panic. Remember, she has her somatic defenses for a reason. Obviously, she isn't ready to recall certain events, and you must pay honor to her fortress wall. She built it because she couldn't suffer more and go on living. Now you're asking her to give up her protection. You invite her to hurt all over again."

"But what she feels is remembered suffering, not real. Not like the first time."

"How much do your painful memories hurt you, Roberta?"

In session, I want to move on to deal with Rachel's daily life, but she cannot stay present. She is getting better, so perhaps she is right. I cannot imagine allowing any other client to live in the past this way.

Once more she lies in trance. She needs no induction from me. All I need to say now is "Hello, Rachel," and she is ready. Trance is extremely easy, for someone who is a multiple.

I sit quietly on the floor beside her, watching her prepare to do her work. I may never know where she goes, or why she suffers so. I only know that during these sessions, I too, become exhausted.

"Will you be here when I come back?" Rachel asks.

"What do you think?"

"I think you will. Will you hold my hand?"

"I will count backward," she says, squeezing my fingers.

"100, 99, 98, 97, 96, 95, 94. Thank God I'm not in the room with the picture. 93, 92, 91, 90, 89, 88."

This room is coolly comfortable, blue and cream. Rachel feels safe she tells me, as safe as she can ever be. She has tested my potency. She trusts I will be able to bring her back to wrest her from demons. My power, over the unknown enemies from Rachel's past, is strong enough for both of us, because Rachel believes it so.

"Protect me," she says, "I must not remain locked in my life's polluted yesterday. 87, 86, 85, 84, 83."

The afternoon sun shines through the wood grain venetian blinds. Two walls are lined with Rachel's friends, books.

"8, 7, 6, 5, 4, 3, 2, 1," Rachel speaks in the voice of a young girl, breathlessly.

I see the bleak ,industrial town crouching beside the icy Atlantic. In the street, dirty sleet melts under the heavy shoes of the workers. Snowfat clouds hang over red brick buildings. They are stained with salt. Through a window, I recognize dim young faces, from which frozen breaths exhale, through rotting teeth.

Row upon row of sewing machines, ritualistically, drone their chant. A foreman manages to get a factory girl alone. He moves his hand inside her shabby dress.

The noon whistle shrills. I feel the sharp sting of salt spray on my cheek. It is carried on the invincible wind. Reflected in the brown and silver frozen puddles, the sweatshop workers drudge their youth away. They wait for their next ten minute break or, as now, their scanty lunch. They cannot bask nor chatter long, for the day's quota must be made.

Mother works in Stateside Sleepwear, until the jarring night she stabs Auntie with the screwdriver.

Angry Mother is so strong, it takes two first floor foremen and the Townski girls to hold her. After that, it is the staying home that makes her so fat, so cruel.

I never see Auntie again, but I am told that she heals well. She is scarred around the puckered puncture mark in her stomach.

Look! There is the fish pier, surrounded by boats of the fleet. See the masted sloops, and the squatty tugs, all black and red. The air is dirty, like the unpainted buildings and the shriveled people, compressed with cold.

Rows of condemned tenements rise up before me. They are the barren shells, where mill workers once lived. In this project, among battered empty semistructures, a singular building slopes upward. Like the others, it is rusty, loose and splintered from the snowy wind. Dirt and rat feces accumulate on its battered stairs, yet it seems to shine with a pale, savage light. If it had eyes, it would wink slyly, signaling danger. This building beckons me. It wants me to look inside, but I will not . Not yet.

True democracy arose in little towns like this, with the town meeting. The statue of The Minuteman still stands in the square. It reminds us that Colonial farmers and British soldiers lost their young lives on this ground.

Now contaminated with bloody superstition, this delapidated neighborhood's respect for human life has decayed into scum. Here on tenement row, the dirt between the houses lies bare. Ugly rocks jut upward. The creaking of the wind squeals through flimsy, windowless structures. Building number four is not empty. Inside its secret room, human animals wait.

Mommy tells me to hurry to do my work. She and Daddy have a special meeting tonight, and I am to accompany the two of them. I am not to have supper. I had no lunch and no breakfast. Am I not to eat because I have been bad, or because I have been good? We are to ride in a car.

Together, with a man in black, Mommy, Daddy and I climb the narrow stairs to the meeting place. Holding the railing,

Mommy groans with her gigantic effort. Step by step, she hauls her bulk upward, grasping the weathered railing with her powerful hands and arms. I am both frightened and excited. No, I am astounded.

Look at the altar! I know what it is. Dazzling, it gleams in the light from blue black tapers. More sooty candles burn on the altar shelves, casting wavering shadows over the room. There is a strong odor in the air, berries or stormy nights or wet wood. Looming beside me, Mommy fiercely pinches my arm, to warn me to sit still. Her breath comes out in heaving sighs from her climb. She moves away into the darkness. Daddy too, is gone.

Passing outside in the hall, I see an old grandpa I know, a neighbor , dressed like a devil. Does our house have a devil next door?

I stare at the table in front of the altar, where a shiny golden bowl reflects the shifting movement of the candle's flames. Pictures are engraved around the bowl's golden outside. I cannot see them clearly , but they look like animals and people hugging. This must be a church.

Where are the other children? Looking behind me, I can see people are changing their clothing in the anteroom. They look alarming, like skulking night beasts in heavy black capes with hoods, partially covering their heads. They are joining me on the benches.

I sit silently, forlorn, among the erect, caped figures, until Mother takes me away to a tiny room. There, in the middle of the floor, is a tub of warm water. Tenderly Mother bathes me. Her giggling laugh is gone. She puts perfume in the water. I can see the picture of a white flower on the bottle. It says Gardenia. As she pulls the long white dress over my head, she looks at me in a way I cannot remember. She sees me. She knows I am her own little girl. Mommy?

I wish I knew if I have been bad or good. Left alone in this room with the lone black candle, I wait. I am dizzy and sick with hunger, but I have my hope back. She touched me. My Mommy loves me.

The messenger summons me, dragging me onto my feet. He pulls me along a corridor. The sound of his pounding on the door reverberates. Dizzily, I fall against the metal. Then I am lifted within.

The flock stands with heads bowed. When the brethren begin to chant, the sound rolls across the room like banging on the fire escape with a stick. The reverberating sounds go on for a long time inside my head. I think I hear the singing waves from the ocean of my nightmare. That is part of a bad dream I have had since I was little.

I rest in the arms of the Messenger. He shakes me awake to face the altar.

A diabolic figure slips silently from behind the bank of candles, carrying something on a tray. In his vermillion robe he moves smoothly up the stairs. The room is dark, shadowy, yet I can see above the man's blood red robe, something fluid smeared on his face and in his hair. A high collar shadows his fearsome face. He is scowling deeply. Vertical lines split his forehead into winglike shapes. I am afraid to look, yet compelled. Reverent, I scrutinize this strange man creature.

Beside me , Mommy isn't Mommy. She is not Mother. She is The Witch. In the swirling lights I can see a shimmering black robe wrapped about her chunky body. Although her hurtful hands touching me are familiar, her face is uncanny, alien. This woman's eyes look huge. Her voice is monotone, deep, with a low guttural resonance, rather than the screech I dread. The assemblage mouths a word, softly, then builds to a thunderous shout.

"Beelzebub, Beelzebub."

The Witch has a gold medallion around her neck. Awed, I watch its colors change, the candlelight shining on the gold piece as it sways, gleaming. The embossed picture of Lucifer, carved into the precious saffron metal, terrifies me as its eyes look directly into mine. They are golden, and I watch them turn black, like Daddy's.

The big woman forces into my hand a heavy golden cup, shinier than anything I have ever seen. Automatically, obeying orders from cellar rehearsals, I gulp, strangling and choking, downing the thick and lumpy drink. It smells froglike, tastes sour, foul.

The room constricts around me. The air grows thinner, as a

great hush moves through me. My body slumps against the Messenger, then against the Witch. Her voice is now a whisper, far away. Revolving colors around me are bright orange, yellow and green. The room moves in a spiral. The buzzing grows louder in my head. I feel my body dragged upwards to the altar. The Witch's hands, rough, impatient, powerful, pull my dress over my head. My skin goose pimples.

"No, oh no! Oh, don't do that. Not here!" I am sickeningly cold. My clothes are off in front of all these people.

The evil thing I call Daddy stares at me with glaring, sinful eyes. I remember now. This man hates me. I have known his hate before.

Daddy rubs something thick and sticky into every curve and crack of my body. His hands are arctic. From far away I hear the order to lie still.

My arms and legs will not move. They will not pay attention to what I beg them to do. I am tied. My skin smells like matches. It burns, then sleep comes. Through my dream I see the Devil above me. He has a strained oval face, hollow cheeks and red horns tied with a flesh colored string under his chin. His bony hands with big knuckles and long fingers hurt me. Ghoulish faces look down at me,while demon hands scratch, pinch and poke. I dream of chickens being plucked and disemboweled.

Am I sacrificed, because I am wicked? Or because I am special, the chosen child? Mother has told me so. I am an imp. I am a fiend in human shape. I belong to the Devil."

"Have you forgotten me, Rachel? Your Lilith? I'm here. I won't let them hurt you any more. Go to sleep."

Daddy struggles to perform the ceremony.

It is over. I am alone in a dark room. I have been sick. I cannot feel my body. Have I been bad or good?

"My eyes do not open easily. When they do, I can see my own dingy, pale yellow flowered bedroom. The sun shines through the cracked glass of the window, warming me , where I have lain on a stained striped ticking mattress. My body pains me everywhere. From under my swollen eyelids, I see that my skin is traced with bloody scratches. My arms and legs *are bruised, my heels and buttocks rubbed raw. Why don't I have my nightie? I don't ever, ever sleep naked! I sit up and the sunlight turns black, empty. I put my head down for a while, how long, I have no idea. I try again to get out of bed, but I am too dizzy.*

I must dress to hide these marks. No one must know. I can move my arms, so I put on the good dress that lies crumpled at the foot of the bed. Between my legs hurts. I hear the woman called Mother, stamping through the hall toward her bedroom. She walks heavily, powerfully.

"What's wrong? Why aren't you up yet?"

"Nothing." I totter to the bathroom, bent over like a new mother, supporting myself by leaning against the wall. Seated at last on the toilet, I discover I cannot urinate.

"Lilith, please help me. I need you, now. Please, I can't pee." Pictures start up inside my head. Images flash by me. I can barely see, but Mother and Daddy are in the pictures with lots of people. My head hurts violently, savagely. I cannot live with this pain.

Mother is calling me. I hear my Rachel voice answering.

"I'm coming, Mommy. Right away. Please don't be mad."

I suddenly know I can never trust Mommy or Daddy. They will never take care of me. They will never love me. I have become Rachel 2, who does not believe them.

I do not cry. Instead I... I go into the kitchen to start the day's chores.

Thirty One

"My eyes are blind   My ears are stones The beasts are after me.   Uneasy, I drive the car into town.'Fraid to look into the back seat Because I know the she-devil is riding there. She peers down watching me from everywhere I've noticed I've neglected my toenails.They've grown long and sharp."

Billie Barbara Masten, *Mountain Woman*

I've got to ask Roger's help. Since he graduated from therapy, well again, it is ethical to involve him. Inquiries I have made for Rachel provide little information.

The hospital doctor who treated her for massive injuries is long dead. We still have his notes which simply list the little girl's hurts, the nurse's observations, and Mother's complaints. From the fragments left to us, it is clear he didn't care much for Mommy. He might even have been afraid of her. The social worker who sat with Rachel at the inquest married. That changed her name and she moved away. Records of the inquests are scanty.

There was more than one, it appears, but Rachel's parents were only questioned, then released. We can't find out what suspicions authorities had at that time. But Rachel and I need some truths. Perhaps someday we can go back to the New England villages where the atrocities took place for evidence. Can we someday be brave enough to discover actual dates and places?

"Roger, here are the names of a man and a woman I need to find out about. You know how to do that, and I don't. Please help us."

don't. Please help us."

Rachel's emotional and physical experiences continue to test her, as God tested Job. Often, she comes to share her pain and fear. Resting in light trance on the now familiar carpet of the blue office, she murmurs, pleading.

"No, no! Not the cellar! Please, Mommy!"

Her entreaties build to a scream. Her neck is in spasm. Grotesque muscular lumps appear on either side of her throat. They twitch and turn. Kicking and twisting, muscle spasms restrict her moans. Her cries cease, and Rachel is mute. Only her thrashing body tells of the agony Rachel is reexperiencing.

She does not return to consciousness at the end of the period set aside for her, because, as Sam complains, Rachel's demons refuse to fit themselves into a standard therapeutic hour.

After a long, long time, the Rachel who lives in present time is resurrected, weary and dazed.

Unable to speak, she turns to pencil and paper. For five days her avenue for communication is to be her journal. Though her mouth and throat are proscribed from speaking horror, her hands are still free to write. Staggering, childish scrawls fill page after page.

I must see what Rachel wants me to know, yet I despise what I read.

Thirty Two

"Instead of the educated, thoughtful, dignified, womanly personality, which was usual, worn out with long contained illness and pain, there appeared a bright, spritely, child personality, with a limited vocabulary, ungrammatical and peculiar dialect, decidedlly Indian in character, but as used by her most fascinating and amusing..."

R. Osgood Mason,
Psychotherapist, 1893

"**D**isgusting! Come on, Sam, I hate pornography! I don't want to write it or read it."

"You Feminists are one hundred percent wrong on your pornography issue. When you fuss like that, you and your sisters are putting out the word that you are actually sensitive, weak, susceptible beings, If so you have to be protected from men's dirty stuff. The arch-conservatives will be happy to protect you from real life, anytime. Back up against the wall, Mother! Zap! You lose your power of choice." Sam and I are having another one of our consultations.

"Roberta, you are willing to listen to all the obscenity Rachel relates about her treatment in the past. Her abuse was "disgusting", sexual and shocking. Yet, you pay careful attention to her. For far too long, I might add."

"That's my job!"

"Your job is to desensitize yourself in many areas so you can be an effective sex therapist. You don't stop listening just because something "sounds dirty." Clearly all the smut you hear from Rachel only makes you sympathetic, not turned on. It sounds like you are a 'normal.' If

212

true, Dr. Money claims he could shut you up in a room for five hours, showing you coprophilia movies, and there's no chance you would eat shit sandwiches for breakfast in the morning."

"Ugh, Sam, you're choosing your words carefully to offend me again." Sam's hero is John Money, an unconventional and brilliant sex scientist. Experienced with deeply troubled children, principally boys, Sam agrees with him.

Wholesome sex play is crucial to normal human development. Sam sees too many effects of sexual repression in his young clients. But our "good" citizens are against any childhood erotic rehearsal.

"When the juvenile sex play of monkeys is prevented, they never grow into normal adult heterosexuals. I'm afraid some of my boys aren't ever going to become sexually healthy."

Like Money, Sam thinks puritanical attitudes play a large part in the development of paraphilias. These are what most people call perversions. Sam sees a paraphilia as a biomedical event. Young children, whose brains are particularly vulnerable to sexual learning, undergo experiences that affect them neurologically. Ordinary folks would say they "get twisted." Shock or physical discomfort, having nothing to do with sex for most people, can become permanently linked with erotic responses, lubrication in girls or erections in boys."

"And horniness. What happens to someone who gets off on the wrong foot early?" I ask.

"We know more about males. Because of the mapping of a boy's brain, the way he is wired, he's apt to become a visual paraphiliac. Things he sees become important sexual turn-ons. Remember how little boys need to peek?

As a man, that little boy may need to see himself dressing in women's clothes in order to perform sexually. That's fairly common. Or he may have any of a vast array of visual perceptions, which have become erotic cues for him. Now, a woman tends to be 'touchy-feely'

213

in her sexuality. But, if she is masochistic, chances are she will associate pain with sexual excitement."

Sam and I always learn as much as we can about the sexual childhood of our difficult clients. Unfortunately, their memories are often blocked, and they can't talk about what happened.

I try to apply what Sam tells me to Rachel's parents. They and their "friends" were pedophiles. How did they get that way? How did they get together? Why were they sexually drawn to helpless children? Why did they combine sex with pain and fear?

It's time to talk with Sam about my foolish repetitive thought.

"Here's a creepy sexual notion that keeps popping into my head, Sam. What if Rachel's mother... is really a man." I wait for a reply.

"You're grinning. But I'm not being funny," I say. Sam isn't either.

"I'm smiling at you, not grinning. I've had that same thought several times from your description. But, I don't believe Mother is a man. I do speculate that her gender is confused. Neither Rachel's mother nor her father sound 'normal,' whatever that is. Perhaps Daddy is a feminized male and Mommy a hormonally pseudo-women, a sort of caricature.

She must be physically striking in the flesh, if you'll pardon the pun. And a violent, erratic person, as she is, could certainly be showing evidence of some genetic disorder. Her hypersexuality and hyperreligiosity suggest neurological impairment.

We'll have to see if she has webbed skin between her fingers, or where her earlobes are connected to the sides of her head. Remember, the fetal brain develops at the same time as the skin. Physical anomalies may indicate that her brain has not developed fully. I'd be curious to see the palms of her hands, to see whether she has a peculiar transverse palmar crease."

"Not me, I wouldn't dare get that close! Sam, didn't the ancients worship freaks? Hermaphrodites, and the

214

like. I'll bet her followers are fascinated with her bodily incongruities. No wonder they give her power. Maybe that's why they might have made her a leader in spite of her lack of education. She sounds mystical, wondrous and horrifying.

And Daddy makes me think of a Medieval gargoyle on a cathedral, a mini horned god of the old religion squatting there. Together, physically, Mommy and Daddy could symbolically represent the dark side of human nature."

"They're compelling, all right. Perhaps ugliness and distortion could make them objects of worship."

"Like living symbols of wickedness. I wonder how witch 'head honchos' get chosen nowadays, now that witches are good guys, helping Feminists interested in ecology?"

"With the New Age dawning, I have no idea. More healthily, I imagine. The right kind of witches fit nicely into the ideals of the human potential movement." Sam muses on.

"You know, like the 'friends of Mommy and Daddy's' you've been hearing about, I once connected aberrant sexual behavior with demonic possession. It's an old, old idea. But I lost interest in demons as motivators, when I grew up intellectually. I became involved with the science of sex, not the folklore of sex.

John Money teaches about "sexosophy," religious confusion about sexuality. America embraces scientific investigation in theory, but sexosophy still controls us. Religion, with its notions of guilt, atonement and sacrifice, is a perfect vehicle to be distorted into pathology. It's uncanny how many torturers, rapists and lust murderers come from rigidly religious homes.

I suspect that Mother, like other paraphiliacs, has no ability to form a love bond. From the time of her first sex play, her love somehow got separated from her lust. Love never found its way back, so Mother became dangerous.

Narcissistic Daddy would only concentrate on his own

215

physical gratification. Since he could not be sexually aroused by tenderness, he would turn to shock and pain for excitement.

Your client's mad mother dreamed of sacrificing her child. Poor Rachel."

"A child sacrifice. Did Rachel have a sin, Sam?"

"Being born to the wrong parents," he tells me.

Notes:
Rachel and I have a dilemma. Psychiatrists, like Dr. Fielding, are accustomed to being able to predict the beneficial or harmful effects of prescription drugs with some certainty. They also know which side effects might occur, but not when multiple personality is involved. A genuine multiple is not going to respond in any predictable way to any substance. Depending on which personality or personalities are in control, medication will surely have differing effects.

Personalities, inhabiting one body have demonstrated different handedness, accelerated or slowed healing processes, different allergies, autonomous nervous system effects and differing abilities to control pain. Most psychiatrists familiar with this disorder agree, that drug therapy may at times be absolutely necessary...or not.

The greatest danger is that a MPD person will accidently overdose, (a personality taking the medication may not know that another self has taken it) or an overdose can be used as a suicide or a homicide (a destructive personality intending to kill another). Physical or physiological additions are easily developed. If one of the personalities is a former drug user, sometimes this alter can protect against the effects of the drug so thoroughly, that any attempts to medicate are rejected.

I guess Rachel will have to tough this out with any moral support Sam and I can give her.

The phone rings. Roger tells me what he's discovered.

"The people whose names you gave me, your client's parents? Nobody back East knows much about them.

Only that they were involved in suspicious doings, Roberta. They've gone, disappeared. All anybody knows is 'they went out West.'

There's a sister. She doesn't want anything to do with them or talk about them either. Says they're crazy, and it's a relief they're gone. Sounded scared. 'Went West.' That's it."

"Oh, no. I don't like the sound of that. Thanks, Roger. I'll have to tell my friend. She may need to protect herself."

Thirty Three

"Prior to 1983, stories of ritualized abuse and strange rites weren't appearing in child abuse cases. That I know from personal experience. Between 1983 and 1985 the media wasn't discussing them so there was no media contamination.

However, investigators in the field kept hearing these stories - we kept hearing these stories independently and thought we were the only ones. Then in 1985 stories of ritualized abuse began to surface, and we in the police began to take notice. These children all tell similar stories, describe similar events. I worked with one little girl who drew the ritual itself. In it she was holding a knife over a little child, and above the image she wrote "Praise the Devil."

Sandra Daly Gallant
San Francisco Police Department

"**S**am, how do you decide who's kinky?"

"Well, I become suspicious the moment anyone becomes terribly self righteous. Someone who parades piety. I ask myself 'What's under all that phoniness?' I've been surprisingly accurate lately. Experience is what I've got."

"And you have intuition I notice, even though your cover is so rational. I'm suspicious of holiness, too. Right away I think there is a 'sin' somewhere. Sin to me is only some kind of secret."

"There is only one sin. Ignorance."

"But surely, Sam, even you don't encourage early sexuality for children? Uninhibited sex play?"

"Not since the unbridled sixties, Sweetie. Or should I say the undraped decade? Undiapered? Evidently, sexual freedom can't work in this country. We're not grown up enough. Americans usually fall back on moral right-eousness and occasionally turn out wierdos, like Rachel's parents or the Branch Davidians.

In some ways we create the people who prey on children. It's a price we pay for repression. Of course, I'd like to give out strong, positive explicit messages to children about the usefulness of masturbation.

Young people should be taught early in their lives about its advantages. Instructing people in safe, easy methods for experiencing sexual pleasure seems a reasonable alternative to the secrecy on which we insist. We already have fear, violence, rage, terror and panic available to us.

How about learning to feel good? We already teach how to feel nasty and ashamed. Sexual secrets add to guilt. And guilt is a dangerous feeling for people attracted to cruelty. Dangerous to other people."

Thirty Four

"Don't think of her as a victim. Don't see her as weak, sick, or permanently damaged. Instead, hold the attitude that she's a whole human being going through some difficult struggles. See her as courageous and determined. Concentrate on her strength and her spirit.

Reflecting the survivor's strengths back to her is a gift you can give throughout the healing process...Healing from child abuse is a heroic feat. She deserves your respect, confidence, and admiration."

Ellen Bass and Laura Davis
The Courage to Heal, A Guide for Women Survivors of Child Sexual Abuse.

How can this tormented victim of satanic practice be healed? Her suffering can only be compared to those who lived through the horrors of Auschwitz or Belsen. It makes perverted sense to me, that contemporary satanists have adapted the swastika as one of their emblems.

Terrified Rachel is bombarded with fractured pictures. Her eyes have taken on a life of their own, as if they see all by themselves, without contact with Rachel's brain or her surroundings. Her many beatings left her with the visual consequences of severe head injury. Her imagination, too, has been appallingly hurt. Subjected to childhood abuse so extreme, her only challenge was to survive, Rachel's developing personality was broken and crushed.

Unloved, Rachel drifted in a hostile world. Like a wild animal, she hid inside herself, pretending to be a perfect lady, venturing out only when she dared. Physical damage impaired her functioning for years. From emotional damage she created elaborate defense mechanisms, which allowed her to withstand further torture.

Today she still lives in fear, screaming inside.

Yes, she may be hallucinating, but I don't think so. She is not crazy. Inside, she holds the memories of hurt children bent on survival.

Thirty Five

"In short, what we are dealing with here is mass delusion, superimposed on mass hysteria...unfortunately, there is a segmant of the psychiatric and psychological community that harbors this delusion as well..."

Richard A. Gardner, M.D.

I call what Rachel is experiencing "flooding" or "gating." She is receiving visual information so quickly she is overwhelmed. All at once she has two thousand picture puzzle pieces in front of her eyes and no idea where they fit. Like viewmasters her eyes click away so fast she has no chance to process. Her right eye projects whatever she sees - up close. She needs to back away. In her left eye, the illustrations are distant, only dimly perceived. Rachel clearly feels a stone and mortar wall which runs down the middle of her head. During guided imagery her skull throbs with pain and confusion.

So Rachel writes in her journal with her left hand becoming grown up Rachel's child self. Information from a memory center in her brain pours out of the part of her that is "left hand, left eye and faraway." The message is always the same. Rachel is not to see. Rachel is not to know. She is never to tell. Right hand is an adult self, reminding her to back away emotionally from the images that bombard her. This part of Rachel's brain advises her to calm down and to make an effort to understand what is happening. She thinks well and relates to present reali-

understand what is happening. She thinks well and relates to present reality, but the brainwashed children in Rachel are afraid of everything. They doubt, not only their own perceptions, but their sanity.

"I'm crazy," she hums to herself. Born into a madhouse the little girl inside survived, by adapting to the craziness of the people already living there.

"Where is Mother? Are she and Daddy coming here to Texas to hurt me?"

I have an idea I think may help Rachel. Such a client as she cannot fit into a conventional therapeutic time slot. I gave up that struggle a long time ago, so I'll ask her to spend the night at my house. She can stay in trance, then debrief her experience with me in the morning. I desperately want Rachel to finish the therapy work in which she believes. Can we stand to go on like this? She and I are exhausted. So is Sam's patience.

"Are you working 'round the clock now, Doctor? What happened to the fifty minute hour? Don't you know when to quit?"

Apprehensively, Rachel brings her white cotton night clothes to sleep her night away in the calm, blue office. This will be a recess from her mothering duties for one complete night.

Gallantly, she moves into trance with no hesitation. Immediately, she grows rigid and cold to the touch. Her toes and fingers splay outward as her body arches, then falls back upon the bed. Again she arches and falls. Her white nightclothes flutter with her movements, billowing out around her. Her muscles are as stiff as old leather.

Rachel's long hair flattens into a circle around her head, as she falls repeatedly backward on the bed. Her eyes are squeezed shut, her breath gasping. From my armchair I call her back, but there is no response.

I am more and more insistent. Finally I command her, but in this pattern of exaggerated movement, lifting and falling, Rachel remains, all the long night. Her psychic suffering is beyond anything I had believed possible. She will not return.

Most often, I do therapeutic work that is reality orient-ed. Occasionally, someone benefits from short periods of trance. They relive archaic pain, briefly, but come back quickly, when reminded of the present. If they discover tears on their cheeks, they are more aware of a marve-lously comforting physical and mental relief. As they walk out the door, they laugh and chat about everyday things, unburdened. But Rachel is different and will not be soothed. She does not end her suffering, until the morning sun shines hotly through the glare-blurred East-ern windows.

Rachel cannot eat. Neither can she drink the warm co-coa I hold for her. Resting against the bed pillows, her eyes are blank. She is unthinking, spent, remote. Rachel's perspiring family arrive crowded into their hot, dusty car. Alarmed and worried, I beg them to allow her to rest.

No more hypnotherapy for Rachel. Only grounding in today's reality. I have put my foot down. I watch Rachel here in my living room, as she prepares herself for anoth-er group session. This is her opportunity to stay ration-al, not to "act out." Tonight, she plans to simply put some of her experience into a few words and control her own reactions.

Taking her place in front of the fireplace, Rachel looks around once more at the faces of the warm, sympathetic women who encircle her, waiting. Strong once more, she trusts herself to be clear and brief. I nod to her encourag-ingly.

As she opens her mouth to speak, a harsh sound whis-tles out of Rachel's throat. Her face turns stiff. Rubbing her eyes with her knuckles, Rachel struggles to breathe as her neck thickens. In the flickering light from the fire, visibly swollen, her throat cannot emit a sound.

The next day, a nose and throat doctor diagnoses her infirmity. He calls her complaint laryngitis. Rachel and I know her condition is Mother. For a week Rachel suffers from the fiercely contracted muscles in her painful face, neck and head. Late each night, her left hand fiercely inscribes her chronicle in her journal. She fills a notebook and more. Her right hand trembles in fear, unusable.

"Where is Mother?," a voice inquires in Rachel's head.

"Coming West," is the echo.

Recovered from her "sore throat" and determined to tell me whatever comes into her mind, Lilith calls to request a hypnotic induction for Rachel. All right, I agree, one more trance session, but we cannot continue to work in this way. Rachel must have reality therapy, with emphasis on the here and now. Sam and I agree. Finally, so does Rachel, but only after one more session using hypnotherapy.

This guest room make-shift office has blue wallpaper in an orderly stripe, conservative and trustworthy. Books are in deliberate rows, too, not in stacks as in the office next door that pleases me. Nothing is unsettling here, but having everything in exact order feels unnatural to me. This much neatness is not my style. Rachel will no longer meet in the office with the painting.

Outside the window, the wind is blowing the leaves of the carob tree, increasing its spermy odor. Some people are disgusted by the smell. It reminds me of the power of sex. In my work I am aware of nature working inexorably through the people to whom I listen in this conservative and polite room. I and they are removed by only one thin wall from the aromatic tree and the pulsing wind shaking it. A word comes into my mind. It is "fecund." The world is fecund, fertile, sexual. Its inhabitants deal with the imperative of sex in the best way or the only way they can.

Once more, Rachel lies on the blue carpet, which is a symbol of courage to her.

"I want you to explore to find whatever will help you. What it is you will understand and bring all the way to the surface of your awareness."

Much, much later Rachel returns her attention to the

blue room. She has something of great importance to tell me. Forcing herself to sit up Rachel looks straight into my eyes.

I want to tell Roberta, I know THEY are possessed. Not me. My parents. They are possessed with evil, supernatural powers. No, that's not true. They are crazy! Then am I, Rachel, their daughter, crazy? Am I making this up? No.

Sorcery, black Magic, demons, evil spirits, spells, potions, sacrifice, Lucifer, rituals, chants and coven are all words I have known from babyhood. But all this is just elaborate craziness. Madness. Foolishness acted out..All lies. I will explain that to Roberta. I am Rachel 2, and I do not believe.

Suddenly the word "punishment,""omnipotent" and "all-knowing" blaze in my brain. They freeze my tongue. Then, pain. The pain comes. "Silence, silence!" someone orders. I must not, I cannot speak.

I return Rachel's stare with my heart sprinting. I hold her hand tight. Frightened for her, I try to ignore my own panic, as I see her face growing larger, her right cheek jutting outward. Her jaw balloons, tight and lumpish. When the swelling stops Rachel's mouth is sealed shut once more, painfully, by the tension in her jaw. She is driven home without speaking.

I have to Sam about this newest series of behaviors. Talking to him gives me balance.

"Well, Sweet One, clearly Rachel has a fine case of hysteria, as you might have assumed long ago. Like you, Freud used both hypnosis and talk therapy for hysterics. That's the tradition. Don't look so upset. You, although clearly female, do follow fairly well in the Papa's footsteps... and you are not as radical as you like to believe."

Immediately I am angry, my timidity forgotten. Energy floods me.

"Don't beat that old dead horse, Sam. Rachel isn't Anna O! I understand my client better and treat her more decently than Freud ever would. Sisterhood is powerful, Buster! Rachel is responding positively to

Feminist philosophy, it's just too radical for you and too effective. You're jealous, because you can't identify with a woman's experience, as I can. That handicaps you as a therapist."

His anger provides me with temporary relief from my fear.

"Get this clear, Richards! I've been doing therapy for twenty-five years. You're spending your sleeping and eating time pursuing the rotting trail of some psychotic hag, who cursed a pitiful child years ago. Who do you think I am, Bruno Bettelheim? I became disinterested in Fairy Tales about the time I retired. I'm willing to put my personal energy into long walks, short naps and candle-light suppers, preferably with you. I am not jealous of your clients, I am jealous of your time. And, I had been just about to tell you what a splendid job you're doing with Rachel."

"Oh." I realize I have just been goosed out of my scare. What can I say that won't sound like backing down?

"That's very honest of you, Sam."

"Don't give me any more of that assertiveness horse-shit! Let's take a walk and think of some erotic way to spend the rest of the evening."

He tickles my palm and tells me the truth. "Roberta, I'm concerned. You're getting more deeply involved in something unpredictable and dangerous.

How can Rachel's parents be steeped in traditional diabolic lore, when they have no educational background? They failed to finish even grade school. Was it something they absorbed in the air of New England? Is satanism a folk tradition anyone can learn along that coast? Do legendary ideas like Devil worship "transfer" to other parts of the country? Was this brand of devilishness imported from abroad more than once? Has satanism rerooted itself on our shores once more, or is this home grown?

And the real question is, are Mother and Daddy following Rachel?

"What are you thinking, Sam?"

"Remember Arthur Miller's play, the one based on the witchcraft trials in Salem, Mass.? Adolescent girls were involved, confused and upset over their own emerging sexuality in their deeply repressed society. They went a little nuts. Who wouldn't, if sexual thoughts were genuinely believed to be as dangerous as sexual acts."

"Who's saying anything about sex?"

"You don't have to bring it up. I will."

I will not laugh, I tell myself.

"As usual, I have a hard time getting you to stick to the topic, Sam, when we discuss Rachel's case. I don't want to talk about those adolescent girls. And you can't distract me with sex talk right now, Sam Dear." I harden my expression.

"Today, Rachel thinks that if she gets angry it will destroy her."

"Who says it won't. She'll have to experience overpowering rage sometime, to pull out of her depression. As her therapist, dear Doctor, just stay in a clinch until you hear the bell."

Thirty Six

"Allegations of Satanism - rites involving mutilation, infant sacrifice and devil worship - have emerged in more than 100 child sex abuse investigations across the country.

In four years, though, investigators have found no evidence to support fears that cults are preying on the nation's children. The Commercial Appeal studied ritual sex abuse allegations in 36 cases and found instead that many of the stories labelled "satanic" or "ritual" have the hallmarks of "urban legends." "Urban legend" is a term coined by sociologists to describe fascinating and colorful tales that spread rapidly across the nation, usually with little change in detail, but that rarely can be traced to any actual event."

"The Commercial Appeal", *Memphis*

"You know what the major sin of women witches was, don't you? They had pride. They acted uppity, Massa Sam. Witchcraft was clearly rebellion against the male God, that is, rebellion against men and men's institutions," I say, ready to battle. No answer.

"In Colonial times the "signs" that intelligent, independent thinking women had transferred their allegiance from God to Satan were anything from Sabbath-breaking to objecting to ministerial authority. Blasphemy signified a covenant with the Devil. I think blasphemy meant 'not agreeing with the preacher'," I say.

Breakfast for Sam and me is homemade marmalade on "health nut" English muffins, baked with sunflower seeds, raisins and the fiber Sam insists is straw. He glares suspiciously at the bumpy surface, searching out chaff to prove his point. All right, so I'll change the subject. If I talk about sex I can be sure I will attract his interest.

"Most people, you know, believe debasing sexual fantasies inevitably lead to real-life acting out. But instead, you, Sam, say normal people have wild and rebellious sexual fantasies to keep their actual behavior within socially tolerable bounds."

"You're thinking about Rachel's parents again, aren't you?", Sam says immediately. "Once I was the morbid one. Now its you. You need help, Doctor. Am I going to have to take you to a movie? I recommend 'The Sound of Music' or 'E.T.' Maybe 'Peter Pan'.You can clap your little hands together to make Tinkerbell live. Stop being so gloomy."

"Don't get sarcastic. Mother and Daddy may be in our very neighborhood by now."

"Do we have more of this marmalade?"

"Listen to me, Sam, they may be here in Texas. They've moved West, and it may be possible that they have tracked Rachel down."

Sam is acting cool. I notice, though, he's forgotten to drink his coffee.

"Sam, dear, listen. If Rachel and I write her story will it seem too exaggerated? Will her recovery be unbelievable? What about the symbolic nature of her unconscious life, do you think it is too romantic and nineteenth century? Like the Grand Hysterie literature? Dramatic and corny? Too Freudian, maybe?"

"Now you're getting insulting."

"Well, if she and I decide to write her life story it will be a horror tale. Pretty Gothic. But it might also have some clinical value or just be interesting. What do you think? Sam? I do understand why you tune out when I discuss Rachel. You've been listening to me for seven or more years now and that's a long stint."

Looking up from his paper, Sam gives me his full attention. This is a rare moment.

"You learn from Rachel. That's good. Unfortunately, you are compelled to share everything about her, which has been a lot for even an excellent listener like me. If you write a book with her don't make it too long. You've been furious with Rachel, patient, bored, disappointed, tired of her, hopeful, astonished and frightened. But you still hang in there. You push her away when she is dependent and support her emotionally when she's desperate. Now your long shot is starting to get well. I'm glad for you and I'm glad for her. But when you tell me about her interesting symptoms and her progress just keep it short. I have spoken."

Sam is friendly, patronizing and infuriating all at the same time. Smiling warmly, he returns to his paper.

"What do you think about witches, Sam? In the time of the witch hunts in New England have you ever supposed some of the accused genuinely were witches? That they actually practiced the black arts in order to harm or kill their enemies?

I think the reported vengefulness of the witch could contain enough truth to surprise us. With disagreeable manners and obviously hostile thoughts, do you think some women brought the accusations upon themselves?"

"No, I believe they were simply mentally ill. Other people grew afraid of those poor women, because they fitted the stereotype of the European witch which has been kept around since the Middle Ages. The 'Poisonous insinuations' of witches," old Cotton Mather said," spread like a 'terrible Plague' through communities, ausing them to become 'infected and infested' with evil.' In other words, people grew panicky, and dramatized their fear by acting out."

What do other people talk about over breakfast? Sam is lecturing me again. He does this to help me, he thinks, when I am upset. It doesn't. After I get angry enough it is my turn to lecture him on how he talks down to me. We are off on a new topic, but as usual still related to Rachel.

"Oh, come on! You know child molestation has always been with us, Roberta! Just now it means something to you personally. Stop it! You, like most of us, failed to recognize child abuse until you had to. We have our reasons for being blind. Remember there is no typical child molester and there is a wide, wide range of

abuse from the naughtiness of peeping Tom to your satanic sex-abuse rituals. Pedophiles are drawn to religious
practices that provide easy access to children. What do
you expect? Spirituality? Religious enlightenment?

Now you're having a hard time believing a sadistic les-
bian mother would frightfully abuse her daughter.
'Women don't molest children', you say. I'll never forget
the pictures of the bloody dildos Rachel's internal children draw. That's hideous to me. But you're almost
right. It's infrequently reported and undoubtedly rare.

" Look at you, pacing back and forth while you talk", I
point out. Sam retraces his steps.

"But perfectly nice people you know don't object to
sex between an older woman and a boy. When a twelve
or fourteen year old lad is engaged in sexual behavior at
the urging of an older woman, is that sexual abuse? Or
something for the boy to brag about later?

As parents", he mumbles, "we keep the story of the
malevolent stranger around because it's easier to protect
children from perverts in rain coats, hanging around
around grade schools, than from the harmful behaviors
right in front of our noses. I mean sexual abuse by relatives. Sexual abuse by friends. Those missing children
you fret about probably weren't kidnapped. Many of
them are runaways, escaping sexual abuse at home.

The point is that an imbalance of power in a sexual relationship between an adult and a youngster cannot be
resisted by a child. What little kid can say 'no' successfully to someone insistent and larger.

Someone with personal power over the child. Someone willing to use force?"

There are no more firestorms in Rachel's head, but her
body does not cooperate with calm. She is often physically ill, but her thinking is intact. Is the daily fear she experiences realistic? I believe so. In the form of her parents
insanity may have followed her West. Fearful as she is,
Rachel shows more than a lively interest in her studies
again. Her scholarship is impressive and she is on her
way to becoming a gifted therapist. As Sam says, Rachel

and I share an interest in multiple personality. Only she teaches me.

"It takes one to know one", she says.

Still heckling, Sam plays Devil's Advocate for me and now for Rachel as well. Lately he focuses on satanic aspects of her life story.

"I cut this out of the newspaper for you two clinicians. I know you'll appreciate it. Better still, I'll read it out loud. Right now."

"No, no, go away."

Rachel and I try to drive him from the room by pelting him with professional journals. He only ducks and continues as if we had given him applause.

"Here goes. My Answer is the name of the nationally syndicated column by Billie Graham. I quote. 'Some of my friends in our high school have gotten fascinated with things like witchcraft and fortunetelling with tarot cards. Do you see anything wrong with this?'

Here's his answer. I've found it interesting and you will, too, Rachel."

"'These activities are not harmless because they can bring you into contact with Satanic spiritual powers - which are real, and are totally evil and opposed to God and his truth. Never forget that Satan is real, and that he will try every way he can to keep you from God.'"

"Ho hum", Rachel murmurs.

"Cut it out, Sam!," I shout. "Don't bother us. We're reading clinical stuff, an activity you insisted upon when I was your student. So leave the room and let us work."

Rachel and I sometimes put our heads together on her writing projects. As a Psych major, she easily makes the Dean's list and is aiming at yet another scholarship. Someday she'll write for publication to add to the small store of information about helping the ritualistically abused.

Sam settles down nearby.

"I can't drive you away with a sharp stick," I complain.

"You think we might want your opinion, Sam?" Rachel asks him.

"Why change?", Sam smiles. "Rachel", he says,"when you've finished your search, here's an article I want you to see. Let me know what you think of it."

Sam has clipped six pages from a marriage and family therapy journal that are exactly what Rachel needs for her paper. Her major project on Codependent Women is due. We have been looking for sources to cite and here it is Women Victims of Child Abuse

"Concerns pertaining to self seemed to fit into four main areas: identity, self-esteem, physical functioning and sexual functioning. Concerning identity and self-esteem, many of these women have a very negative self-image, have a sense of being different and distant from "ordinary' people, have a sense of being powerful in a malignant way, express self-hatred, and are depressed and anxious. They may also be self-destructive and suicidal.

Physical complaints include feelings of dissociation, migraine headaches, severe backaches, gastrointestinal and genitourinary problems, inability to concentrate, lethargy, anxiety, phobic behavior, and substance abuse....Sexual identity conflicts and impairment in sexual functioning are also presenting complaints. Sexual problems range from an inability to function sexually at all to promiscuity and masochistic behavior. A range of sexual dysfunction, such as inability to relax, vaginismus, inability to orgasm, and so on, occurs between these two extremes.

Relationships (of women sexually abused as children) are described as empty, superficial, conflictual, or sexualized. The inability to trust is pronounced. Good or pleasurable relationships often increase guilt and shame because they are viewed as undeserved or impossible. Conflict is most apparent in marriage or other intimate relations with men."

Many of these women have very negative feelings toward men, yet at the same time overvalue men and search for a protector. Paradoxically, yet predictably, these women very often end up with men, who, like themselves, have been abused. These men are abusive or neglectful of them, so this type of relationship serves to recapitulate early experience and reinforce a negative sense of self-worth".

Journal of the American Association of Marriage and Family Therapy

"I knew you when, Rachel," Sam says. "Isn't this article a fairly accurate description of you six or was it seven years ago? Eight? If so, you have a niche in the psychological literature. Just like a clothing store saleslady says, 'it's reeaaaally you'. All they've left out is devotion to Satan."

"Read something else if it bothers you, Sam," Rachel says," meanwhile, bug off."

Sam is making sure Rachel can both take it and dish it out. Rachel has graduated to the rank of Smartass. However, she puts the article Sam has given her away carefully in her knapsack.

Without her once chronic willingness to suffer, Rachel's marriage ties dissolve. She is no longer "the sick one." Eventually, her marital charade becomes impossible to maintain. Both she and her husband are forced to look honestly at their relationship, recognizing the truth.

As two broken people they shored each other up to the best of their abilities using every bit of imagination they could muster.

When Rachel was fragile and sick her husband could be strong. He saw himself as protective, powerful, in charge and always right. Like all of us Rachel and her husband wanted a happy ending to their story, but they no longer have stamina nor energy to continue their pretense.

Having grown as individuals, they can now free themselves from their neurotic entanglement. In order to heal, Rachel has discovered a strong, new individuality. She looks squarely at the problem of her husband's alcoholism and her earlier denial.

Rachel has "gotten well," and separated from her husband." One of us had to go first," she says.

Thirty Seven

"Three recent teen-age suicides on the Navaho Reservation have been inked with the growing popularity of devil worship on the nation's largest Indian reservation....all three victims had 666, a number associated in the Bible with the anti-Christ, burned into their skin. The rise of satanic events on the Navajo Reservation is blamed on the heavy metal culture of the young and disenchantment with society's values. Plus, there's already a sense of witchcraft, of darkness, in the Navajo culture.

Arizona Republic, *November 17, 1988*

Life for Rachel has changed. Having grown as an individual, she is free of her neurotic entanglement. In order to heal, Rachel has discovered a strong, new individuality. She looks squarely at her husband's alcoholism and her earlier dependency.

She is not the damaged goods she believed herself to be, for she is awake at last.

Generally now, her mind is clear, and she copes well with her new job in a counseling clinic. But antibiotics cannot permanently subdue the smarting, stinging bladder infections she develops each two or three weeks. Her sick kidneys are at serious risk, plagued by vicious bacteria and toxins. When ill from infection, she can become disoriented of time and place, returning in memory to her tortured past. She wants to take no chances on becoming "crazy " again.

Still, another doctor has given up on her insides. He recommends she see an expert urologist. This impersonal doctor's words are the same as those of the physical therapist, who grew impatient years ago, tired of massaging spasms in Rachel's neck.

"I'm sorry. I've done all that I know to help you. I'm referring you to a specialist."

Another run-around. That expert, too, wanted Rachel to go away. How many specialists did she see? Rachel endured cortisone injections into the base of her skull, which required her to lie quietly for eight hours. That was meant to relax the muscles in her neck. It didn't, of course. When constrained, she descended into terror.

Her brain was X-rayed for the presence of tumors. A CAT scan and an electroencephalogram found no invasive tissue, but her excruciating pain went on and on.

Rachel longed to hear a doctor say, "You have XYZ, lady. Take ABC and you will be fine."

Instead, her reality is still a comfortless uncertainty about her health. At least urology will be a new area for the medical exploration of her body.

"Heads to tails, Roberta," she tells me, trying to be both clever and brave. The waiting room checklist requires intimate answers. Yes, she feels pain when she urinates, which she does many times in the night. She's more honest than she used to be, even on this medical office form. SEX: Intercourse has been bothersome, a nuisance. She gave it up years ago. NO: she can't remember if sex was physically painful. During coitus, Rachel felt nothing and pretended it wasn't happening. That made it easy to forget. YES: leaking is a constant annoyance during the day.

Rachel's new doctor comes back into the midget room, where she waits, awkward in a scratchy split-up-the back nightshirt. He makes his examination.

"I want to look at you once more, and then I'm going to schedule you for tests in the hospital. After that, we will have a better idea of what to do."

This man is civil and affectionate. Tall, balding, wearing steel rimmed glasses, he is reassuring somehow. Rachel trusts him. Clearly, therapy has helped her remember Grandpa. She knows that old man loved her, and now this old man wants to take good care of her.

"Roberta, it's strange, but I haven't been out of control with apprehension during the exam. I was sure I would be, especially since he was looking at my 'bottom,'" she tells me.

"What's this 'bottom' stuff, Rachel? You know what that part of you is called." I won't put up with any more "wee wee and poo poo" language from Rachel's internal children.

At eight the next morning, Rachel is in the hospital. The lab technician describes the small incision that will be made into her abdomen, into which a tube for the scope will be inserted. With her feet in stirrups, Rachel fights her chronic terror, archaic and habitual. But this time she wins. Rachel can keep her panic under control. The doctor directs the tiny electronic eye, to see deep inside her.

"You've had many forceps deliveries, Rachel."

"No."

"Are you sure, Dear? I can see adhesions. There are large areas of scar tissue and old tears in muscles and soft tissue. Would you like to see?" She would.

The doctor adjusts an eyepiece on a long tube so Rachel can peer inside her pelvic and genital area. She tries to understand what he describes. Untrained, Rachel can see only differences in color. Pink turns to purple between bands of healthy tissue. What is that she sees?

Gently the doctor points out puckered scar tissue and the torn areas. He treats Rachel with dignity and thoughtfulness, taking his time and thinking quietly to himself before he speaks.

"Dear, there are a number of holes and fissures in your internal walls." His voice is hushed. "A great deal of repair work must be done, my lady."

When he inquires about the scars on Rachel's outside, she doesn't know what to say. She, too, has seen the marks, but only when she couldn't help but look.

"This one on my stomach is about as long as I am wide," she says, "I know I'm skinny. There are some white lines on my wrists and streaks, that look like pink

ink sketches on my arms. My hands have patches of crumpled silver and lilac colored skin. I haven't paid these marks any real attention. I've had work to do. I guess I look out toward the world and not down at myself."

Rachel remembers how concerned I was, about the dents in her skull and the brand marks on her arms.

"They don't show much because my hair and my sleeves cover them. My therapist acts as though they are important," she admits, "I used to think she was tactless to mention them."

The old doctor covers Rachel with a sheet and a soft blanket. She remains meditatively on the table, as he outlines his plan. His tone of voice reassures her, although his words are alarming.

"I am going to schedule you, immediately, with a surgeon."

Thirty Eight

"Certainly in many cases there is a halting flow of thought of the principal intelligence, indicating that the activities of the secondary intelligence tends to inhibit the untrammeled flow of the former."

Morton Prince, *Psychopathologist,1904*

D r. Blake tries to be funny. An eminent surgical expert, he twitches his mustache, endeavoring to put Rachel at ease about her "plumbing problems." Levity is wasted on her for she is suspicious of him. He is too engrossed in her so something must be amiss. The doctor sounds ill at ease and downright silly. A sharp crease in his pants, or a military brush cut would reassure Rachel. But this man is plump and too jolly, although his reputation declares he is the finest surgeon in this state for a women's reproductive system. And Texas is filled with medical specialists.

"But famous or not", Rachel tells me, "this doctor has dandruff on his shoulders. Under his seersucker suit jacket his belly protrudes over his belt. He needs a haircut. Saying he will do a partial hysterectomy he wants me to keep my ovaries 'where they should be'. He will 'look around', my bladder will be 'tied up', 'propped into place', 'good as new'. The operation will take an hour or so and I will need approximately two weeks for recovery. The anesthesia will be sodium pentathol."

Looking back, I believe Dr. Blake when he claims he

had no idea of the implications of that last choice.

Rachel wakes, vomiting green bile from deep inside. The day is Thursday. Her surgery was at seven in the morning.

On Monday. If she could read her chart, she would find the wall between her anal region and vagina has been rebuilt. The surgeon found there was no thickness of tissue inside her so that light shone through the mutilated apertures. Patiently removing waves and tangles, Dr. Blake smoothed a labyrinth of built-up scar tissue, where Rachel's abdominal wall was meant to meet her uterus. The hysterectomy had to be total, of course.

The untangling and rebuilding of extensive bladder repair, tissue replacement, and ligature took eight hours.

Thirty Nine

"302.20 Pedophilia:

A. The act or fantasy of engaging in sexual activity with prepubertal children as a preferred or exclusive method of achieving sexual excitement.

B.I f the individual is an adult, the prepubertal children are at least ten years younger than the individual. If the individual is a late adolescent, no precise age difference is required, and clinial judgement must take into account the age difference as well as the sexual maturity of the child."

Diagnostic and Statistical Manual III

I want to visit Rachel to tell her what I have decided. When she is well, I will go "back East" with her, to investigate. She's right, we need to know more.

I wait, hour after hour, for her to regain consciousness. Today, I have come to the hospital, even though she is still "out." What shall I do? Go home?

I pick through old magazines, filled with distaste for the yellowing marbleized plastic table, the phony flowers in fake baskets. I wish I were back in my office, and yet, I cannot leave. The coffee cups here are plastic foam that I can taste through the pale brown liquid. Dismal, I cannot entertain myself or work today.

I can only wait, staring at the granite floor. I am shocked at what the doctors have discovered. I hate what happened to Rachel.

In crumpled periodicals and magazines on this dusty coffee table, fate has arranged for me to find the kind of articles I try to ignore, but always read. Shall I pay attention to more " information"? Sure, I will.

The first magazine tells me that police and psychologists are discovering evidence of devil worship in criminal cases. Professionals are taking seriously tales of satanist rituals. No one knows, however, how to bring suspects to trial in cases like this, because survivors of ritual sacrifices live in fear that members of the cult may follow and punish them.

I have a sudden strong urge to push on, through the heat, to my house with its cool patios and lockable doors. There I can comfort myself, borrowing from Sam's ready skepticism. He has clinical explanations for everything, including evil, and he sticks with safe scientific language, I understand. His air of intellectual sanctity protects me from my own fear.

Right now, reading this ugly magazine in a grey, big city hospital, I am gloomy. I admit I am also frightened. Stories of ritual murder and sexual abuse of children are bizarre tales, but absolutely believed by the psychiatrist interviewed by these investigative reporters.

He says that we are dealing with a religion. People who believe in it are extreme, just as there are fanatic believers in Christianity, Judaism or Islam. Crimes are committed for the sake of religion, as in holy war.

A woman tells of horrors she has only just remembered, from the time she was three years old. Her mother was a worshiper, who gave her up to the cult. She was physically perfect, a worthy gift for Satan himself. But her twin sister was born with a club foot and was therefore murdered.

As a child, the survivor believes she was always in the care of a satanist, moved from home to home. Drugs kept her quiet and obedient. The power of post-hypnotic suggestion controlled her, until at seventeen, she woke up and ran away. She had no memory of her ghastly experiences, but she had lost months and years from her life. Because she was so confused, she was given counseling in a homeless shelter.

Visual images of black robes returned to her, uninvited. Her counselor heard all about the familiar symbols

we expect to find in horror literature: processions, ceremonies, fire, the altar, candles, naked bodies, chanting
and women as sacrifice. Her descriptions were full of
trite imagery: goblets containing the blood of cats, cattle,
chickens and humans, formaldehyde used to preserve
human flesh, in a place where dead cats hung from an altar.

But this was not a low budget movie. It was the experience of a woman, who moves pitifully among us today,
scarred mentally and physically, deep within. She is another Rachel. Her counselor did not believe her. Neither
did the next. Or the next.

This is June. It's as if this is the month when news
magazines have decided, together, to describe cults. This
one tells about ritualized, satanic cult sexuality, how it
moves swiftly into orgy, with sex between men and
women, men and men, women and women, women and
animals, men and children. Hymns are said to be perverse parodies of Christian songs, turned inside out.

These gruesome ceremonies are supposed to take
place in settings like ordinary grain fields, wooden
barns, middle class homes or even in crowded city apart-
ments, where the Devil's festivals celebrate the spiteful
side of human nature. The articles describe all the ugly
details, then sumarize the skeptiic's position: "it can't be
so."

Carl Jung would appreciate this, I think. When I get
home I'll have a drink, or swim laps in the pool.

"Runaways from satanism are always afraid that they
will never be forgotten by true believers. Surely they
will be found out and punished. Satanists are good at
finding people," the other magazine concluded.

That makes me think! I ponder Rachel's mother and
father's overripe pathological imaginations for a while.

Why is satanism featured this month? Is there generally this much interest, or is it because I now notice?

Someone has to help the victims, I say to myself. Other
professionals are disgusted by descriptions of ugly
events and grisly descriptions, that are too bizarre to be

believed. But so am I. These accounts are too superstitious, too childish and too...too extreme.

One detective takes confessions seriously.

Was that Roger? I hear him urging me to believe satanic horror lives around the next corner in my own neighborhood. But Roger was sick. I argued forcefully with Roger, when he was so morbid.

I tell myself , this is just another urban folk tale, picked up by Newsweek or Life. Folklore spreads. It is always repetitive, developing in cycles. Remember how jokes pop up all over the country at the same time. Then variations appear, over and over, every five or ten years. The same old stories about satanism have gone round and round for centuries.

I put the magazine back on the gritty table to rest my head. To pass the time, I remember how Rachel and I played at tennis. What a silly time we had. Of course, Rachel couldn't hit the ball. Her eyes didn't work together well enough. I had no excuse, I'm just clumsy.

In ninety degree sunshine, we sweated into our eyebrows from under our head bands, chasing out-of-court balls until we were exhausted. Each day, we spent long minutes searching the dusty oleander bushes to find the orange Spaldings, that belonged to us.

Finally, serious about learning tennis, we enrolled in a class.

"We'll get better in Tennis One", we assured one another. Mr. Glassman, the gentle coach, had a friendly, but neutral smile. His hair was gray, so he was safe for Rachel to be around. She was still afraid of most men.

"He has nice legs, Roberta."

"Rachel! You never used to notice things like that. What's happening?"

"I'm getting well."

Mr. Glassman practiced patience, while we practiced running and picking up. Three times a week we continued to play. We were hopeless. No one wanted to play doubles with us.

"Good morning, class. You ladies take the furthest

back court."

Mr. Glassman nodded to us. He knew what to do with incorrigibles. On Wednesdays he would walk out to where we were, to see if we were progressing. He found us looking for balls in the oleander hedges. It was all we could do to keep leaves and stems out of our mouths, knowing they were poisonous. Dusty and prickly, we stumbled back onto the court, to bang more balls over the fence. After watching a few minutes, Mr. Glassman would shrug slightly. He contined looking kind as he directed his tan, smooth legs back to the students, who could benefit from his presence. A gentleman, and never one to hurt our feelings, he must have talked to Nora about Rachel and me.

Out of the blue she volunteered to help Rachel develop coordination and to let me stay the way I am. You would think a team teacher would try to develop her partner. But Nora left me clumsy.

"Crawl, Rachel," she yells. "We gotta all learn to crawl before we walk. You'all had a bad start, thas' all. Com'on, Honey. Give yourself a chancet."

Every day for weeks, Rachel crawled around the gym. When she could get her arms and legs to go together, propelling her forward, Nora taught her to walk. Rachel's heels were to hit the floor first, then the balls of her feet, followed by her toes. Her arms learned to swing with her stride. Next came walking backward. Finally, Rachel did cross-overs.

"You'll never dance like Zorba, but you'all are doin' good, Honey. Keep goin'." Rachel labors.

With perseverance she trained her body to do what her brain said for it to do. She even learned to skip.

Her tennis stayed rotten. Was it because she played with me? When the weather got even hotter, I made a therapeutic decision.

"It is more important to concentrate on overcoming your water phobia, Rachel, than on tennis."

Teaching her to swim was cooler, and besides, I already knew how.

I bring myself back to the hospital. Well, I'll read a little further in this out of date glossy.

Psychotherapists in California say satanic abuse is 'coming out of the woodwork,' because therapists, at last, can recognize signs of satanic abuse. How terrible, yet how good it is not to feel alone!

I feel an inward shock. Lately, in therapy, Rachel remembers children penned in a stockade. She is terrified for them. She has an image of them, too, pale from "the draining," lying in white faced rows. "They die," she says,"because their throats are cut and they are hung upside down over buckets to catch their blood." Can it be these things are true?

Proving satanic abuse is close to impossible, Sam has told me. Most professional people respond as Sam did, especially doubting any stories small children tell. I can imagine what happens in a court room, when a little girl like Rachel tells of being assaulted.

"First I am drugged," she might say, "kept in a cage with snakes or rats, forced to eat feces and drink urine and blood. Then I am raped in a bloodlust ceremony."

Almost any district attorney will tell you, going to court with a child witness under five is next to impossible. The only thing worse is a child who is blaming the Devil.

I think about how Sam mentally "reframes" what he is told by a child. Extreme stories appear to him to be exaggerated pleas for help.

"An admission ticket for getting help in our society is to display a gigantic problem. Kids can lie purposefully. They learn satanic stuff somewhere. If not on TV, then they learn it in horror movies or comic books. Just as Satan lives on in our culture, he becomes a part of each child's imagination.

Certainly, there are people who are satanists and who commit ritual killing. They maim and abuse children. But tales of cabals spanning generations of highly intelligent people, carrying out psychopathic acts, are incredible. Psychopaths are too unstable for any durable associations. Stories of them doing so are fantasies."

I want to believe Sam. I don't much care for this network theory, either. Please, God, make Rachel's parents a couple of random nuts, rather than part of a sophisticated criminal system, out to get Rachel and me.

Personally, I resist authority figures, especially Sam, probably too much. Someone turning to the Devil as an authority must have a desire for humiliation, belonging and servitude, and an urge for power, a strange mix.

Satanists must rely on terror and the effects of drugs to separate parents from a natural impulse to protect their children. According to Rachel, children are taught that their parents will never love them.

I'm vulnerable, today, to the message that satanic foolishness has real consequences for all of us. I have a heavy feeling in my chest. What becomes normal for satanically abused kids is not normal for you and me. Does this mean Rachel will always be compartmentalized and in pain?

The ritual abuse of children is not sex abuse, for sexual gratification, but to gain absolute control of the child. The purpose in using drugs is not to get high, but to exercise power.

I hold my back straight and force myself to reread a horrific ritual about a little child, put into an open coffin and lowered into a grave. Dirt is thrown down with a great noise. The child's mother is present, watching. The child may call out to mother. If so, the head priest removes the little boy or girl from the grave to perform sexual acts upon the little one. There is no question, who has power. Who will help? No one, not even mother.

Only a few psychotherapists dare vouch for the truthfulness of their client's stories like this, I read. I enjoy a small wave of self pity. Treatment for Rachel has demanded time and long, careful attention. I have had to have a strong stomach. I only thought I had heard disgusting things, until I met Rachel.

I will walk around the outside of this shabby pile of worn marble and dirty windows called a hospital, and

Forty

"Satanism is to a drug cartel what New Age training is to a lot of corporations.
It creates a magical worldview filled with abso-lute terror and the most macabre forms of cruelty and violence in order to ensure loyalty..."

Carl Raschke, *Professor of Religious Studies*

The nurse is eager to tell me why I have been called. Rachel, not yet out of anesthesia, is watched and monitored in the recovery room. Still raving, she has been delirious ever since the surgery.

"She is suffering a psychotic break, Dr. Richards. She's screaming about blood and babies burning, children cru-cified, ugly things."

The staff has strapped Rachel's torso to her bed and tethered her hands. They are afraid she will tear open her newly stitched incisions.I hold Rachel's hands when-ever I can catch her fingers, which claw at the straps that hold her wrists. I steady myself.

"Cold! Shut in the box. Can't breathe," Rachel screams again and again."Oh, oh, oh, no more", she begs. "Get him off!"

Time drags. Rachel suffers on and on doing her emo-tional work. Rachel is "feeling".

"Under the water. Help me, pull me up! I won't tell."

Next day, vomiting a thin, greenish fluid, Rachel is awake at last. Bathed by the nurses she does not speak.

My chant goes on and on in my head as I purge myself of Mother, Daddy, and their perverted religious system.

I am sick with the knowledge that my parents never loved me. I empty myself of the memory of blood sacrifices, cleanse myself of dark closed-in places, in which I am locked with dead things. I rid myself of the power of evil and of Lucifer. I am not powerless.I am no longer the enabler that allows the torture. I am Rachel 2.

The squawky voiced nurse again calls me to come to the hospital. When the phone rings, I know who it is before she tells me. I've been waiting days for this call. It means Rachel is conscious. Driving to the hospital I am hot and cranky in this blistering summer afternoon. There are long waits for left turns. My city hesitates to spend money for green arrows. Confused tourists hold up traffic while they try to decide how many cars should go first. Impatient, I worry.

"Who will I find in Rachel's hospital bed?"

When I finally collapse on the straight chair next to Rachel's stiff, white sheets, I am sweating and rumpled. I look at Rachel's crazy stare, her pale strained face. My friend is not present.

"Take your time, Rachel." I'm still foolishly trying to tell her what to do. "You don't have to talk right now."

It's a long, sticky drive home again from the hospital.

The ugly, angry howling begins that night. I don't believe I have ever been so frightened. From the alley behind the house the voices blend in obscene song, celebrating Beelzebub, the Tempter.

"I saw movements along the fence and shadows shifting in the bright moonlight", I tell Sam. "Two painted white faces with sooty eye sockets rose up above the fence line. Now they are gone."

Days later, Rachel rests quietly on hard hospital pillows, eyes open.

"Do you remember any of my visits?," I ask. She smiles a tiny smile. Her voice is flat and faint.

"Yes, I took you with me into the long tunnel where Mother beckoned to me."

250

Rachel closes her eyes.

"I am there now. You walk behind, close to me. There are two little girls with their backs turned to us. You and I pass them by. At the end of the tunnel there is a shadow. It is a person, someone I cannot recognize. I think it may be Daddy."

Rachel's voice trails away. She sleeps, her face as pale as her cotton pillow case. She looks small in this crisp hospital bed, like a little child who is severely ill.

During the next visit she speaks to me from somewhere far away.

" This Purgatory has thick damp walls of New England taprock. It is dark here, clandestine, like a temple or a prison. It is a cellar. I will stay in this place until I decide to be live up there with you...or not."

Rachel sighs. As I ready myself to leave, Rachel makes another effort to speak.

"I know you are out there, Roberta. But I want you to understand that I am so deep down in this cold place I cannot come out. Once more it seems I will not live, nor will I really die."

Solemn, sloppy Dr. Blake and the other doctors confer.

"I'm surprised," Blake tells them. "No, I'm annoyed. Not one of her sutures is healing. Damn! She is a first."

Unmindfully, he spills coffee on his wrinkled pants. Noticing I am listening, he becomes cautiously understated.

"Certainly unusual."

Rachel is carried home to her narrow bed. Silver nitrate painted on her stitches does not help. Vitamins, protein drinks, chocolate malts, vanilla egg nogs, food supplements, all day bed rest and chicken broth make no difference. Only the presence of the girls brings a response. Their mother smiles vaguely at their antics. In her soft voice she tells them how much she appreciates the way they take care of each other.

Back in a medical office nine physicians confer about Rachel. They are angry at the refusal of her body to repair itself. There is no healing in Rachel all summer.

As August ends its dusty days, slapdash Dr. Blake announces there is nothing left to do, but repeat the surgery.

Notes:
As always, Dr. Blake is scrupulous about his work, and delapidated in appearance. He is no longer optimistic or cheerful in manner. Weeks ago he stopped trying to be amusing and folksy, refusing to listen further to explanations from other specialists. Today, he simply falls silent, looking deep into his discolored coffee cup.

The bougainvillea riots in purple bloom outside Rachel's hospital window. Rachel sentences herself to confront her past once again. She asks for a hypnotherapy session before her second surgery, her next ordeal. This hypnotic ritual seems more a prayer meeting for two friends than a clinical intervention. It is the night before she confronts again pain and fear and I invite Rachel into trance. Understanding her task, she quietly closes her eyes. She and I are deeply moved by the seriousness of her mission, the crucial importance of this reverential moment.

I want to be worthy of Rachel's valor.

Goodbye, Roberta. I have left you now. Long cool streaks of fog lie over the river where I am.. Bubbles slowly wind their way along the banks. They are caught on stones for a moment, then pulled along by the gentle hypnotic insistence of the moving water. Just as I am pulled into the past.

There are the cranberry bogs and marshes, where I wanted to wade like the other children. Some of the white houses along the river are giants.They are neatly painted every seven years.The mansard roofs are reshingled whenever they show wear, and the shutters are black, dark green or the color of clay

Decorated with pots of scarlet geraniums, the windows look beautiful. There are no windows in the cellar at home.

Daisies grow in these gardens. The lawns are mown all the way down to the water's edge. Gigantic maples line the wide cracked streets in front of these family houses, pushing up the sidewalks. There is the gray house I loved the most when teacher took us on our field trip. Its color is dove and that means peace. The family who lives there sits peacefully on the porch. Now they wave to us. When I grow up I will be like them. I will be happy and friendly and at ease.

But now I must go.... home. Home is a big house too. Many people live here and the hall has a bad smell. The yard is hard packed dirt and there is the fence I must stay behind if other people come around. The cellar belongs to my family. I am to go there now.

Next morning at seven, as the blazing Texas sun begins to heat the white concrete walls of the hospital, unconscious Rachel is wheeled into the operating room to meet her Devil.

This time there is no sodium pentothol. Truth serum is far too dangerous for someone with "leaky margins" like Rachel, someone who can become emotionally out of control. On this journey to the inside, Rachel will choose life or death. Will she transcend her torture and her torturers? Or will Peeper have her chance at last.

Forty One

"Satanism is the basement of the occult. The only reason I'd say there is some kind of network is the amount of simularities in ritualistic signs that crop up, like the Goat of Mendes mask - the old goat's head symbol - the black robes, the way rituals are reported. There are some fundamentalists out there that run dog and pony shows and never give any substance. They claim there are satanists behind every rock..."

Mark Roggeman, *Denver Police Department*

Rachel chooses wellness. In the white operating room once more she travels to the end of the tunnel. This time she crawls, as Nora has taught her, then rises to walk gracefully, alone.

The fearsome tunnel is long, but no longer exhausting. It is white light itself, ablaze with florescence steaming from the ceiling. Above Rachel comes the sound of human voices. Deep within the place of whiteness, the woman waits. Close now, Rachel looks steadily at Mommy. She understands that Mommy is also Iris, Mother and the Priestess; one woman only, cruel and thoroughly mad. It is safe for Rachel to look away, for now the woman has no power.

Rachel moves on, hearing Peeper and Lilith whispering together where they sit with their backs to Rachel. They are arguing. As the two little girls turn around, Rachel can see that each of their faces is her own.

At the far end of the tunnel Rachel passes directly through the thin shadow with the burning eyes that is Daddy, and emerges into light and air. She breaths easily

She breaths easily and dozes.

When Rachel's early selves agree to get well the doctors are even more confused than they were when Rachel's tissues refused to mend. Now rapid healing takes place at a deep cellular level of Rachel's body.

I can't explain it, but I can be glad. Together we celebrate the magnificence and mystery of the human mind/body.

Forty Two

"'..investigating satanic crime may be a growth industry...the crime of the 90's.' He's led more than 200 seminars for law enforcement professionals on how to spot the earmarks of the occult in everything from church robberies to child abuse...he gets calls from colleagues around the country perplexed over headless hens, spray painted pentagrams - and worse."

About Robert Simandl, *Chicago Police Detective*

I remember how Rachel once insisted her husband was the most important person in the worldto her.

Notes:

She arranges her thinking to make him fit the role of rescuer. Submitting to his boyish seduction behind the factory storeroom door, the caustic smells of the solvents used to clean the sewing machines smart Rachel's eyes.The tears she sheds are not from passion or from joy. As her dry tissues smart from his fierce proding, the pain drives her downward into darkness and deadly cold. She is lost in time.

Rachel disappears, and someone takes her place on the oil slick plank floor.

Because she has produced only one scanty period in the four years since she was thirteen, she has no idea she is pregnant, until her coworkers tell her. They can see the tiny, but distinct bump, pushing its way out of her faded t-shirt. The band of her drooping skirt rises to ride above the protuberance.

Mother leans out of the window to see the boy, as he whispers with Rachel on the tenement steps. The gigantic woman warns him.

"You are making a foolish mistake, talking to a bad girl."

But no one watches as Rachel and her sweetheart escape into the summer night. A newly married lady on her way to Texas, Rachel declines the brown bottle that sustains her new husband on their long, hot ride.

Years later, I deeply regret the necessary turmoil in Rachel's marriage, inevitable as she becomes well. I know her alliance is distorted, based on illusions that cannot maintain themselves in the clarifying light of emotional honesty. But even in the service of mental health, it is sad to watch the painful unraveling of a relationship, no matter how full of pretense it is. People in any tangled connection feel terrible pain, when the knots can no longer hold.

This year, Rachel's once childish dependence on exteme, overly rigid, conventional religious ideas has turned into a genuine spiritual yearning. I admire Rachel's intellectual and emotional courage, as she grows more authentic. She is not a bad girl. She is not a good girl. She is a real woman.

Today Philip, fallen away satanist, comes to my office. He wants me to know he's the newly elected President of the Latin Club at High School. His big-eyed girl friend is the new secretary. She carries Philip's sulfuric skin cream in her purse and reminds him to apply it morning and evening. A head taller than when he first frowned his way into my office, Philip is more like his age mates. He walks like a boy instead of a stick. His skin is "acceptable." Cylindrical glasses add to his severe expression, so he is still considered "a serious fellow."

Devotion to Latin and the rules of the club dominate his thinking. Together, he and his girl are planning the banquet at which there will be orations. The primary one

257

will be Philip's, of course. Club members will recline on pillows borrowed from lawn furniture while dining, and Sophomores, serving as slaves, will minister to the Junior's needs.

Philip still loves ritual and ceremony. He will always be his father's son and obsessive /compulsive, but perhaps he will no longer be handicapped by the insistency of his thoughts. If Philip's repetitious habits intrude on his life too much, as he grows older, there is medication available that can help him.

Philip's girl gently demonstrates that there is life beyond the Ciceronians. With Philip at her side, she looks forward to becoming a wheel in Campus Crusade. Fortunately, she also likes picnics, Christmas, clothes, too much make-up, other kids and family, as well as power.

I'm invited to be a speaker at the banquet. My topic is to be "Mental Health in the Roman Republic."

Philip apologizes. "I'm deeply, deeply sorry, Roberta. I should have stopped them."

"Who? For what?" I try to keep down the betrayed, lonely feeling that affects me as I listen. Philip spilled our therapy secrets to his ghoulish adolescent friends.

"I told them, I shared our satanic secrets with you. So they were warning you with the fetus and the cat's head and that other stuff. You were supposed to know that was to keep you from talking to the police."

Of course, he had to tell them about me, I remind myself. He couldn't have been expected to keep a confidence.

How could those creepy kids have known how frightened I was? The fear I suffered, thinking Mother and Daddy would find Rachel and me was physical. And mental. The frightful scenes I imagined, making movies in my head of Rachel, Sam and me, caterwauling in horrible panic, as our bodies tumbled about in agony. In my fantasy we heard only satanic chuckles and our own savage cries. Over and over, I invisioned fury and revenge.

I must forgive Philip for being a jerk. He's a kid. Like him, his half-baked occult buddies have turned to other interests now. Girls.

When I give Philip his hug, I notice he has changed more than I first guessed. He washes his hair and uses aftershave. He's going to be all right.

Forty Three

"Dear Dr. Graham-

Do you think there is really such a thing as Satan? If so, why does God allow him to exist? I've always thought that evil is real in the world because you see so much of it, but I don't think I can accept the idea of a devil who runs around with horns and a red suit." -K. M.

"Dear K. M. - Satan is not a myth nor just a symbol for evil. The Bible makes it clear that Satan is real. Rather than some imaginary idea or picture, Satan is the master of disguise and, according to 2 Corinthians 11:14-15, can even transform himself so he appears like an angel of light."

Billy Graham,*" My Answer," August, 1988*

At her mental health clinic, Rachel works with psychologically and physically battered children. It's a good thing she has so much training in human behavior, because she needs it. She values her own daughters, a red haired spirited brood, but her oldest daughter is drinking. She's genetically loaded. The kid might be more out of control with someone else as mother, but Rachel keeps a tight rein, monitoring and guiding this rebellious adolescent.

Rachel knows her girls are at risk. Their father was clearly alcoholic, and her own parents were addicted to far more than drugs or booze. With so many biological strikes against them, Rachel's children must not raise themselves. And yet, Rachel must work long hours to support them.

When she can take time for her children, Rachel teaches herself how to show affection and respect to her youngsters. Little by little, every day, Rachel heals herself through her work with the children of others.

Her difficulties with her own girls are ongoing, as they test her and Rachel's many emerging selves. Family therapy is only partially helpful. The girls and Rachel's alters have to cooperate more than they are able, to make that happen. There is uproar at Rachel's house.

She comes to Sam and me to complain, because she has no one else. Rachel has stopped abreacting so easily, that is, reliving old traumas. It doesn't seem necessary nowadays. Her present is difficult enough, to take all her time and energy.

More and more, I learn to appreciate the intimacy therapy demands and the special relationship in a working therapeutic match. It is stronger than anything but family, yet more objective than friendship. Only Sam and I are aware of the ferocity of the daily battle Rachel wages internally, struggling to trust, to forget, and to learn to love the world.

Today, Roger and I eat Thai lunch with his wife and children, saying goodbye in style. Growing away from therapy was easy for Roger, when he found his equilibrium once more. Instead of further treatment, he created a healthy outlet for his need to protect kids... from his own fears.

He claims his own two children stay alive on noodles that slip down their throats without chewing.

"Both kids are in braces. My orthodontist is delighted, I've been promoted, of course. I can pay him more each month, since my consulting work earns me a good deal of fame and a very good salary. I like important people treating me with respect, Roberta."

Roger is darkly calm. He looks taller in his businessman's gray suit, his new leather briefcase adding to his aura of importance. His book emerged from the presses as only a pamphlet, yet well enough written to be distributed by the Feds. Roger appears casual, yet deliberate.

"You're still spontaneous," I tell him," and at the same time, urbane."

"I have presence," he tells me. His wife and I laugh. I will miss this man when he moves his family to Washington. He is my impressive friend, the reformer, rapidly climbing the ladder of success.

So that's how it is, I tell myself. All of us are growing up. Philip, Roger, Rachel, Lilith and Roberta. Everyone but Peeper. Sweet, crazy Peeper is not dead as a doornail. Her dependence on Grandpa, who cared for her was greater than her love of life, but she is, thank goodness, integrated, along with Lilith, and Rachel is no longer in thrall to a wraith.

The sweet gingery aromas in this tiny restaurant have lost their compellingness. Leaning back in my chair after plum wine, assorted vegetables, shrimp with snow peas and coconut ice cream, I am feeling warm, sleepy and philosophical. All is well with my body and the world.

"Roberta, tell your friend I have some information about her parents," Roger says. His words cut through my steamy contentment.

"They're here in town, and wanted for questioning. We suspect them of being involved with those kids that desecrated the cemetery over on the West side. One of the juveniles took the head of a corpse home. Had it in his room. If you want to, you can tell your buddy she can see her folks in the waiting room of our police station, out on Thirty Third Avenue. Her parents won't even know she's there. Tomorrow. First thing in the morning. Eight o'clock. The plan is that they'll be driven in by van. They are definitely on the list of people to be questioned."

The sky is lavender. Rachel, Sam and I wait in the outer office of the Westside Police station. Breezeless, it is still too early for the white Texas heat, but I am sweating. Rachel is trembling and pale. As I watch her struggle to compose herself, I remember who she once was, a guarded woman, bound in tangles within herself and hampered by secrets. She craved love, yet was unloving.

Withdrawn, Rachel was distorted by pain, like a wounded snail in its shell, dying slowly, alone and unaware.

The round dark glasses she wears hide her eyes. It is eight twenty. Dust coats the wrinkled glass of the doors and windows. The worn linoleum shows dirty foot prints.

"So they aren't coming," I finally say.

"Let's go, Women!" Sam tries to sound cheerful. He is being forceful and hearty, something he does when he is particularly uneasy. Our caretaker this morning, Sam insists on driving and feeding us.

"I'll take you to the Pancake House. We'll have strong coffee and a big plate of flapjacks."

"Give me a minute, Sam. I can't walk. My knees are all water," Rachel admits.

We are looking the wrong way, toward the front of the building, when it happens. With a crash, something that looks like a snowman in a wheelchair jams its way out through the inner door. It dwarfs the black eyed, knotty little fellow behind. He struggles, side stepping, to maneuver the oversized chair. A uniformed policeman comes to his rescue. Together they heave and shove.

In the chair, piles of snowy skin are topped by short gray hair, floating upward from an oversized head. Rolls of pale fat cascade from Mother's face, neck, shoulders and arms.The chair-creature mutters and yelps.

Word salad spills from her open mouth. Sound piles upon sound with no coherence. As she howls, her heavy tongue pokes forward, through the round vowel noises.

The creature's eyes are vacant. She gazes in the direction the chair faces, her head unturning. Now, she spits the sliding, hissing sounds of consonants. Her mouth stretches widely from ear to ear, her thick tongue pokes from behind her grinding teeth.

Rachel crouches like a grouse in tall grass. Hiding behind her glasses, she bends inward, clutching her purse in front of her. I can't hear her breathe and have a sudden fear, she will hold her breath until she dies. I too, am terrified. Beside me, someone gasps. It is Sam, protectively reaching for my hand.

The woman in the chair raves wetly, seemingly unaware of anything but her inner dialogue. Her bulbous fingertips draw pictures in the air with sharp cutting movements. As the policeman opens both glass front doors, to allow the passage of the giant chair, Mother's grinning mouth tightens. She turns her massive head toward us.

"Imp of Satan!" she shouts. At the sound Daddy giggles.

Creaking, the doors slowly close behind them. Early morning sunshine slants into the echoing, dusty room.

The policeman shakes his head. He turns to look back once more, through the glass panel at Mommy and Daddy, then walks past us into the inner rooms. Behind him, the heavy varnished door swings shut. I can see the gold letters.

I tell myself, I detest the ugly and the monstrous, yet Sam is right. The hideous has a macabre fascination for me. I will always remember with a thrill of horror the shock of Mother bursting upon us, propelled by Daddy.

An anomaly, epicene, bizarre, she was draped in her own flesh. It is the sheen of evil about her I do not forget. I see her tiny glittering eyes almost hidden behind the giant mounds of her cheeks.

And yet, the tiny man with coals for eyes is the person it would be wiser to fear.

Roger calls me to tell why Rachel's parents were released.

"They're both too crazy to worry about, I guess. No one knew what to do with them, so the van took them back to the Group home. They appear to have a lot of friends there. This report says the woman's a burned-out, uh, schizophrenic, all gone in the head. Ugly. The man doesn't know what's what, either. Definitely some bricks missing. Relax, Roberta. They're just a couple of crazy old folks some street people think well of. Tell your friend not to be concerned. How can they be dangerous?"

The Women's Therapy Group enjoys Irish coffee. They continue to meet informally to talk dirty, encourage, validate and love each other. These women buddies call themselves "shirt off my back friends." Rachel never misses a session.

"Your laughter is no little snicker. You've got a real belly laugh, Rachel, but no belly," Lydia points out. "That is, to speak of. "

"Bullshit", Rachel shouts, sticking out her newly rounding abdomen.

Why should anyone be convinced Rachel's story is true? Perhaps someone will believe because of the new findings in the professional literature, or the hundreds of therapists working to discriminate between false memories and the painful truth of abuse.

"What do you think of when I say 'the devil next door', Sam?"

"Sex."

"No, no, stop that! We're thinking of calling Rachel's story, 'The Devil Next Door.' What do you think? Sam? Answer me! Sam. Sam?"

Forty Four

"I am also concerned with further distortions of religion occurring when a parent reinterprets it for his offspring. Though such distorted concepts may resemble the original beliefs only slightly, they continue nevertheless to be someone's idea of religion. And while a particular religious practice may be beneficial or harmless when unaltered, it may take on a new and destructive meaning in the hands of a parent bent on using it as a means to his own end."

Eli Chesen, M.D.
Religion Can Be Dangerous to Your Health

Rachel sits at her desk, wondering if she can go on learning about herself. Lilith , Peeper and Rachel 1 no longer exist as separate entities. They were fused through a ritual, a ceremony, into a highly developed grown up Rachel. Will more alters let themselves be discovered as a result of her desperate need to know about her inside world?

Once only pain and confusion belonged to Rachel, though she pretended perfection. She knew anger, fear and nightmare sensations, living with terrible anxiety.

Now she experiences uncertainty, sadness, friendship, excitement, sexual tension, fun, quiet joy and occasional pleasure. Just like people.

In the Spring Rachel and I will fly back to the scenes of her despair. Can she make herself touch that soil again? Look out across bay water. See the moon? Walk through woods. Follow shabby streets? Find the cellar?

Rachel and I remember how her life was ten years ago, when we met:

Notes:
Rachel merely exists from day to day, telling herself this is being alive. Persistent physical pain tortures her, yet emotionally she is numb. Now her body can no longer tolerate pain from muscle spasms, headaches, bleeding ulcers, colitis and constant bladder and kidney infections.

Rachel's medical doctor tires of getting nowhere.

"Too much stress, Mrs. You need biofeedback. You must learn to relax."

Rachel senses her perfect world is falling apart. She is unable to fiercely, yet politely, control everything and everybody, but she knows no other way to relate. With skill and all the energy she can muster she acts out her roles as wife, the mother of a large family and a striving college student, but in reality she is a hollow, hardworking someone called Rachel. Period.

"Busy, I have to be busy. Doesn't the doctor understand? What is relaxation, Dr. Richards?"

She has no idea. How shall she begin? Somehow she must make a start , even though the voices in her head are shouting and whining. Inside, the babies are all crying at once.

Rachel hurries out my door to where her protective husband waits in the the fading light that streaks through dry palm trees. The hulking man is hunched over the wheel, her rescuer, waiting to drive his tormented wife home through the darkness.

Fearful, making herself open the car door, Rachel listens to the wind's rattling sound. The night air is oppressive. Whatever her pain, Rachel twists her lips into her idea of a smile. She must try harder, she tells herself. She must force herself to go on.

QUOTATIONS

Bennett Braun, director, Dissociative Disorders Program, Chicago Bush-Presbyterian-St. Luke's Medical Center,
Newsweek, April, 1993, pg. 58

Frank W. Putnam, "Diagnosis and Treatment of Multiple Personality Disorder", The Guilford Press, 1989,pg.VIII

Father John Navone," Life Magazine", June, 1989, pg.50

Anton La Vey," Newsweek", December 5, 1988, pg. 29

Sigmund Freud, "The Life and Work of Sigmund Freud", Ernest Jones Basic Books, 1957, pg. 34

Ric Masten, "I Was A Teenage Creature", "Even As We Speak", Nichols and Dimes, Odessa, Texas 198, pg. 16

Jim Mattox, "Life Magazine", June, 1989, pg.48

Pierre Janet (1890) quoted in Rappaport, 1942, pg. 201

Father Gugliemo Lauriola, "Life Magazine", June , 1989, pg. 51

David St. Clair, "Say You Love Satan!", Dell Publishers, New York, 1987, pgs. 93-95

Mark Galanter, "Life Magazine", June, 1989, pg. 55

Anton La Vey, "Life Magazine", June, 1989 , pg. 51

Mark Roggeman, "Life Magazine, "June, 1989, pg. 55

Journal of Marital and Family Therapy, American Association for Marriage and Family Therapy, April, 1982, Volume 8, Number 2

Carl Jung, "Psychology and Religion", Princeton University Press, 1969, pg. 93

Eli S. Chesen, M.D.," Religion Can Be Dangerous to Your Health" , Collier Books, New York, 1972, pg. 6

Freud, Sigmund, The Origins of Psychoanalysis, New York, Basic Books, 1954

Freud, Sigmund, "Breuer and Freud", 1893-1895,pg, 49n.

Freud, Sigmund, "A Difficulty in the Path of Psychoanalysis , 1917a

John Paul II, "Life Magazine", June, 1989, pg. 51

Eric Berne, "What Do You Say After You Say 'Hello'", Grove Press, 1972, pg. 115

Reverend William P. Nye, "Life Magazine", June, 1989, pg. 50

Colin Ross, " Mutiple Personality Disorder", John Wiley and Sons, 1989, pgs. 55 and 212

Billie Barbara Masten, "Billie Beethoven", Sunflower Ink, Carmel, California, 1983, pg. 17

Erich Fromm, The Anatomy of Human Destructiveness, New York, Holt, 1973, pg. 332.

Mason, R. O., Duplex Personality, Journal of Nervous and Mental Disease, 18:593-598,1893

Sandra Daly Gallant ,"Newsweek", December 5, 1988, 29

Harvard Mental Health Letter, Harvard Medical School, May, 1993, Volume 9, Number 11

Ellen Bass and Laura Davis, "The Courage to Heal, A Guide for Women Survivors of Child Sexual Abuse", Harper and Row, New York, 1988, pgs. 345-47

Morton Prince, "Dissociation of a Personality", Longman, Green, 1929, pg. 45

Dr. Carl Raschke, Professor of Religious Studies, University of Denver, Life Magazine, June, 1981, pg. 55

Robert Simandl, Newsweek Magazine, December 5, 1988, pg. 29

Richard A. Gardner, M.D., "Sex Abuse Hysteria: Salem Witch Trial Revisited", Creative Therapeutics, New Jersey, 1991, pg. 52

Diagnostic and Statistical Manual of Mental Disorders (Third Edition) American Psychiatric Association, 1981